American Nightmare

ALSO BY JERROLD M. PACKARD

Victoria's Daughters
Farewell in Splendor
Neither Friend Nor Foe
Sons of Heaven
Peter's Kingdom
American Monarchy
The Queen & Her Court

American Nightmare

THE HISTORY OF JIM CROW

Jerrold M. Packard

ST. MARTINS GRIFFIN ✺ NEW YORK

www.stmartins.com

ISBN 978-0-312-30241-2
ISBN 0-312-30241-X (pbk)

Contents

Preface

Having never seen a set of *three* rest rooms before, I was shocked that first time. It was February 1962, and the Illinois Central Railroad had just a few minutes before dropped me at its station in the center of Montgomery, Alabama. There were, to be sure, a good many things in the world that might have amazed an eighteen-year-old, newly minted member of the United States Air Force only a few months out of high school. My father and a couple of uncles had told me about some of the exotica with which I'd be confronted among the strange, to me at least, customs of the Deep South. But three rest rooms—marked Men, Women, and Colored—muddled the blueprint covering such commonplace arrangements with which I'd grown up in the Pacific Northwest. That four-decade-old incident has, in a persistent and uncomfortable way, remained a staple in my stock of essential experiences, a check on a young man's incredulousness.

When I told friends of my plans to write a book on Jim Crow, the first question many asked me was *Why?* That was commonly followed by some variation on *How come you want to write about something* most *people have, thank God, forgotten?* About half the time though, especially if the questioner appeared to be under forty, the response was simply a blank stare followed by something like *And now just who was Jim Crow again?*

It's easiest to answer in reverse order. Jim Crow wasn't a *who.* It was, at its core, a structure of exclusion and discrimination devised by white Americans to be employed principally against black Americans—though others felt its sting as well, not least Hispanics and Asians, and even whites who opposed it. Its central purpose was to maintain a second-class social and economic status for blacks while upholding a first-class social and economic status for whites. Jim Crow discrimination against African-Americans existed in every state in the nation. But it was codified in statute and *lived*, every minute of every day, in the southeastern quadrant of America, in what had for four years in the mid–nineteenth century been the Confederate states. In the South, Jim Crow discrimination at its height existed not only by statute but by custom and racial "etiquette," and it was rigidly enforced by both the law enforcement agencies and courts as well as by ordinary white citizens who were neither policemen nor judges but who often took the law into their own hands as though they were.

As for the part about *something most people have forgotten*, I'll concede the forgetting is, if hardly universal, widespread and maybe even understandable, perhaps representing the end Jim Crow best deserves. Why, after all, write about horrors that died a richly earned death, and many of whose worst details are almost beyond comprehending today and whose retelling would be painful?

There is, I think, a good reason, and it bears mainly on understanding the background of the race attitudes that infuse modern America. This nation's racial ills are far from having healed, or even from having ended. But though we can't guess when America will enjoy genuine universal justice, we can, at the very least, take a lesson in the fact that statutory Jim Crow has ended. As you'll read in this book, Jim Crow was a disease that once permeated every fissure and fold of American society. And that "once" isn't so very long ago—a generation or two, depending on how that imprecise term is understood. Until recently, for black Americans almost every part of life was governed by Jim Crow's humiliations. For white Americans, enormous chunks of life, and of wealth, went into maintaining the delicate, brutal, intense business of control. We should not forget where we once were in such business, and how we got there, and how we ended it.

And then the *Why?* This is my eighth book on social institutions, but it's the first time I've written about my own country's civil rights history. At the outset, I'll admit that this story is not about the good in America, but about the bad. It is, in fact, a book about the worst of our country's memories. I hope, of course, that writing about Jim Crow directs light on this dark corner of our past. My intent is not to try to explain every kind of racism or to analyze the merits of affirmative action or of racial reparations that have in large part been the legacy of Jim Crow. But I don't think we should forget what Jim Crow did and how far we've come since these events transpired, or even how it was that rest rooms once came in threes.

For reasons I'll soon try hard to satisfactorily explain, this is, in the main, a Southern story. So I went to the South to research it, traveling by Greyhound through the region whose pulse was until the mid-1960s taken by the beat of Jim Crow. My first thanks go to my fellow Greyhound passengers, largely African-American, who told me of their own memories of life in the Jim Crow South, or—perhaps more often—what their parents or grandparents had told them about those days. My thanks, too, to the young ones who said they didn't know what the term *Jim Crow* meant—which in itself told me something I needed to know.

And a few special thanks by name, all to people who helped me with kindnesses and advice, but none of whom, of course, bears the slightest responsibility for whatever errors or misinterpretations I've made. Janice White Sikes at the African-American Research Branch of the Atlanta-Fulton Public Library. The Reverend Willie Rogers Sr. at Morehouse College in Atlanta. Mary Glenn Hearne at the Nashville Room of the Public Library of Nashville & Davidson County. Janie Morris at the Duke University Library in Durham. Two ladies of Reston, Virginia—Thelma Calbert and Bernice Tate. Johnnie Carr in Montgomery. John Egerton in Nashville. Mississippi assistant attorney general Jim Fraiser in Jackson. Former governor William Winter in Jackson. Professor David Gochman in Louisville. Professor Mills Thornton (of the University of Michigan) in Montgomery. Professor Charles Reagan Wilson at the University of Mississippi in Oxford.

My thanks go to my editor at St. Martin's, Charles Spicer, without whose confidence the book wouldn't have happened, and whose encouragement lifted me. And thanks, too, to my literary agent, Natasha Kern, who said yes from the beginning.

American Nightmare

Prologue

COMING HOME

Wendell Tandy didn't exist in flesh and blood but, as a metaphor, was as real as the Jim Crow he faced. What happened to Wendell was similar to what thousands of African-Americans endured, servicemen and servicewomen who, in countries not their own, fought a war against racism only to return to the same scourge at home.

t was December 1945, and the United States Army of Occupation in Berlin was sending Wendell Tandy back to Mississippi. For eighteen months First Lieutenant Wendell Lawrence Tandy III had served his country and had done so with notable valor. With so much valor, in fact, the army had given him a Distinguished Service Medal for obliterating a German tank in a maneuver his commanding officer had in the award citation described as "heroic and damn near suicidal." Wendell had also picked up a Purple Heart in tribute to the meatball-size chunk of bone and gristle one of the panzer's smaller guns had blown out of his left thigh.

The slender and soft-voiced infantry officer had begun the last eighteen months of his army life by facing a cataract of German artillery shells hurled at him across Normandy's Omaha Beach. That ordeal was succeeded by a bloodily fought slog through France and Belgium and Germany, Hitler's Thousand Year empire breathing its last as the exhausted unit crawled through sniper fire in Leipzig. Three months later, on the same August day the Japanese were surrendering on the other side of the world and putting an end to the Pacific war, a colonel had pinned the DSM on Wendell's first-class blouse and a moment later handed him the silver insignia of a first lieutenant to replace his old gold bars. Happy to have gotten through the fighting in one piece, Wendell had ended up in Berlin, in charge of a minor portion of the boring duties of an occupying army.

But for every mile and every hour of his journey, another enemy, one wearing the same uniform as his own, had taunted the twenty-three-year-old lieutenant. This foe was pure American, and it came his way solely because of the color of his skin, which was a shade of gingery auburn. For Wendell, Jim Crow had been as much a part of army life as his K rations—and was, for that matter, in many ways indistinguishable from what he had survived growing up in Mississippi.

In Berlin, the greater part of Wendell's time had been spent living—sleeping, eating, working—with fellow blacks in segregated barracks that had not long before housed a regiment of *Waffen-SS* troops. It had not, of course, been merely happenstance that his unit consisted entirely of black soldiers. That was the way it was in 1945 in just about every corner of the U.S. army. As an officer, Wendell nonetheless often interacted with white troops, though few of them seemed entirely unmindful of his color. In fact, a good many of them occasionally voiced the petty racial innuendos that were second nature to the greater part of white soldiery. Still, a few, especially the Yankees or the Westerners, treated him as just another GI, sometimes even ungrudgingly acknowledging his rank and deferring to his officer's status.

Though the officers' club was off-limits to Wendell for simply hanging out, just as it was to every other black officer, he was nonetheless required to attend the club's official weekly gathering. These officers' calls included a sit-down dinner, where he dined with white officers on what were the first occasions in his life that he had eaten at the same table with anyone other than blacks. He took it for granted that officers who got up and moved when he joined a table were, likely as not, Southerners. Everyone expected Southern soldiers, both officers and men, to bring their back-home race prejudice into the army with them, and the army fully accommodated such expectations. Beyond these dinners, few other social or recreational opportunities were extended to the handful of black officers in Berlin, and Wendell understood that nothing was to be gained by dwelling on this reality.

Sick of looking at and, especially, *smelling* the wasteland that had once been a splendid and orderly metropolis, Wendell gladly signed out of Berlin on December 5, his orders directing him to final outprocessing at home in Jackson, Mississippi. The European part of his long journey back to the States would end at Le Havre, on the Channel coast, and that meant he'd get to go through Paris, the transportation to the French capital by duty train, a U.S.-requisitioned French locomotive pulling a few battered German carriages, heading west through a devastated landscape on the last remaining set of the defunct Reich's still-usable tracks.

Like just about everything else involving the army and race, Wendell found that the duty train, too, was segregated, the white officers and men provided with coaches, sleeping cars, and a dining car, while black enlisted men were quartered in a single separate carriage, in which together they sat, ate, and slept—the latter sitting up—arrangements befitting the status of black troops and the customs of Jim Crow. Wendell's commissioned status complicated these matters. Though military protocol frowned on any of its handful of black officers sleeping in an open coach with enlisted men, it nonetheless yielded to the white officers' refusal to share their own accommodations with *any* blacks, even fellow officers. To get around the impasse, Wendell and the one other black officer on the train found themselves assigned a compartment at the rear of the white officers' sleeping carriage, a closed-off four-foot-by-seven-foot space in which they were expected to remain, unseen to white American eyes, for the entire sixty-hour journey from Berlin to Paris. Visits to the "colored" latrine meant stepping out of their compartment directly into the passageway connecting the coach to the all-black enlisted coach behind. As for eating, a German steward would wordlessly bring boxed meals to their cubicle.

His itinerary gave Wendell seven hours to spend in Paris before his next train—a French one, *and* civilian—left for Le Havre. These brief hours in the City of Light represented the first of his life during which he had been entirely free of Jim Crow. For an almost-whole day, he met no white man's glance hardened by contempt, no signs telling him a toilet or a water fountain or a café was barred to people of his color. A waiter seated him at a table smack in the middle of French diners, *white* French diners, and, except for difficulties with language, served him with precisely the same Gallic self-importance he begrudged the other patrons. Later that afternoon, a shop assistant had smiled when she'd sold him perfume as a gift for his mother and, when he'd departed, had thanked him in poor English but with a respect the exact likes of which he had never been shown by a white countryman of his own. Expressing admiration for the United States, a fellow browser in a bookshop proffered an unexpected and gravely formal handshake to the young American dressed in the uniform of an officer, a bid Wendell knew would be unimaginable from any Mississippian wearing a white skin.

The train that would take him to embarkation in Le Havre unsurprisingly overflowed with American troops. But it wasn't an American train, and he was free to take any seat of his choosing, still another first for Wendell, to sit where he wanted, without reference to his own country's racial etiquette. He spotted a pair of empty seats and took the one by the window. Before he had his army blouse unbuttoned, an elderly Frenchman asked if the aisle seat was unoccupied.

From Paris to Le Havre the two men talked, tentatively as the train pulled out of the Gare du Nord, but as the French countryside overcame the clutter of Paris, the conversation grew animated as the elder's halting but correct English warmed up. Wendell told the Frenchman about Jackson and his mother's cooking and about how much he missed his Mississippi home. And he told him, too, about Omaha Beach and his run-in with the panzer and the friends he had lost. The Frenchman in turn showed Wendell a prewar snapshot of his own family, including his two sons, one a pilot killed in the 1940 invasion, the other a *résistant* shot in Lyons a few weeks before D day by a German firing squad. Skin color seemed inconsequential, nowhere in the conversation needing to be mentioned or in any way acknowledged. At Le Havre, the idyll ended.

The converted troop ship was, decidedly, not French. And just as the army's script demanded, Jim Crow kicked back in the moment Wendell entered the pier shed. Directed to the gangplank "reserved" for Negroes, Wendell presented his embarkation orders to a black NCO and a white boarding officer, the unmistakable disdain in the latter's face and tone of voice a foretaste of the next seven days at sea.

Like the Berlin duty train, the ship, too, was segregated, painstakingly so. Quarters for black troops were aft, a symbolically rich location that Wendell knew hadn't arisen accidentally. Black officer quarters were laid out around the curve of the hull and consisted of small four-man cabins that at least afforded a semiprivacy nonexistent in the enlisted men's large open bays covering what had once been the converted liner's third-class dining room. At every point where corridors and companionways connected the "colored" areas to the far larger white areas, foot-square chained signs blocked traffic between the two: there was no mistaking the curt military lingo announcing Off Limits to Colored Personnel on Wendell's side, Off Limits to White Personnel on the other.

For Wendell, the voyage passed in a fog of tedious days and sleepless nights interposed with spells of vomiting brought on by seasickness that was aggravated by the heavy, greasy, and monotonous rations. The army evidently assumed black men were uniformly raised on boiled meat and greens, some mutation of which was served at almost every one of the twice-daily meals. Normal army procedure, extended where possible to black officers, meant that Wendell's duties consisted of little beyond supervising black work details as the enlisted men laid into twelve-hour fatigue shifts. The high point of the voyage came at the end. As the ship skimmed past the Statue of Liberty, Wendell wordlessly breathed in the symbol of freedom from his vantage point in the black exercise space on the poop deck. A struggling winter sun was just coming up as the liner-turned-troopship swung into its Hudson River pier.

After wrapping up three hours of paperwork at the military pier, Wendell set off to spend a day and a night in the city before entraining for Mississippi. He walked out of the quay onto West Street, hailed a black-driven taxi, and told the cabby he needed a hotel room. The driver recommended the Theresa, on 125th Street in Harlem, and explained to his fare that even though most of the midtown hotels didn't take colored trade some "bighearted" clerk might afford a room to a bona fide black *officer*— but then added that he'd face a lot less hassle and be a lot happier putting up with his own folks. Getting into the subject, the cabby advised that by confining his eating to Harlem, Wendell would also avoid much of the petty grief that'd be sure to come his way in most of midtown's white restaurants. Wendell agreed to the hotel and tucked away the advice about restaurants for later.

The Theresa—racially integrated only five years earlier—was a time-scarred but still impressive building, and it sat at the busiest corner of the greatest African-American neighborhood in the country, squarely in the center of America's black soul. But judging by the crowd streaming in and out its doors, it also looked to be discouragingly jammed. Filling the lobby was a mélange of prosperous-looking blacks *and* whites as well as colorfully dressed types who might have been Malays or Hindus or almost anything else peopling the international entrepôt New York had become since the war had altered the city's face. Fortunately for Wendell, the desk clerk found him a room after glancing deferentially at the officer's insignia that was still far from common on black servicemen.

Within thirty minutes Wendell had stowed his bags in his cubbyhole quarters and was back out on the sidewalk. On the near-freezing but cloudless December day, for the first time in two years he finally drew a first genuinely deep lungful of American air. That it was *Harlem* air made it sweeter, for these few square miles were the freest, most welcoming place in the entire nation for men and women of color. The simple truth was that for black Americans in white America, Harlem came about as close as it got to freedom from the stench of Jim Crow.

Yet even here, on streets crowded with purposeful-looking black people, true freedom for those who shared Wendell's African heritage remained nearly as much illusion as reality. Even if this young Mississippian thought he had landed in paradise, Harlem's residents well understood that a few blocks away from the sheen of 125th Street lay a different reality, one in which overcrowding and unemployment and untreated illnesses ranked Harlem among the most squalid slums in America, a city within a city where the vast majority of the restaurants and hotels and stores were white-owned and where African-American customers were banned by many of those businesses—even, and most famously, by the world-renowned nightclubs and theaters that permitted only white trade to enjoy their black entertainment.

Before looking at the rest of New York, one item of business remained for Wendell to attend to, namely buying a train ticket to Jackson. So a second cab ride took him back to midtown's Pennsylvania Station. Via the next morning's Pontchartrain, the crack New York to New Orleans express, he reserved coach accommodations to Jackson. The ticket clerk had told him the purchase of sleeping space would be a waste of his money, explaining that even those blacks who had bought valid sleeper tickets in the North were often barred use of them after Baltimore, where legal Jim Crow took effect. Wendell would certainly have preferred his own compartment but deferred to reality. The white clerk, clearly sympathetic to a soldier in uniform, finally advised him to buy enough food to get himself to his destination because he'd get hungry after Baltimore, in which city African-American access not only to Pullmans ended, but where admission of persons of color to the dining car became difficult and, more often than not, impossible.

Disheartened but still eager to drink in this astonishing city for the few hours he had left to see it, Wendell walked out of Penn Station and headed straight down Thirty-fourth Street into the heart of the metropolis. Even though he was hungry, he wasn't sure of Northern race etiquette and, remembering the cabby's advice, decided to skip the white restaurants that liberally dotted the midtown streets. Instead, he bought a paper-wrapped baked potato from a vendor's cart and took it to the park behind the big library on Forty-second Street to eat it. Afterward he walked up Fifth Avenue, looking into the treasure-laden windows of the classy shops. On the busy street he couldn't help brushing past white women who dexterously stepped out of his way as they clutched their purses extra-carefully while shooting him looks that implied astonishment that he should be wearing an officer's uniform.

Later in the afternoon he was back in Harlem, where he happily roamed the broad avenues, occasionally turning onto the quieter side streets and everywhere scrutinizing the scores of Negro businesses and storefront churches, peering up at the stoops of brownstone apartments, returning the glances of passersby. Wendell broke off his wandering long enough to eat dinner in a big neon-lit restaurant on Lenox Avenue. His fellow diners were all black, the only reality he'd ever known at home and one he found comforting even in New York.

The Pontchartrain's departure was scheduled for eight-thirty the next morning. So Wendell was up at 6 A.M. and checked out of the Theresa thirty minutes later. For breakfast he bought a bag of pastries at the bakery down the block from the hotel, where he also got himself a big bagful of cookies for the train. A taxi delivered him to the station in plenty of time to stop at the tobacco counter and pick up half a dozen of his favored Hershey's bars, added sustenance against the expected Jim Crow hunger.

Grinding out of Penn Station, the Pontchartrain's coaches remained unsegregated. Wendell thought the passenger mix looked to be about three-quarters white, the remainder mostly native blacks and a few dark-skinned foreigners. Except for the aisle seat next to his own, his car was completely full as the train started to move. As it picked up speed, a white woman wearing a preposterous feathered hat appeared at the end of the coach. Passing Wendell's seat, she hesitated for a moment, looked embarrassingly pained, and walked on. A moment later the conductor was leaning over Wendell. In a cross between asking and ordering, he explained that some "seat rearranging" was necessary. Wendell found himself moved to a seat next to a white man that until a moment before had held a white woman, the latter now being directed to Wendell's former seat— next to the feather-topped white woman, who still looked pained but now slightly less so.

The tornado-like winds of Jim Crow didn't take long to arrive, legally kicking in as the train crossed the Pennsylvania-Maryland line. In Pennsylvania, black people had been, at least in theory, ordinary citizens; entering Maryland, they ceased being ordinary and became, with the unlimited majesty of Maryland's race laws, *second*-class citizens. Accordingly, during its Baltimore stopover the Pontchartrain's carriages were rearranged to square with the demands of racial segregation. From here to home, Wendell would either sit behind movable screens in a colored section of a white car or in a coach wholly "reserved" for people whose race was, like his own, second-class.

When he crossed that boundary—the so-called Mason and Dixon Line—more than seating arrangements changed for Wendell. Civility toward blacks on the part of the train's personnel mutated into insolence, with conductors sometimes even calling blacks "nigger," an indignity directed at any African-American for deportment deemed by whites the least demanding, or "uppity." By Southern states' law, train conductors possessed many of the same powers as police officers, and few hesitated to use them in the furtherance of Jim Crow. Wendell now found that the main waiting rooms in stations were off-limits to him, coloreds being required to keep themselves to segregated and almost always shabbily inferior areas. Station restaurants below the Mason and Dixon Line served only whites, though some of the larger ones came equipped with an inconspicuous pass-through window or rear platform from which blacks were allowed to buy food to be taken away and eaten elsewhere, which was to say away from whites. The tobacco or magazine shops were routinely located in the white areas, and a dash across a white lobby to buy a pack of cigarettes could, for Wendell, end in arrest—or, worse, a policeman's club brought down on his head.

From the moment he entered Maryland, Wendell would have one small chance of obtaining food on the train itself. If an agreeable diningcar porter were to permit two or three tables to be sectioned off behind a screen or a curtain at the end of the diner, African-Americans would be fed. Even though the law required "equal" dining facilities for whites and blacks, the railroad companies negated such "protections" by invoking the omnibus put-off of "wartime shortage," an excuse for stiffing blacks used long after the war itself had come to an end. Sometimes blacks were allowed to eat either at the end of the regular meal service, which meant after the last whites had vacated the car, or at "first call"—for breakfast that translated into 5:30 A.M.—ensuring they would be out of the way when white passengers dined at the more reasonable hours.

Crossing the Carolinas and Georgia and Alabama, Wendell finished off the last of the cookies from Harlem and followed them with his supply of Hershey's bars, the sugary sustenance preferable to hazarding the humiliation of groveling for a curtained-off seat in the diner. The further the Pontchartrain sped toward its destination, the deeper it penetrated the Old South and the more crowded Wendell's Jim Crow car became. But even though fully half the nation's blacks lived in these eleven southeastern states, the railroads refused to provide anything like equal or proportionate space or facilities for them.

Since it was close to Christmas and its crowds of holiday travelers, at no point in the trip did Wendell profit from the luxury of an empty seat next to his own. He consequently found himself forced to sleep upright in an old and thinly upholstered chair, and each station stop easily jolted him out of his intermittent dozing. Early on the second morning of the journey he awakened under a brightly lit train shed, a large sign hanging from its rafters proclaiming, Birmingham—The Magic City. Looking out his window and into those of a motionless dining car on the adjoining track, he saw dozens of men, all dressed in gray uniforms, sitting at cloth-covered tables where black waiters were politely serving them. The uniforms were the same Wendell had seen from Normandy to Berlin. The breakfasting German war prisoners were too busy feeding themselves to glance across the narrow platform into the window of their former enemy.

The National Association for the Advancement of Colored People had named Wendell's state the most segregated in America, a recognition most white Mississippians esteemed. Likely the only consolation this lent Mississippi's black citizens—about half of the entire population—was that discrimination elsewhere must be at least a fraction less forbidding. White Mississippians arrogantly bragged that the state's bare-knuckled racial climate "differed more from North Carolina's than North Carolina's differed from Ohio's." And from the executive mansion in its capital city, Governor Theodore G. Bilbo had not long before jubilantly proclaimed for anyone who didn't know that "the best way to keep a nigger away from a white primary is to see him the night before." Not all white Mississippians favored Bilbo's implied violence, but their silence made the vast majority complicit in the governor's attitude.

Gliding into the Jackson station, Wendell was too exhilarated to think about the underside of the place in which he had grown up. Leaning out over his car's open platform, his eyes and those of his parents met. After leaping down the steps and embracing first his mother and then his father, the young lieutenant threw his bag over his shoulder—blacks routinely carried their own luggage for the simple reason that porters weren't allowed to serve them—as his parents happily placed their arms around his waist and led him down the platform, toward the waiting-room entrance prominently marked For Colored Only, and through it to the busy street.

A few steps more and the family was at the bus stop, where the three Tandys automatically joined the Negro waiting line. Separating black riders from those with white skins was a steel railing, extending back about five feet from the curb, whose purpose was to make sure the two queues did not merge, which might, of course, lead to the impermissible touching of white skin by black. Whites habitually ignored blacks on the other side of the railing, but Wendell's uniform excited notice from two or three of the whites, whose surly scowls precisely spelled out their disgust for what they regarded as an "uppity nigra" who had gotten too far above himself with his fancy silver lieutenant's bars. Wendell knew most whites fundamentally saw him as more than anything else a sexual predator, and he was quietly pleased at the contrary notions his obvious education and unmistakable commission elicited from whites.

When the Farish Street bus arrived, the one headed for the Tandys' neighborhood, the driver stopped precisely where the open front door would permit those in the white queue to board first. When the handful of white riders had gotten on the bus, the colored riders were allowed to step up to the fare box. There they deposited their dimes and immediately stepped back down to reboard by the rear door. Wendell knew anything like a "sassy" look from a Negro was enough to motivate the white driver—there were, of course, no black drivers in Jackson or, for that matter, anywhere else in the South—to pull away before the paid-up customer could make it to the back door.

The Tandys did make it, and Wendell spotted the last three empty seats—two together and one directly behind it—on the Colored side of the adjustable overhead sign dividing the races. Wendell and his father sat together, Mrs. Tandy in the seat behind. Here they faced yet another potential humiliation: riders in these forward-most colored seats would be the first ordered to move back if more whites got on than there were seats available to them in the white section. Which is what happened to the Tandys three stops after leaving the train station. Two young white girls, faced with a full white section, returned to the driver and quietly but unambiguously claimed their rights.

Without hesitation, the driver half-turned toward the rear of the bus and curtly barked to the affected blacks, "You niggers in those first seats gotta move back." That the rest of the black section was full was immaterial. Wendell and his father stood and moved toward the rear, then the teenagers slid the movable Jim Crow sign back a seat's length on its rail and quickly sank into the seats that had a moment before been occupied by the Tandy men. The uniformed lieutenant and his sixty-six-year-old father stood the remainder of the journey while the teenage girls hunched down in their newly won seats and began giggling about something not known to the Tandys.

Even if he hadn't grown up in this city, Wendell would have had no trouble recognizing the approach of the black neighborhood: paved sidewalk turned to dirt path where the white homes petered out and his own colored district began. When Mrs. Tandy arose as the family's corner approached, she told her son that their friends had for days been eagerly awaiting the chance to welcome back the neighborhood's war hero. Wendell smiled, but asked if they could keep the hellos short so he could treat the two of them to a quiet restaurant dinner to mark his homecoming.

A "celebration" for Jackson's blacks was very different from what it was for the city's whites. Celebrating for African-Americans generally meant doing so at home, the reasons for which were uncomplicated: blacks were barred from setting foot in any of the city's white restaurants or white cafés or white soda fountains or white cafeterias—anyplace, in fact, that served white people food or drink. No black could enter a white bar or a white nightclub or a white dancehall or a white bowling alley or a white skating rink or a white public park or a white auditorium or a white golf course or a white swimming beach or a white public lending library or—God forbid most of all—a white church. Of the city's downtown movie theaters, only two allowed access to blacks—and in both of these blacks were permitted only in the balcony, what whites called the buzzard roosts, or nigger galleries, and to which entry was gained through a side door, or an alley door, followed by a steep climb by way of open steel steps to the top of the theater. When an especially popular picture was showing, when more whites wanted to see the movie than there were first-floor seats, the management simply opened the roost to whites and turned away blacks.

Delighted with their son's surprise offer, Wendell's parents allowed as how they *would* enjoy a restaurant dinner. On what Mr. Tandy earned as a schoolteacher in a colored school, which was about three-fifths of what a white teacher was paid for teaching in the city's far better equipped and staffed white schools, Mr. Tandy had rarely been able to give his family such a luxury.

The South's taboo on a white person and a black person eating together was, excepting only interracial sex, the most potent precept of Jim Crow. But, fortunately, the Tandys' community possessed its own commercial heart, albeit a small heart. Farish Street provided Jackson's blacks the kind of downtown that the "real" downtown a few blocks away gave the city's whites. Though entirely enclosed by the larger and far more elaborate Anglo-Saxon city in which blacks were almost wholly excluded except as menials and servants, this African-American community provided the Tandys with a happy place to celebrate their son's return home from war.

A short walk through the Christmas-tree-scented night air delivered the family to a street that gave them the unique joy of moving freely among their fellow human beings. Free from an "etiquette" that never-endingly alluded to the inferiority that black skin represented to white Americans, the Tandys walked together as ordinary human beings, passing other ordinary human beings, not having to step aside for white pedestrians, free to enter any store or café or theater, and enter in dignity, and where, uniquely in the entire city, they would hear themselves addressed as "mister" or "missus" instead of "boy" or "auntie" or "you" or simply "nigger." For Wendell, the journey from Berlin to Jackson ended in the only reality he had ever known. It was 1945, and life wasn't going to change much for a long time. Not, in fact, until another entire generation had grown up enduring America's own apartheid.

The remainder of this book will describe how America got itself into this situation—how, and why, this nation's people built such a structure. Jim Crow really happened. Americans really lived like this imagined Wendell Tandy, who stands for so many others. Under the standard of white supremacy, for the greater part of four centuries blacks endured all this— and much more that was far, far worse. What follows is why it happened, how it came to be, how we justified it, and how we finally ended it.

A Note

The origin of the term *Jim Crow* lies in the early-nineteenth-century minstrel show, a form of popular stage entertainment that can be thought of as the predecessor to vaudeville. Minstrelsy consisted of white song-and-dance performers crudely mimicking African-American dance steps and rhythms, generally for the enjoyment it gave to white audiences while demeaning the blacks whom the white entertainers tried to resemble by covering their faces with burnt cork. One of the earliest and most famous minstrels was Thomas "Daddy" Rice, who devised a strutting dance character supposedly suggesting a prancing crow, and the character thus came to be called Jim Crow, an act for which Rice gained nationwide fame.

How the vaudeville character called Jim Crow came to be the general term for American racial segregation and discrimination is not known. But at some point in the nineteenth century, the term ceased to have anything to do with minstrelsy (whose popularity had by the end of the nineteenth century greatly waned), instead signifying what it meant throughout the twentieth century, namely the legal, quasi-legal, or customary practice of disfranchising, physically segregating, barring, and discriminating against black Americans, virtually the sole practitioners of such practices being white Americans.

The full range of the Jim Crow of this book is, admittedly, difficult to define with precision. Think of it, though, as being a little like pornography. That, too, can be hard to define, but as Supreme Court justice Potter Stewart once remarked, you know it when you see it.

1

STARTING FROM THE
VERY BEGINNING

We can, of course, little more than hypothesize how our racial passions first began to overtake us, how humankind's obsession to embrace the similar and despise the different got stuck in our communal psyche, and why, most pertinent to this book, white people have seemingly forever assumed an innate superiority over black people. As to the latter, right through at least the last couple of millennia white dominance has been ascribed by white-skinned societies to God as his—or nature's—plan, and that has seemed to many such ascribers to make it a righteous thing. Some have held that the power of white over black is simply the natural order, a kind of instinctive reality of the way human beings should relate to one another. Many have been convinced that the low station of humans whose skin is other than white is a universal reality, a postulate sensible men and women shouldn't challenge. The rationales have been legion, primordial, and heartfelt.

But racial ordering of white over color is neither natural or providential—the will of "providence" or of "God"—nor outside the remedy of reason. The creation of color-based caste was accomplished in lucid steps by groups more powerful than their prey, for reasons both social and economic. Its survival has been nurtured over numberless generations by, among others, Christian and Muslim clerics and slavers, by historians and the learned of science, and by ordinary people whose purses have grown through its perpetuation.

Complicating any account of racial prejudice is the hurdle we face in precisely defining the meaning of "race" itself. Assuming, as much of science does, that we all descended from the same progenitors, the same set of monkeys or of first parents of whatever genus or species, where did our differences in skin shade and eye shape and hair texture and lip size come from? What exactly constitute the degree marks on the scale of race? Why have human beings doggedly used the superficial construct of race as, second only to gender, the most important separator within our common humanity? Why in the United States did race become caste, as it had in many other cultures, and why has it consumed America's national consciousness to an almost bottomless degree since Europeans' earliest contacts with this land?

It is useful, unsurprisingly, to look for answers at humankind's beginnings. Or, at least, at one of the two concepts of what constitutes the beginnings, which is to say the biblical version. The Bible story varies in its details according to whose Bible you're taking it from, or which theologians or politicians supervised or commanded a particular interpretation or translation of the original writings. But the following should serve as a reasonable condensation of early Judeo-Christian theological ideas on how racial division began. Central to all versions is a character named Noah, the tenth patriarch in direct descent from Adam, and of whom it is written that his family, and his family alone, survived the Great Deluge That Cleansed Man of His Sins.

The biblical legend of Noah has it that he fathered three sons, whom he called Shem, Japheth, and Ham. Shem, the eldest and accorded a sort of tannish skin, became the ancestor of Abraham, from whom Shem is separated by eight generations. Abraham is regarded as the father of the Semitic world, from which sprang the historically consequential tribe called the Jews. Largely undisputed is what later happened to these Jews, which was to lose their ancestral lands and then suffer two millennia of Diaspora, or dispersement, a history culminating a mere half century ago in both the Jews' greatest calamity and their greatest triumph, in that order.

Japheth, the middle boy and lightest of skin shade, became father to the generations that eventually settled in the "Isles of the Gentiles"—

interpreted by scholars of these matters as Europe—and which people became the prototypical Caucasians, or "whites." Japheth's and his progeny's fates have excited relatively few theological emotions. But central to the story of Jim Crow is the legend of Ham, which *has* stirred a great many emotions.

The darkest-skinned of the three brothers, Ham was his family's habitual troublemaker. As accounted in Genesis, this youngest son badly irked his father when Ham expressed to his brothers contempt for Noah for having gotten drunk and fallen asleep, naked, on the ground, symbolic of moral lapse on Noah's part. But as patriarch, Noah resented both his son's impertinence and the inference of wrongdoing. During this episode Shem and Japheth threw a rug over their father and thereby preserved his dignity, and he thus gave them his blessing—and more important, he gave it to their descendants as well. But for Ham's disrespect, Noah put on him and his descendants a curse, one unto perpetuity, and further declared that Ham's descendants would forever be the servants of the descendants of Shem and Japheth.

Though Genesis doesn't specifically say it was Ham who ended up in Africa and thereby fathered that empty continent's peoples, generations of Jews living in the early first millennium encouraged this scenario until it became an oral tradition, one that over generations hardened into literal "truth." Thus the "accursed" Ham and the "accursed" generations that flowed from Ham's seed became the blacks of Africa, "facts" taken up over the ensuing centuries as a biblical, and thus an unimpeachable, truth. In short, it morphed into a theological justification for European domination over black Africans.

None of Noah's story is based on empirical historical evidence, even though much or all of it was, at least until the twentieth century, still widely believed, particularly by conservatively observant Christians and Jews. But throughout modern Western societies whites have willingly, indeed eagerly, adopted religious mythology as the moral grounding for their beliefs in white superiority and its corresponding certainty of black inferiority, including the foundations for racism in America's early political and social development. What lends substance in social terms to this phenomenon is that such biblical inventions are intimately connected with notions of afterlife and salvation and thus for many outweighed a moral cosmology based more on reason and scientifically observable experience.

Societies that developed apart from the West's Jewish-Christian model created their own versions of where everything came from, many of which accounts are as fanciful as the stories found in the Bible. And pertinent to the point of this book, like their Western counterparts they have generally involved some kind of divine social ordering, separating the "good" insiders from the "bad" outsiders. The Han Chinese, for example, wrote of blond and green-eyed people-creatures who looked like the monkeys that had supposedly spawned them; included was an explanation for the lowness of non-Chinese borderlanders based on the notion that they were the progeny of interbreeding between dogs and men. The brown-skinned peoples of South Asia came up with Hinduism, whose practitioners came to espouse a sort of mega–Jim Crow caste component still practiced in Indian society today. In a more realistic approach, Islam distinguished between fellow monotheists—Jews and Christians, who generally look pretty much like Muslims and whom Muslims were directed by the Koran to respect—and the barbarian polytheists, who usually looked conspicuously different and whom True Believers in Allah were permitted to deal with as circumstances warranted.

What in scientific terms actually accounts for the differences in mankind's vari-hued and vari-sculpted physiognomies has long been pretty much understood, though the timing and many of the details of the deviations are either fuzzy or debatable, especially that which constitutes the point in time when prehumans morphed into modern humans—though the latter issue is as much philosophical as it is scientific. One body of thought has it that creatures definable as humankind kicked off at some point a couple of million years ago when what had hitherto unarguably been animals began to pick up bits of stone to serve as extensions of their paws and slowly found to their undoubted astonishment that those bits were unexpectedly useful as weapons and tools. Another school places the crossover point with the beginning of speech, taken to mean discrete wordlike utterances as opposed to simple grunts of alarm or murmurs of satisfaction. Still others set the beginning of true thinking humanship at the point where protohumanoids' forefingers could be made to precisely oppose their thumbs, a milestone that marked a revolutionary change in dexterity by enabling the earliest humans to accomplish what animals couldn't. One notion seems as valid as the other, and none seems non-sensical, and in any case, whichever or whatever happened, it most certainly didn't happen overnight.

But the issue of race, a matter of extraordinary weight to humankind throughout history and the issue upon which Jim Crow turns, is something that would seem to be entirely extraneous to our origins as sentient human beings. We—meaning we human beings—possess obvious differences in our individual physical appearances. But if *race* as we today use the term posits a large enough degree of *substantive* dissimilarity between humans to rightly justify all the grief it has caused over the centuries, then the notions of its importance simply don't logically hang together.

Though many religious conservatives continue in their opposition to the scientific theory of evolution, the combined consensus of scientists and academics is virtually unanimous in their stand that man—what we regard as a human being as opposed to merely an advanced ape—sprang from a single point of origination. No credible physical evidence points to a shift from primate to man as having happened at more than one point on the planet, which multiple originations would provide the only logical support for a theory that different groups of contemporary humans (which is to say, different races) descended from unrelated forebears. All but surely, one and only one species of creatures became the ancestors of every human being now living. If another humanlike species did emerge in a separate jump from mere animalship, that group did not, evidently, survive. What's more, massive and mounting evidence verified by carbon dating of bones places the animal-to-people transformation in what is now Africa, specifically in the Great Rift Valley of the central eastern part of that continent. In the ultimate sense, one supposes that makes us all "African" in origin—African-American or African-Chechen or African-Japanese. Go back in your lineage far enough, and eventually you're going to get to your African ancestors. Which is not, however, to say those ancestors are necessarily going to have looked like modern sub-Saharan Africans, today's black Africans.

So when and how did humankind become so varied in its physiognomy? One, perhaps obtuse, observation might be made at the outset. Actually, we're not *really* quite so different as might be supposed. Of course, the bookends of human appearances are, on the face of it, pretty far apart. Look at the differences between a five-foot-two, blond, blue-eyed contestant in the Miss Sweden contest and a four-hundred-pound African-Hawaiian-Japanese sumo champion. One's short and petite, the other's a high mountain; one is about as light-skinned as we get, and the other's skin might be a kind of burnished mahogany. But just about all the other differences are environmental, internal and external sex and pro-creative organs the main exceptions. Miss Stockholm and the wrestler are perfectly capable of producing a healthy child, they stand a one-in-three chance of sharing the same blood type, and their organs line up identically with every other woman and man, respectively, in the world.

It takes a *very* long time for differences that are environmental—things that happen to us because of where, or how, we live—to evolve into genetic differences, the kind we're born with. We have family traits such as re-semblances in behavior or appearance (the famous Hapsburg jaw, for example), but in generational terms these tend to fade in and out fairly soon. Yet slowly and for reasons that must have had to do, at least in part, with adapting to the climate or to different levels of physical exertions, early humans in their African home began to look increasingly like we do today. Although lots of other species died out for various reasons—think of the dinosaurs—these first humans instead multiplied and got stronger and increasingly able to master their environment. And after an aeon or two, some of them began to migrate, eventually going ever farther away from Africa. A million or so years ago, the first great human emigration began when these now fully upright beings moved northward, into the Eurasian landmass. By one or two hundred thousand years ago they had covered vast parts of the planet, many having done so by routes and land bridges that have since changed or disappeared in the earth's continuous process of remaking itself via continental drift and altering sea levels.

As groups of migrating humans settled into their various domiciles on the planet, they became subject to new or different natural forces. Those who remained in Africa's equatorial regions experienced the greatest amount of direct sunlight, and over time their environmentally darkened skin became genetically darkened skin. Other groups, farther north or south from the most direct rays of sunlight, experienced the process in reverse, possibly to better produce vitamin D from less direct sunlight. Secondary racial characteristics also began to set in. Eastern Asians, for instance, developed—for reasons unknown to us—their own characteristic eyelid fold.

But what no group anywhere developed was a body mechanism that would cause any of the migratory and physically changing populations to become creatures that were genetically unequal or noninterbreedable. Instead, humankind everywhere shared everyone else's genetic composition. The vast majority of the bits and pieces making up a human being remained identical, including the brain and its *potential* abilities. Skin color, hair consistency, nose shape, lip size, height, weight—these variable characteristics are in the overall cosmos of the body the merest of incidentals. Yet what we today term "race" attaches to them a mountain of importance.

For as long as we've recorded human actions, the signs have been unmistakable that individuals and societies have judged each other on how closely or how differently one resembled the other. And because members of a community have for all sorts of reasons required the trust of one another to function successfully, it's difficult to see how things might have been otherwise. The opposite side of the same coin means that it's natural to be wary of others who don't speak, act, or believe like you—and, perhaps most of all, who don't look like you.

Only a few hundred years ago the most powerful white-skinned descendants of the Rift Valley prototypes, adventurous people from the Northern Hemisphere who called themselves by such terms as Frenchmen and Englishmen and Spaniards, happened to find what was for them a new hemisphere, one they called the Western Hemisphere because they sailed west to get to it. Unsurprisingly, these Europeans brought their peculiarly homegrown outlook with them, an outlook we could classify as subgroup Hispanic in the southern part of the "new" hemisphere, and—primarily—as subgroup Anglo in the northern part.

Though highly politically contentious with each other, the European subgroups comfortingly shared each other's whiteness and secondary bodily characteristics. Though the skin complexion range differentiating the European tribes was considerable between, say, the relatively light Scandinavians and relatively dark Iberians, this generally did not in the overall *European* outlook make the latter any the less "white" than the former. Almost all sneered at almost all the others in matters having to do with cultural differences—politics, religion, language, ambitions—and went to war over these subjects on a lethally repetitious schedule. But in their sense of a shared "racial" pedigree, Europeans have been deeply allied since the beginning of the notion of "Europe." Europeans of all stock existed inside their own self-defined Pale, while the physical characteristics distinguishing non-Europeans placed them irredeemably outside the boundaries of this Pale of race.

On the plus side of the balance sheet for today's Americans, the social beliefs of the subgroup Anglos, the men and women who sculpted a new nation out of the aboriginal-inhabited eastern seaboard of North America, were in many ways far ahead of their time. The constitution written by the political leaders of the new United States contained notions of such progressiveness that still today many of the world's nations have not adopted like ideas: the worth of the individual, the notion of government serving that individual rather than the other way around, the spectacularly bounteous guarantees involving political representation and jurisprudence and religious freedom—all were taken to heights that very few peoples had ever before seen. But as to these Founding Fathers' belief that the state of "whiteness" created by their God represented the highest form of humanity—well, there is little reason to think that the George Washingtons and Thomas Jeffersons and Patrick Henrys would have been, in spite of their intelligence, anything but men of their place and time. And the place and time of which they were a part accepted white supremacy without so much as any really serious twitter of doubt. The institution of slavery that they accepted—at bottom an outgrowth of their racial beliefs—meant profit and national growth, and so they justified such institution, and the majority of the American community fell in line with their justifications.

The Europeans who settled their newly "discovered" hemisphere faced their first problem with the people whom they found had already taken possession of these lands, the "Indians" who had beaten them to this side of the globe. The Europeans' sense of discovery and even of ownership was deeply felt, despite that thousands of years before Europeans found their "new" world, the "new" world had, of course, already been found. Nonetheless, the newcomers inevitably claimed as their own every square inch of what they had stumbled onto. Equally deeply felt was their reluctance to share it with those already here, especially since those already here were dark-skinned human beings who knew nothing of European deities and displayed little appreciation for or inclination to learn of such things. In this situation, the certainty of their own religious beliefs, combined with greed and hubris, gave the Europeans all the moral justification they needed to simply overwhelm the indigenous Americans. This or that group of European settlers would occasionally make a halfhearted stab at "civilizing" the natives, which is to say Christianizing them, but most Europeans found that simply isolating or murdering them represented the most efficient ways of dealing with what they viewed as an obstacle. And because their Judeo-Christian belief system regarded the people who were already here as "heathens" or "savages," their white-oriented consciences were little, if at all, troubled.

At the time white-skinned settlers found themselves encountering native Americans, the relationship between Europeans and black Africans— the latter the descendants of those who had remained in the Rift Valley and the continent surrounding it—hadn't been much of a problem for either group. Oddly, before the Europeans had left their own shores to come to the new world, comparatively little sense of white supremacy over black Africans had existed in Europe. Europeans were largely physically separated from black Africans and, in any event, long preoccupied instead with other concerns, many of which involved the developing of Western civilization for good and bad. Among the latter was their anti-Semitism, a prejudice motivated by distaste for what they considered a false faith and the belief that Jews were responsible for murdering their Christian God. Secondly, they had engaged in a centuries-long series of wars called the crusades, bloodletting aimed at regaining control over what Christians considered "their" religious sites and which bloodletting would, probably more to the point, push back or at least stop the Islamic tide threatening Christian Europe's political integrity.

The ancient institution of slavery is likely the deepest foundation for modern Western views on racial ordering, and thereby to the Jim Crow practices that came into a substantial existence in eighteenth- and nineteenth-century America. Forms of enslavement of humans of every skin color had long existed in virtually every major social group on earth, the practice of chattel ownership of humans (the equivalent of what was called slavery in America) or of keeping men and women in involuntary labor bondage (what was called peonage, or serfdom, in places such as Russia) having existed for at least five millennia, a span that far antedates any current religion except perhaps primitive Judaism. From classical times up through the mid–nineteenth century, white Europeans—most numerously Russians and Greeks and inhabitants of the Balkans—were kidnapped or captured in battle and taken to be sold in slave markets scattered over North Africa and the Middle East. Asians, too, practiced slavery on a massive scale, from India, through China and Japan, and into the Pacific islands, one Asian group often taking into bondage humans from another Asian group and sometimes even from within their own extended communities.

But no continent has been so exhaustively victimized by slavery as has Africa, particularly that part below the Sahara and commonly known as black Africa. Long after Christian and Islamic societies had become too powerful to themselves be seriously victimized by slavery, they in turn became the principal tormentors, the slave capturers. The tribal societies of black Africa were rarely strong enough to defend themselves from these powerful outsiders and, over the last half millennium, have been bled in three directions: about 11 million of these people have since 1500 been captured for the transatlantic trade—to North and South America and the Caribbean; at the same time slavers seized another 14 million or so for the largely Muslim markets of the Middle East; and finally, unknowable but vast numbers of blacks were enslaved in Africa itself, by other tribes and by European colonists for use in their African colonies.

For the three centuries prior to 1800 the flow of black slaves to the Western Hemisphere exceeded by roughly four times the concomitant white immigrant flow westward across the Atlantic. When the first blacks arrived in the Western Hemisphere, the color of their skin was not yet an innate mark of slave caste, something it would, however, quickly become. The main reason that a large proportion of blacks did come to be seen purely as involuntary and "natural" laborers was in large part due to their inability to resist or defend themselves (in itself not caused by an intellectual deficiency but a result of the disorientation of being violently uprooted from the familiar surrounds of their own civilization) and to their status as non-Christians. Secondly, slavers quickly realized their prey's extraordinary value as a relatively easy-to-obtain commodity. And by the fact of distance from familiar surrounds, Africans became grossly disoriented by their new existence in the Americas, contributing to a docility the whites who purchased them found helpful in controlling their chattels, the wresting of the riches America possessed almost in glut requiring just such trouble-free labor for its extraction. By comparison, native "Indian" populations were by virtue of their familiarity with local conditions far better prepared—especially in North America—to resist European control than were the enslaved Africans.

Thus the purchase of slaves almost everywhere in the New World came to represent the simple couplet of white European owners and black African captives. For these Europeans, slavery was a racial phenomenon: as whites came to a religious and moral understanding that enslavement of other whites was somehow degrading to the meaning of whiteness, their concept of the fundamental quality of slavery became entirely one of blackness, with blacks perforce excluded from white notions of common human brotherhood lest whites' consciences suffer from the cruelty of the system they were so assiduously constructing. Montesquieu summed up the conundrum of racial slavery with biting irony: "It is impossible for us to suppose these creatures [black men] to be men, because, allowing them to be men, a suspicion would follow that we ourselves are not Christian." And as a consequence blacks came to stand for one thing above all else: slavery. Before very much time was to pass, general beliefs about blackness would be shaped by the need to defend the institution of slavery, with blacks being viewed by whites as "natural" slaves and, a step further along this line of reasoning, all persons with *any* amount of black ancestry as being themselves not partially white but instead solely black.

But at the beginning of the African-American presence in what would become the United States, the nightmare of black-on-white racism still stood a bit over the horizon. In August 1619 blacks arrived in Anglo-settled North America, some twenty African men tucked in the cargo of a Dutch man-of-war that landed at Jamestown, in the colony called Virginia. Their journey to America hadn't been voluntary. Though their precise provenance within Africa isn't known, they were certainly seized somewhere on that continent and were then likely bought in barter by one of the tribes along the so-called Slave Coast, probably in exchange for trinkets or rum, and finally sold for export. The Dutch captain who transported them westward offered these twenty men to the first white Virginians he happened on to, settlers badly in need of labor to keep their crops healthy and thus their families fed.

Though the practical status of these Africans was as slaves, this initial American transaction in human cargo actually specified that they were to *legally* be held only as indentured servants, the same sort of contractual labor arrangement that then bound many whites to service in the New World. Indentureship signified that the bindees' services were, in theory at least, freely sold to their masters for a specified period, at the end of which the contract would expire and the bindees would go free. Indentureship did not mean that settlers actually owned the physical bodies of those bound to them. But because there was no end date on the contract of indentureship for these Africans, for them the difference between slave status and ordinary servitude was, in practical terms, largely moot. Tragically, such mootness would set a prophetic precedent.

More captured Africans soon joined this first group, and over their initial half-century in America the status of blacks brought on a succession of slave ships (carriers that were far more often owned by Northerners than they were by Southerners) sank from a watery uncertainty to a barbarous legality. In the first place, blacks quickly came to be distinguished from any other kind of indentured servant. Within five years of the first Jamestown deal, the colony's courts began to lay the legal groundwork irreversibly transforming Africans from indentured servants into chattels pure and simple. Finally, in 1670, a Virginia court decreed the status of non-Christian African men and women coming to America "shall be as slaves for their entire lives," and the line between blackness and slavery essentially disappeared in white estimation. Further legal refinements in Virginia rendered immaterial the morally delicate matter of black Christianity wherever or however long before acquired, which further cut off blacks from white consideration as fellow human beings. Other colonies, including those in the North, soon adopted much the same legal stance.

Importantly, none others but black Africans would meet this fate—slave status was never applied to any nonblacks whatsoever. Indentured whites could have their terms of labor extended for failure to perform or for legal infractions, but there was never a question of regarding such persons as chattels. Most remarkably, no serious attempt would ever be made at enslaving indigenous Americans—what the colonists called Indians in perpetuation of the early explorers' belief they had found India and the natives must therefore *be* Indian—nor was any effort ever made to even declare them "eligible" for slave status. In any case, the prospect of enslaving people who still enjoyed a high degree of martial prowess could hardly have been attractive to the European settlers. Though Indians were often nearly as dark-skinned as Africans, they placed on the social color scale as merely "brown." Slavery thus attained an ironclad synchronicity with blackness and Africanness.

At the same time the nascent legal system was fixing its position on slavery, the wider white lay society was setting the black man's social status. The primary tenet of such status held that no black could under any circumstances be the social equal of any white. One reason was that the white upper classes wished to keep the white lower classes content in their own varying degrees of lowness and deduced this goal would best be served by giving such lower white orders something over which they themselves could claim superiority, namely all black human beings. From this initial simple logic would eventually spring an entire universe ordering black-white relations.

By the second decade of the eighteenth century, the South Carolina colony's government had decreed a thirty-five-section "Act for the Better Ordering and Governing of Negroes and Slaves," a document setting into law that a child of one slave parent would always be, regardless of the race or status of the other parent, a slave as well. The act further required slave owners to keep weapons "in the most private and least-frequented room of the house" on payment of a three-pound fine if one was caught in violation, which violation was regarded as more easily facilitating deadly mischief on the part of slaves. For slaves committing any act of larceny, the legislators of South Carolina gave the slave owner the right to punish his slaves in virtually any way he saw fit, all the way up to and including the actual murder of his miscreant chattel.[1] Though all colonies ordained slave codes, it was the Southern colonies—most heavily populated with Africans—that from the beginning most intricately regulated these measures of black control.

Thus by the time the Revolutionary War victory allowed the transfiguration of Britain's American colonies into a union of American states, blackness of skin indisputably represented the new nation's lowest social condition. Though the Founding Fathers with their "all men being created equal" rhetoric might conceivably have forestalled such a tragedy, they didn't. Instead they chose to placate by now long-standing white views regarding blackness and, probably more important, the labor needs of the Southern states as well as the social sensibilities that had already achieved a standing as the South's "heritage." Being black was thereby confirmed as being low, lower even than the condition of white criminals, since those affected by a racial stigma could never escape such a blemish by serving out a mere sentence of incarceration. Black skin automatically made a human being's status lower than that of a white murderer on, for example,

---

[1] Fishel, 25.

the logic that the worst punishment any court could inflict never took away the freedom of the murderer's child—as it did the child of a slave. In a sense blackness was held as a state lower even than that of a draft horse, toward which creature cruelty could and fairly often did represent a punishable offense. Finally, blacks weren't even held as whole beings for census purposes: to count the number of inhabitants in forming congressional districts, the new nation's constitution specified that a slave would represent merely 60 percent of a person.

The most consequential change in the status of the African-American was the eventual near-total confinement of slave status to the Southern states. In the first decades of American independence, Northern slavery died a comparatively quick death, even though slavery had played a major part in the North's economy in the decades before the Revolution; as an example, out of New York City's total population at that time of seven thousand blacks, nearly a quarter were slaves, many of whom had been purchased on Wall Street's trading block. The institution retreated southward and remained there less because of North vs. South morals than because slaves simply weren't needed in the North: an economy that relied far more on factories than on farms required talents more grounded in skill and formal education than in mere strength. It thus was relatively easy, in an intellectual sense, for Northerners to indulge their region's growing moral unease with the principle of humans owning other humans and to put a legal end to the practice.

In the South, a single overriding factor made for an entirely different reality. In an age when the vast majority of cloth was woven from either relatively cheap cotton or relatively expensive wool, the importance of the former is self-evident. Cotton production represented the South's economic glory. But the ingredient that the growing of cotton required in greater quantity than any other was labor. And uneducated, unskilled labor was the best kind because anyone smart enough to do almost anything else wouldn't pick the stuff. So that meant slaves, people conveniently bereft of education and the ambition education produces because to educate them was illegal, and besides, as chattels, they were unfree to choose to do anything else.

So long as slavery as a legal conception existed in America, this "peculiar institution," as it was famously called, morally preoccupied people both for it and against it, while the other and less obvious issues regarding African-Americans and their association with European-Americans remained in relative shadow. But many such ancillary issues and considerations existed, even in the North.

After slavery settled southward, blacks carried many special and often deadly burdens. Not merely in the South but in every one of the Northern states as well, the fact of a black skin more often than not meant its possessor got the tailings of whatever resources America had to give—or Americans had to take. Blackness meant poverty, want of education, social ostracism, degradation, and early death from malnutrition and disease and lack of medical care. After the passage of the Fugitive Slave Act, requiring the return of escaped slaves to their owners, it meant that if a slave did manage to make it to the North, he or she could legally be handed back to a Southern master. That some seventy-five thousand slaves did achieve lasting freedom through escapes to the Northern states and to Canada represents almost as much a miracle as it does plain testament to the human yearning for freedom.

Though slavery became in very large part a Southern institution after the North legally abandoned it, responsibility for the condition extended throughout the *entire* American establishment, both during the colonial era and after the colonies achieved independence from Great Britain. Not only did America's Founding Fathers—its historical icons—own slaves, so, too, did ordinary businessmen in all parts of the country long profit from the slave trade through ownership of shares in slave-trading companies. When the young nation's plutocrats were writing the Constitution, these men *could* have stopped slavery then and there. But the political and economic price was too high. What the authors merely did instead do was write a constitution by whose provisions slavery could, and of course would, *someday* be ended. But never in America's early decades, not even in the North, did the melting-pot myth apply to persons of African heritage: the vaunted national cauldron only made room for whites of different ethnicities. Blacks were the enemy of all and, ironically, eventually a common nemesis that served to draw the white tribes closer together. In the event however, it was the South's adherence to slavery that settled the most tragic part of the nation's destiny, leading to internecine war as well as to a drawn-out postbellum racial nightmare from which America has still not healed itself.

By 1860 the United States had become two almost distinct nations: in the South a largely one-crop agrarian society with little immigration to invigorate its economy, no expansion room, almost no real cities, and little education to strengthen the masses of white people; and elsewhere, in the North and West, an industrialized people rich in railroads and metropolises, a society that, if often only grudgingly, welcomed shiploads of immigrants to work its factories, the possessor of a vast frontier it considered its own, and a community in which education was available to almost anyone who sought it. And overarching all these fundamental differences was the presence of slavery in the southern half of the nation and its prohibition in the northern—the Northern states having liberated their slaves shortly after the Revolution, even though most withheld equality from them, including the vote. The path that was pointing the nation's way to insoluble conflict and to the early deaths of six hundred thousand of its young men could have been altered but for the last element. That element—slavery—proved intractable to anything so plain as mere reason.

Casting the dilemma in stone was the economic reality that slavery was no inconsequential thing to the South. The region's 4 million slaves had by 1860 become indispensable to maintaining the cotton empire the Southern states had made of themselves. Where at the turn of the eighteenth century many thought the "peculiar institution" would, even below the Mason and Dixon Line, eventually die a natural death, a clever invention of a Massachusetts inventor named Eli Whitney changed any such prognosis. The device Mr. Whitney called his "gin" transformed what had been merely a region's lucrative cotton growing into a true culture unto itself. The gin—a device that efficiently performed the hard work of separating the cotton plant's seeds from its fiber—appeared just as the world's appetite for cotton seemed bottomless. All that was needed by the South to make its crop easy to pick and itself rich was an abundance of cheap labor to work the notoriously difficult-to-pick plant. From $5 million gained from cotton exports in 1810 (7 percent of the world's cotton exports at that time) when the gin had first been used, by 1860 the Southern states were exporting cotton worth $191 million, fully 57 percent of the world's total production. Any humanitarian talk of abolishing the labor system that made this wealth possible had by 1860 long since ceased. Not only did the South have some $2 billion in equity invested in its human chattels, many of the region's influential spokesmen earnestly believed the South's economy would collapse without this slave-based agriculture.

Though slavery profited the North as well as the South, many Northerners were becoming decreasingly sanguine about the morality of the institution that underpinned these enormous profits. By mid–nineteenth century, Northern unease had tightly coalesced around men and women calling themselves abolitionists, a few of whom were inordinately eloquent and a few others of whom harbored violent intentions in their laudable common desire to end slavery in America. As the Northerners' protestations against slavery grew ever less temperate in the face of what they viewed as unwarrantable Southern iniquity, white Southerners grew correspondingly more defensive about what *they* held as their honest and legal way of life. The ethical and learned institutions of the South—the churches and academies—had long since built a moral defense of slavery that absolved the region's practices and practitioners from wrongdoing. When the national constitution was written in the late 1700s, the writers had frankly admitted slavery was an evil, albeit necessary and probably inescapable given the country's economic and social realities at the time. But a century later the white South baldly characterized slavery as a *gift* to the black man. Didn't both God and Reason, they explained, declare the Negro inferior to the White Man, and wasn't the Black Man thus fulfilling his proper even though lesser station in life by serving a superior class that was at the same time providentially providing him with work and shelter and protection and, could it not be concluded, even bestowing a positive benevolence on such black vassals?

By the 1850s no middle ground seemed possible in the controversy. Pushing almost every other issue straight off the map, slavery increasingly preoccupied the nation—at least its Northern states—in those last ante-bellum years. In describing the engrossing effect it had on the American people, Missouri senator Thomas Hart Benton used the analogy of a biblical plague: "You could not look upon the table but there were frogs. You could not sit down at the banquet table but there were frogs. We could see nothing, touch nothing, have no measures proposed, without having this pestilence thrust before us."

Compromises, such as that forged in 1820 and named for the state of Missouri, were with supreme and heroic efforts worked out, arrangements that provided for one territory to come into the union where slavery was forever outlawed while another territory would retain its people's right to vote as to whether to permit the institution within its borders. When such measures seemed to give needed time to cool overheated tempers, Congress would upset the status quo with something like the Fugitive Slave Act, a law requiring captured runaway slaves who had reached the North to be returned to the South—and the palliatives would implode. As would, soon, the nation.

The man in whose name the rock of slavery rolled up against the hard place of legal resolution was Dred Scott, a slave. The immediate issue in Scott's colossally important—and colossally complicated—case was the freedom of one black man, while the obviously larger question was the spread of slavery into the territories. But likely the deepest theme was the moral worth of the African in America and the attendant inability of the law to resolve the conundrum of slavery itself.

The man at the center of one of America's most rancorous legal tempests was in reality the docile instrument of other and far more consequential plaintiffs in the case that nonetheless turned the humble plaintiff himself into a historical symbol. A slave from Virginia whose master had in the 1840s taken him into the state of Illinois and the then territory of Wisconsin—locations both free of slavery—and then brought him to slaveholding Missouri, Scott sued his owner in the latter state's courts with the intent to be declared a free man on account of his earlier entry into free territory. The real plaintiff—the abolition-minded owner—utilized the black man in hopes of obtaining a precedent-setting court decision that would grant Scott his freedom, though, ironically, he could himself have freed his human property simply by signing a document of manumission. After years butting through the Missouri courts, tribunals that consistently ruled against Scott, in 1856 the case reached the Supreme Court. Its significance to the issue of slavery was by now widely recognized in both North and South, the entire nation hanging on the court's decision. That decision, delivered by Chief Justice Roger Taney of Maryland, a slave state, stunned the nation and made war over the issue of slavery nearly inevitable.

What the court said was complex, but it boiled down to simple political dynamite. As to Dred Scott's status as a slave or not, the justices ruled Missouri law governed the issue from the moment Scott's owner returned his property to that state, and since Missouri courts had already clearly stated that Scott was in fact a slave and not a free citizen, Scott was thus disbarred from suing. Taney added in a legal aside famous for its moral brutality that Scott himself possessed no "rights which the white man was bound to respect." This decision alone would have legally satisfied the case as it was brought before the court. But Taney went on to remark that the framers of the Constitution meant, even if they hadn't precisely spelled it out, that Negroes were persons of an inferior order, despite Jefferson's famous dictum that "all men are created equal," and therefore weren't due the right of citizens to sue in a federal court. This factor in itself barred Scott from suing his owner or anyone else in a federal court.

But then the real bombshell exploded. Though not a part of the suit, Chief Justice Taney personally believed the rapidly growing country needed a decision on the larger issue of the spread of slavery as more states joined the Union. Here the court said that Scott's physically being in a slave state or a free state was in itself immaterial, the reason for such immateriality arising from its finding that the Missouri Compromise, an act of Congress, was itself unconstitutional because it impinged upon a citizen's right to hold property—*including slaves*—wherever such citizens wished. In short, Taney ruled that Congress had no right to exclude slavery from any territory, leading to the legally inescapable conclusion that, as the laws then stood, slavery could spread anywhere in the nation;

conceivably, it could even return to the Northern states where state legislatures had decades earlier made the practice illegal. In fine, the court decided that only a constitutional amendment, not merely an act of Congress, could outlaw slavery. And such act is precisely what it eventually took, together with four years of war, to end the peculiar institution.

With the Dred Scott decision, the nation's glue of compromise came undone in a giant rending of Northern disgust. If the Supreme Court had meant to lay the issue to rest, its action achieved precisely the opposite result. In late 1858, Abraham Lincoln summed up the outcome of the Dred Scott case perfectly. It meant, according to the politician in his "Housed Divided" speech, that no slave or his descendants, meaning just about every black person in America, could ever be a citizen of any state as the Constitution used the term *citizen*. Taney would later defend his decision by saying that "the African race in the United States even when free, are everywhere a degraded class, and exercise no political influence. The privileges they are allowed to enjoy, are accorded to them as a matter of kindness and benevolence rather than of right. . . . They were not looked upon as citizens by the contracting parties who formed the Constitution. They were evidently not supposed to be included by the term 'citizens.' " From those words to the Civil War was drawn a line as straight as a die.

Though historians heatedly dispute the war's provenance, make no mistake but that slavery was what the Civil War was about. It was not *at its core* about tariffs, nor about states' rights, nor about any other dispute between the then two great groupings of America's states. Without the issue of slavery, it is inconceivable that such other issues or disputes as existed could ever have led to the tidal flow of blood that was the War Between the States. Yet the man whose person, presence, and policies were the heart of the Civil War famously termed it a struggle not to end slavery but instead to preserve the republic.

Whatever Abraham Lincoln's personal beliefs regarding slavery or blacks, his wartime statesmanship was aimed not at emancipation or abolishing slavery but at denying success to the Southern states in their attempt to free themselves of membership in the United States. "My paramount objective in this struggle," he wrote, "is to save the Union, and not either to save or destroy slavery." He made clear, however, that this represented his *official* view and equally clear that his *personal* wish was that "all men everywhere could be free," expressing his belief in public and in private of the evil of "one man owning another." Yet if early in the war the president could have bought peace for the price of continued slavery, he would have done so without a moment's hesitation. Even the Emancipation Proclamation—today held by many as the supreme icon of his life—has been misrepresented as something more altruistic than the military necessity that Lincoln considered it.

Though much has been made of the fact that the Emancipation Proclamation was a gradualist measure that neither banned slavery nor even freed slaves in the non-Confederate border states—Delaware, Maryland, Missouri, and Kentucky—where the institution remained legal throughout the war, it did nonetheless represent a death blow to the principle of holding humans as chattels in America. Furthermore, it is unimaginable that slavery could have long endured anywhere in the country after the war ended in victory for the North, even in the nonseceding slave states.

Yet if the Northern emancipationists hoped for a presidential edict that would bestow freedom on the nation's 4 million slaves, they were deeply disappointed with what Lincoln gave them. In mid-1862, with the war only a little more than a year old and Union forces suffering significant battlefield defeats, Lincoln feared that slaveholding border states that had remained in the Union despite their sympathy with the aims and ideals of the Confederacy would, if pushed too far, join the rebellion. But to undercut a sweeping congressional drive to free slaves that would not only provoke these border states but also harden the seceded states' resolve to press the war, Lincoln finally acted on the slavery issue in September 1862. Helpfully buoyed by a just-won major victory at Antietam, the president on the twenty-second day of that month signed his Emancipation Proclamation, its terms to take effect the following January 1. Those terms, though, were not nearly as encompassing of black freedom as they have been imagined in the document's roseate historical afterglow.

In what he called a "fit and necessary war measure," and while declaring his desire to compensate slave owners for their losses, the president's executive order freed slaves only in areas "in rebellion against the United States," leaving in bondage those slaves in the border states and—in a historical oddity—in specific portions of Virginia and Louisiana as well as a few other oddments of territory considered technically not to be in a state of rebellion against the United States. Lincoln had freed slaves (knowing, of course, that his writ could extend only as far as Union armies could back it up), but he had not abolished slavery in America. The president also well understood the order could not withstand constitutional scrutiny, a point of some moment what with Roger Taney of the Dred Scott decision still reigning as chief justice of the United States.

Congress, too, understood the fragility of Lincoln's decree as well as did its author. In consequence, a groundswell arose to create an amendment to the Constitution to make that document color-blind, to provide that America's laws would tolerate neither legal recognition of the whiteness or the blackness of its citizens' skins nor of any hue in between. It became the first—and the last—attempt Congress would make to legally prohibit racial classifications in the Constitution. It failed primarily because the implications of such a notion were plainly too overwhelming even for a Congress resolved on the eradication of slavery. Instead a constitutional amendment—the Thirteenth—that merely abolished slavery passed the Congress some three months before the war's end and was ratified by the end of that same year. Resolving the slavery issue through the force of arms had cost some six hundred thousand lives, but the enormous price meant the former slave states would remain a part of the United States.

For all its cost, the Civil War gave Americans from Africa and their descendants nothing so provocative or progressive or magnificent as a nation whose laws would in fact be color-blind, nor a nation in which racism and white supremacy might conceivably have been forced to an early death through wiser and stronger postbellum governance. But it did at least enable their release from chattel bondage. They would no longer be owned. It didn't give them suffrage or compensation, and it left fundamental questions as to the caliber of their citizenship. But it reendowed them with their bodies, with rights, and at last, with some control over their lives.

2

SLAVERY TRANSFORMED
INTO PEONAGE
1865–1896

Horrified by the changed status of blacks, before the war's cannons had wholly cooled Southerners began a long counterattack aimed at re-subjugating their former slaves. Their efforts culminated on a calamitously historic day in 1896 when, after three decades of fattening, Jim Crow came to maturity armored by the Supreme Court with the full force of the Constitution. To placate white America's prejudice, the nation's highest court held aloft its collective forefingers to the winds of the time and, abasing the principles on which the nation had notionally been raised, gave its imprimatur to the perpetuation of racial caste.

It seemed obvious to the American people in the spring of 1865 that mere peace had not resolved the greatest dilemma in American history, that of race. True, after four years of combat and six hundred thousand war-related deaths, the national fratricide had finally come to an end. But sprawling southward from Appomattox, the dusty Virginia crossroads where General Lee had surrendered his gray-clad armies to General Grant, limitless vistas of social chaos and of devastated cities and farmland eloquently condensed the conflict's legacy. The defeated Confederacy lay paralyzed, the Union armies' scorched-earth tactics having ensured that the South's infrastructure—its factories and farms and schools, its roads and shipping and rail systems—had been rendered largely unusable. The

German-born journalist Carl Schurz wrote of what he saw by likening the land to "a broad black streak of ruin and desolation . . . lonesome smoke-stacks, surrounded by dark heaps of ashes and cinders marking the spots where human habitations had stood . . . with here and there a sickly patch of cotton or corn cultivated by Negro squatters."[1]

Most consequential, more so even than its broken stones and lifeless fields, the South's human relationships had been turned upside down. A public order that had for two centuries framed a huge part of Southern social intercourse was that spring suddenly unlawful, the old relationship of master to slave now dead. But while few white Southerners could imagine a life based on equality with their former human property, a significant number already envisaged a future for African-Americans not altogether different from the way such things had always been.

Before the moon rose on the first night of peace, freedom was already proving more illusory than real for the millions of black men and women spread out all over the eleven defeated states. The South's roads were bursting with homeless former slaves suddenly cut off from the only roots most of them had ever known and few of whom possessed the slimmest notion of where they could go or what they should do. Many simply roamed directionless, bereft of a home for the first time in their lives and moving for little reason other than that they now had the *freedom* to move. Educated in little other than how to work from first light to last in their masters' homes and fields, for these black millions President Lincoln's freedom meant in real terms little other than a "right" to fend for themselves. Frederick Douglass saw the truth of their liberty, writing at the time that the former slave had "neither property, money, or friends . . . he was free from the old plantation, but he had nothing but the dusty road under his feet . . . he was turned loose naked, hungry, and destitute to the open sky." What was needed for the freed black more than anything, needed greater even than the legal protections of the federal government, was the means with which to survive. Food and clothing and shelter, the

[1] Latham, 27.

fundamental prerequisites of life itself, existed, if at all, in disastrously short supply.

But if the South's blacks found themselves bereft of direction, the former beneficiaries of their labor quickly began to regain their own social bearings. The vast majority of the region's whites had no doubt of the need for a racial relationship to replace what their military defeat had cost them. Almost immediately whites began to map out a new master-servant relationship, one they hoped would look as much as possible like the old— excepting little other than its element of actual human ownership. Still morally certain of their own racial superiority, whites instinctively believed the only way they would keep from drowning in a black sea was to reestablish iron control over their former slaves, what would effectively evolve into a system of serflike peonage.

It isn't hard to understand white Southern behavior in the aftermath of the war. More than any other factor, Southerners' immediate anxiety amounted to a well-justified fear of black retaliation for two centuries of enslavement, dispossession, corporeal and psychological cruelty, and social and familial fragmentation. White Southerners saw clearly that the North and its legislature possessed neither a grand vision nor even a practical plan as to how to manage the newly freed slaves. What was more, any notions of recompense for the value of the South's lost slaves had long since been put aside in the bitterness of the war's last years and the finality of the Confederacy's defeat. Southerners also saw that the North's once ardent abolitionists seemed to forget about black concerns once their overarching principle of destroying the *institution* of slavery had been achieved. In fact, most Northerners stood squarely against voting rights for blacks, judging them too uneducated to vote intelligently. (In 1865 only six Northern states—New York, Maine, Massachusetts, New Hampshire, Rhode Island, and Vermont—allowed African-Americans to vote, which fact not unreasonably elicited Southern charges of hypocrisy.) The federal government's newly established but underfunded Freedmen's Bureau, an agency set up mainly to help blacks get on their economic feet, made little more than a dent in meeting the needs of the former slaves. Nor was talk of granting blacks homesteads in the Western states and territories acted upon, the notion instead vetoed by racist interests in Congress determined to keep the West white.

In a spirit of reconciliation, the North allowed the Southern state governments to continue in operation, with ex-Confederate officers and officeholders leading most such administrations. These largely freewheeling provisional legislatures set as their first task the establishment of laws controlling life for freed blacks, statutes that effectively resumed prewar patterns of black exclusion from the South's public life. The measures controlled nearly every aspect of black life, with whites allowed to employ draconian remedies against recalcitrant blacks. These laws soon became known simply as the Black Codes.

There was nothing complicated about this strategy, actions whites viewed as necessary for their own safety as well as to any hope of rebuilding the South in its former prosperous image. The lately rebelling states intended a return to—perhaps *continuation of* is more accurate—virtually the same social relationship between whites and now-freed blacks as that which had existed before the Confederacy's defeat. To achieve it, the Black Codes were deliberately designed to be restrictive and harsh in their application. One famous tactic involved convicting blacks of some crime, usually a minor one, and when such victims were unable to pay the fine—which was, of course, just about always—they were classified as convicted "vagrants" and sentenced to hard labor to pay off the "debt." While under sentence, white keepers were empowered to apply corporal punishment as judged necessary.

What would a few decades later harden into a systematically and formally legislated Jim Crow system saw many of its particulars first spelled out in the Black Codes. For example, almost all barred African-Americans from testifying against whites in a court of law, or from serving on juries. Many forbade blacks from entering towns and cities without police permission, and others prohibited them from remaining overnight in a given locale. The Codes often required public transportation to segregate facilities for blacks or even to bar them entirely from trains, carriages, and omnibuses. Thousands of the region's theaters, parks, hotels, restaurants, and shops were closed to blacks under the Codes, and they were even barred from admission to the region's insane asylums and poorhouses and orphanages. As was the case with serfs in czarist Russia, blacks were prohibited from moving from one location to another without their employers' written permission. Whites refused to share the vote on the rationale that African-Americans were largely uneducated, though this reasoning was never raised to disfranchise equally illiterate whites.

Most intimidating to the future of African-Americans, though, was black exclusion from proper schools. Georgia, Arkansas, and Texas allowed only whites to attend schools, and some states that had managed to retain their prewar schools now closed them entirely because of fear they would be forced by the federal authorities to admit blacks equally with whites. Even the Northern missionaries, men and women who in the chaos left from the war fanned out over the South to set up schools for freed blacks, met with fierce resistance from local whites. One startled Northerner commented that whites acted as though "the blacks at large still belong to the whites at large." He was in fact not far off the mark: underlying every facet of the Codes and of Southern behavior was the presumption that blacks possessed no rights whatsoever that any white person could be forced to respect.

It should be understood that many of these same attitudes and not a few of the same laws had long existed in the Northern states and would continue for many years after the war ended to plague blacks living in the North. In light of this, Southerners were quick to charge Yankees with a double standard for their own generally still-deplorable state of black civil rights. But the Southern variants aimed squarely at any notion of true emancipation for the region's newly freed slaves, men and women who in 1865 formed the vast majority of the nation's total African-American population. Southerners adamantly maintained that freed blacks were unfit to assume the civic responsibilities and attendant rights that had at least theoretically come with emancipation, a stance that at the time and in light of blacks' lack of education (which, of course, had been due to no fault of their own) was not entirely illogical—though the logic was not, to repeat, extended to uneducated whites. But whites strove to hold back the former slaves from the education necessary to *ever* give them the founding on which to cast a considered ballot, taking from the white stance any conceivable justice it might have borne and placing it squarely in the clothing of racial bigotry. Melville Myers, a South Carolina newspaper editor, justified his state's Black Codes by declaring the Negro race "had always been excluded, as a separate class, from all civilized governments and the family of nations . . . doomed by a mysterious and divine ordination." More moderate but no less sincere was the former Confederate general Benjamin G. Humphreys, who added his own voice to the debate: "The Negro is free, whether we like it or not . . . to be free, however, [that] does not make him a citizen or entitle him to social or political equality with the white man."

For the two years following the war this state of black debasement went on virtually unchecked in the South, the Black Codes becoming ever more exhaustive in controlling life for the region's African-Americans. While Southerners defensively insisted what they were doing wasn't reenslavement but instead merely the bringing of order out of chaos, Northern Republican politicians increasingly angrily deplored the behavior of their former enemies. In fact, legions of ordinary Northerners—farmers, city dwellers, the uneducated as well as the learned, people who regarded their own dead as having died *specifically* on the altar of black emancipation from slavery—were furious at their former enemies for annulling the expected emancipation that had been won at the cost of four years of national butchery. The *Chicago Tribune* spoke for this Northern view when it editorialized that "the men of the North will convert the state of Mississippi into a frogpond before they allow any such laws to disgrace one foot of soil in which the bones of our soldiers sleep and over which the flag of freedom waves."[2]

Preoccupied with simply winning the war, Lincoln had left much of his postwar planning in limbo, evidently intending to get around to it after victory was finally achieved. His death thoroughly confounded the situation. In truth, Lincoln's most egregious presidential fault likely *was* his

[2] Ginzberg, 137.

failure to establish a clear image of what the South would need for recovery, especially in light of the dimwit who was to be his successor. When Andrew Johnson inherited the presidency days after the last shots of the conflict had been fired, the new and woefully incapable chief executive was presented with a desperate need to establish such policies. And as Lincoln had been aware that nothing could be accomplished independently of Congress, even Johnson was able to understand this reality. The tragedy for the nation's future was that where Lincoln possessed the sensitivity and skills to work with an often-cantankerous legislature, President Johnson quickly showed himself wholly inept at either negotiation or conciliation. Within months of his accession, the chief executive and the legislature had become locked in an impasse over the handling of the defeated South and its millions of destitute and desperate former slaves.

Andrew Johnson was a Tennessee Democratic senator—albeit one who had obviously remained politically loyal to the Union—who had been chosen by the Republican Lincoln mainly to balance the latter's wartime coalition administration. Not surprising given his home state, Johnson was a committed white supremacist and his Tennessee roots lent him a deep vein of sympathy toward the South's misery. Alas, it was a sympathy little shared in the wake of the war by a Radical-dominated Congress out to show the Union's four-year-long enemy exactly who had beaten whom.

Johnson as president initially made sincere efforts to nudge Southerners into bringing the freed slaves into something like a place of their own in their region's social system. Specifically, he tried to convince Southern leaders to enfranchise at least those blacks who were either educated or owned property or businesses, a segment of the South's black population that began to increase in this early "Reconstruction era" (the term referred to the rebuilding, or restoration, of the South in the wake of the Civil War) over which Johnson was shakily presiding.

But Southern leaders showed themselves either too shortsighted or too prejudiced to consider any course that might even marginally further black social advances, and they firmly rejected the president's recommendation. This rejection in turn deepened the enmity of the congressional Radical wing, disgusted with Johnson's inability to force rights for blacks on the

white South—rights, to repeat, that many in the legislature understandably believed had already been won through force of arms.

Johnson was tragically confounded by his failure to persuade the South
to ameliorate its stance. Never genuinely sympathetic toward black aspirations in the first place, his efforts on their behalf fell off sharply as he
adopted the simplistic attitude that, since the former slaves were now free,
they could either take care of themselves or, incredibly, look for help from
the racist-dominated provisional governments ruling in the former Confederate state capitals with their noxious Black Codes. When Johnson
shockingly vetoed a bill extending the life of the Freedmen's Bureau (he
tried to justify himself by explaining that the position of the freedman in
the South wasn't "as bad as may at first be imagined," as though he were
unaware of the spreading and ever-fiercer Codes), the discord between
Congress and president would within the year culminate in the former
impeaching the latter.

Most legislators understood that the Thirteenth Amendment's abol-
ishment of slavery left unanswered almost every question dealing with how
4 million newly freed slaves were going to fit into the national polity: the
amendment had forbidden slavery itself, but the issues of rights for
African-Americans *beyond* the now-settled matter of involuntary servitude
remained virtually terra incognita. Though sympathy toward African-
Americans was by no means universal in Congress, many legislators were
determined to protect the South's blacks, and in 1866 they undertook to
pass a bill they hoped would accomplish that goal.

Congress started by approving a civil rights bill whose intention was
unmistakable in its floridly hopeful title: "An Act to protect *all* Persons in
the United States in their Civil Rights, and furnish the Means of their
Vindication." Repudiating the Supreme Court's calamitous Dred Scott
verdict, the act first of all declared African-Americans to be *citizens* and
thereby committed the power of the government to protect their rights *as*
citizens. But the president foolishly vetoed Congress's bill, reasoning that
federal law should remain out of such issues, areas in which it had been
thought by the Southern states—and by some Northern legislators—ex-
pedient to discriminate between the two races.

In his refusal to legislate black equality by granting African-Americans citizenship and the rights attached to such status, the president was not, to be sure, without supporters, even from the North. But the majority of Congress clearly equated Johnson's policy with the South's suspect tactics, his ideas dispiritingly similar to those that had led the Southern states to secede five years earlier. What was more, Northern outrage at the South's snowballing Black Codes had come to the boiling point. Congress thus overrode Johnson's veto—by a single vote—and, for good measure, re-passed the Freedmen's Bureau bill, which Johnson revetoed, but which second veto Congress overrode as well.

Congress was now faced with the reality that for a guarantee of civil rights for blacks to withstand partisan assault, it must eventually take the form of a constitutional amendment: a mere act of Congress could, and likely would, be overturned by a simple majority vote of some future Democratic-controlled Congress. Achieving such an amendment thus went into the hopper as the paramount and critical hurdle facing the post-bellum federal legislature.

In truth, the agenda in the mostly Republican Congress was not *entirely* founded on simple altruism toward the newly freed slaves. At stake also was the Republican Party's preservation of congressional control based on a new legislative arithmetic that had come hand in hand with the end of slavery. Slaves had hitherto, as we've seen, counted as three-fifths of a person for purposes of representation in the House of Representatives. But with emancipation, each suddenly counted as a *full* person. That meant that when all the former Confederate states reentered the national legislature, together they would be entitled to an estimated twelve to eighteen additional seats in the House of Representatives, not to mention a like number of additional electoral college seats, one of which went with each congressman, and this paradoxically meant these lately rebellious states would have *more* power in Congress than the already considerable clout they had enjoyed before their secession. And with blacks kept from the ballot box in the South, it would be the white Southern Democrats and their (mostly Democratic) Northern allies who would benefit, not the Republicans, who considered, with justice, that the war's outcome should obviously favor the foes of those who meant to keep blacks in their current state of civil debasement.

The majority of Congress, though, agreed the country needed an amendment providing a safety frame under which blacks would be blended to the extent possible into America's democracy. The discord in finding a workable formula hung on the question of scope. The more radical ("liberal" in today's reckoning of the term) members of Congress—by and large its Republicans—forcefully demanded a guarantee of "nondiscrimination" in the treatment of blacks. That would mean that the nation's laws should essentially be color-blind, a concept not then found anywhere in the Constitution. The Democrats (the "conservatives" and Southern-leaning) opted for a less-embracing formula of "equal protections under the law." In short, the latter won, and the resulting constitutional amendment would, with savage irony, become at once the most important civil guarantee in the nation's history while also managing to plant a hole in the Constitution big enough for the Jim Crow juggernaut that would soon come roaring through it.

In its first and most important section, the amendment—the Fourteenth—met Congress's minimum goal, namely that of defining citizenship and including African-Americans within that definition. Equally important, it proclaimed that no state could "deny to any person within its jurisdiction the equal protection of the laws." The remaining sections were more addressed to the needs of the moment: the second gave Southern states the choice between black suffrage or losing seats in the House, which all but forced them to extend the franchise to the freed slaves; the third disbarred from office Confederate leaders who swore an oath of allegiance to the United States and its Constitution and later rebelled; and the fourth wiped out—"forgave"—the U.S. government's responsibility for the war debt of the Confederacy.

Infinitely less radical than the notion of a color-blind constitution, the amendment's concept of "equality" under the law did effectively destroy the worst of the Black Codes, the proto–Jim Crow statutes that were so offensive to liberal Northerners, to say nothing of the harm they inflicted on Southern blacks. But where color blindness would have meant just that—in other words, that color, or race, would be an irrelevancy to the law, and that discrimination based on color would therefore be illegal—mere "equality" in the Fourteenth Amendment would mean nothing of the sort. This was no error or accident in wording: Congress understood perfectly the distinction it had made, and what the legislators in 1866 believed the nation would support was what it gave the nation. They did not grant a guarantee that the black man would as a result of prohibiting discrimination be fully included in the national polity. Instead, the states—their courts and governments—would in practical terms retain the power to decide precisely what constituted such "equal protection under the law." Which really meant the states would be allowed to discriminate by race as they themselves saw fit.

Further marking the Fourteenth Amendment's provenance was the showdown to which its passage had led between the power centers at the opposing ends of Pennsylvania Avenue, a battle ending in impeachment, which fundamentally translated to a case of America's North vs. America's South. The crux of the collision was based on President Johnson's bitter personal opposition to the Fourteenth Amendment, the chief executive being convinced its provisions would be unacceptable to the South and thereby end up destroying any hope of reconciliation between the late belligerents. Johnson urged the Southern states not to ratify the amendment, a position earning him virtually universal detestation from the congressional Republican majority for rejecting what it defiantly held as its "minimum terms." But every Southern state except, paradoxically, Johnson's own Tennessee did in fact vote against passage of the Fourteenth Amendment, during which voting Southern atrocities against blacks were being widely reported in the North and inciting furious indignation along broad swaths of the latter region's public opinion.

All of this convinced Congress that what was needed was another, less gentle, approach to the former Confederate states. And what Congress decided on dramatically changed the victors' treatment of the vanquished that had stood as the norm for the two years immediately following the war. In the spring of 1867, Congress quashed the South's self-installed provisional governments and turned the former Confederacy over to a far less indulgent regime under the direct control of Union armies and Yankee military governors.

Congress designed military control to achieve a single and extremely focused outcome. Before the former Confederate states' representatives would be readmitted to the national congress, each legislative body would be required to write a new constitution categorically granting the right to vote to blacks. After doing that, each state would then be required to ratify the Fourteenth Amendment. When, and only when, these two conditions were met, could each state again send senators and representatives to Washington, where, now representing *all* their people (that according to Congress's line of reasoning—of course no woman of *any* color had the vote), the delegations would be duly seated.

Congress installed one more safeguard. To deny the president the opportunity to thwart Congress's intent by removing one or more of the military governors or other officials upholding these new policies, the Senate came up with the so-called Tenure-of-Office Act, requiring the chief executive to obtain the Senate's approval before being allowed to oust officials whose appointments the Senate had previously concurred in. With some logic, Johnson believed that giving in to what he viewed as such unconstitutional coercion would effectively equate to the emasculation of the office of the presidency. The president unsurprisingly vetoed the bill, and the Congress unsurprisingly overrode the veto.

The broad outline of what represented one of the few truly explosive government crises in American history was drawn as follows. The president threw back Congress's gauntlet—the override vote—by firing officials he believed were "Africanizing" the South, which is to say were being overly sympathetic to black aspirations for equality. Congressional leaders immediately threw it right back. For the specific act of firing Edwin Stanton, his own secretary of war but a close ally of the congressional Radicals—a deed by which the chief executive unquestionably violated the trap-setting but, at least in constitutional terms, highly problematic Tenure-of-Office Act—the House of Representatives impeached the by now deeply unpopular as well as probably unhinged president (Johnson's many enemies had taken to calling him "this offspring of assassination").

The dramatic climax of the Senate trial following the impeachment is one of the most familiar stories in American history: the upper chamber failed by a single vote to gain the required two-thirds majority to convict, this in spite of the Radicals' threat that any senator voting to acquit would face "torture on the gibbet of everlasting obloquy," rhetoric emblematic of the white-hot rage aroused by this Washington passion play. In the event, the actions for which Johnson was impeached were certainly not criminal (however stupid they may have been), at least not in the required sense of "high crimes and misdemeanors" required for the removal of a president. The whole affair was, rather, a highly dangerous test of whether the legislative branch could get away with removing a president for political differences between itself and the executive branch. Nonetheless, as a national leader, Andrew Johnson was effectively destroyed by these goings-on. And the long-range effects on Americans of African heritage would be far more catastrophic than merely how Johnson would be viewed by posterity.

Two years after the war ended, the proud and obstinate white population of the defeated Confederacy was given its one serious crack at acquiescing to the Northern concept of racial justice or, if that was beyond possibility, at least to a racial modus vivendi containing a modicum of justice. Either option if even halfway successful would have meant a happier future for the South than what actually came its way. In 1867, Congress sent to the South military-backed governments to make this all-important facet of Reconstruction work, which meant somehow achieving black suffrage over a deeply ingrained tradition of white supremacy.

One of the more iniquitous myths of American history relates to the breakdown of Reconstruction, particularly the supposed failure of African-Americans to make good on their golden chance to participate in government. Bookshelves sag under the weight of portrayals of carpetbaggers and scalawags and their uneducated black puppets who together misgoverned the South in a legislative orgy of incompetence, venality, and corruption. But what really transpired bears little connection to this white-inspired construct.

What was meant to happen was this. Because for the two years follow-ing the war powerful Southern whites so plainly demonstrated their in-tention to keep blacks in a state as close as possible to rightsless peonage, the federal government would step in and rectify a situation that had gotten legions of Northerners into a state of high moral outrage. The Constitution was at the time bereft of any provision that would allow the federal government to actually dictate suffrage requirements, but Congress cleverly declared that since the structures they had set up to govern the South in lieu of the normal individual state governments—namely five military districts, each containing a portion of the former states of the Confederacy—were not themselves states, therefore specific suffrage terms *could* be dictated by the military governors of these districts. Congress's requirements stipulated that all adult males should be registered, both white and black, and such was therefore what the newly installed military governors set about doing. After accomplishing this registration, the Southern states were to be formally readmitted to the national Congress, but only *after* their own state legislatures, elected by universal male suf-frage, ratified the Fourteenth Amendment. This sequence of events in fact took place, every one of the ex-Confederate states eventually complying, the last to do so being formally readmitted to the Union in 1870.

But white Southern interests twisted this hopeful scenario, while Con-gress shortsightedly and tragically neglected its substance. Alien Repub-lican Party governments largely controlled the South as a result of these grand tactics, governmental bodies largely composed of three elements. First were the "carpetbaggers," Northerners, mostly white, who came South and were stereotypically accompanied by satchels fashioned from scraps of carpet stitched together and into which their meager belongings were stuffed. Many were honest, idealistic, and competent politicians and bureaucrats, and many were dishonest, venal, and utterly untutored in government. The "scalawags" were Southern whites who openly sympa-thized with the new federally imposed order. Many were honest, idealistic, and competent in their contributions to governance, and many others were, as was the case with carpetbaggers, just the opposite. And filling out the ruling administrations were black men elected from the South and, in fact, most of whom had before the war been free rather than slaves. Many were honest, idealistic, and—again—competent, and some were just the opposite. These white aliens and black Southerners gained their legislative seats largely because the bulk of the South's whites boycotted elections they knew they could neither win nor control.

A little-discussed element of social tragedy went hand in hand with these events. The right to vote that was gained by blacks at this time was, of course, equally gained by poor whites, who before the war had widely been disfranchised by property-qualification requirements. Thus for the first time for this latter group, too, the ballot box was free and open. A small fraction of this class actually threw their lot in with the white Northern reformers and blacks and was accordingly lumped by Southern Democrats in with the overall "scalawag" element.

But ignorance compounded what would become the ultimate tragedy of Reconstruction. Centuries of assumed superiority was buried as deeply in the majority of poor Southern whites as it was in their economic betters who lived in the substantial houses of the cities and gracious mansions of the plantations. Had the exploited whites ever been led to a realization that political cooperation between themselves and blacks in voting against the moneyed classes' control might have opened undreamed-of opportunities, the postbellum South might well have avoided a century of social injustice and its place at the bottom of the American economic ladder.

But in the real way history played out, the vast majority of *all* Southern whites viewed the blacks amongst them as dangerous competition for political power that the latter would if allowed to—at least in the realm of white fears—monopolize in revenge for two centuries of enslavement. Furthermore, such deeply ingrained white prejudice simply could not countenance an outcome suggesting social equality between the races. The result was that wealthy whites reaped a bountiful harvest from the reality of race prejudice: not only did poor whites not cooperate with blacks, but their racial hatreds deepened ever further as they watched blacks gain political power under Reconstruction's federal patronage at the same time their own acquiescence to the control of rich whites settled into stone.

African-Americans elected to the Southern state legislatures (a handful of blacks were also sent to the U.S. House of Representatives, and two—both from Mississippi—to the U.S. Senate) and to local offices represented, of course, only a minuscule fraction of Southern blacks. But in the short years of black participation in the franchise and in Southern legislation, historic and substantive gains were made in the region's governance. Notably, the rights of minorities and of women in many of the former Confederate states were secured for the first time in history. Suffrage without any property requirements was extended to all adult males, as contrasted with the property-ownership ballot restrictions that had existed before the war. And free education spread right across the South, in some parts of the former Confederacy for the first time.

Perversely, despite the Reconstruction-era efforts to enfranchise Southern blacks, no similar efforts or equal enfranchisement came anywhere near reality in the North. Southerners took comfort, perhaps with logic even if with little moral justification, in the Northern hypocrisy that forced black suffrage on the South when the majority of the Northern states continued to prevent blacks from voting at home. To respond to this very real duplicity, the Radical-controlled Congress passed the Fifteenth Amendment, guaranteeing that "the right of citizens of the United States to vote shall not be denied or abridged by the United States or by any state on account of race, color, or previous condition of servitude," an amendment Congress added to the list of requirements the Southern states were required to meet to be eligible for readmission to the Union. Most Southern state legislatures did ratify it, even if California, Delaware, Kentucky, Maryland, Oregon, and Tennessee did not. Congress's good intentions aside, it wouldn't take the South long to find a detour around the Fifteenth Amendment's putative intent.

What many historians have emphasized about black participation in Reconstruction were the failures of that participation. After the Southern states regained control of their own affairs, the region's mainstream historiography—written, of course, by whites—routinely omitted mention of positive African-American contributions while at the same time failing to explain the barriers whites had erected against black success. In truth, the failures of this short window in which blacks participated in Southern politics represented more than anything else a white-engineered catastrophe.

The great majority of Southern blacks were starting their post–Civil War normalization as a citizenry at a sort of ground zero. Yet many of their political allies expected quick progress from a state of political infancy to one of political maturity while affording little training along the way. Owned until 1865 as though they were livestock, fed, housed, and clothed by their masters, excluded from citizenship and voting, from socialization, marriage, travel, or even movement from plantation to plantation or from one town to another, barred from forming the normal family ties that other Americans procured simply by right of their status as human beings, in those fleeting years it is not at all remarkable that blacks weren't able to build all of the same skills and elements of citizenship whites in America had been busy crafting for centuries.

Many blacks in Reconstruction-era positions of authority admittedly succumbed to the seductions and temptations of whites who, often for reasons of personal gain, pretended to befriend them. Not all of the Northerners who came south to participate in the building of a more just society were the stereotypical carpetbaggers of myth, but many *were* far more venal than honorable. Not all Southerners who allied with blacks were "scalawags" motivated by personal enrichment, but many were. And not all black officeholders and officials seized upon what was the first chance any of them had ever experienced to partake in the same graft and misused power whites had always before monopolized. But many blacks did perform less than honorably, even if—almost predictably—they themselves rarely profited from corruption, becoming instead dupes for the more sophisticated, fast-talking white con men who often made fortunes on schemes they engineered.

But the blacks did get the blame from outraged Southerners forced to foot the tax bill rung up by Reconstruction-era corruption and misuse of state funds, outrage that was rarely directed at those who most deserved it. To white Southerners, the experiment's fundamental shortcoming was that blacks were wrongly participating in what was perceived as *white* business—Southern governance of any sort had simply never before experienced black participation. Most ominously, Southern whites especially hated the many blacks who proved indisputably competent in bringing about the valuable achievements that Reconstruction gave the South. But in their doing so lay a conundrum: comforting white notions of black inferiority were given the lie, and that was something whites would not allow under any circumstances whatsoever. Whites didn't want improvements if blacks helped bring them. They wanted African-Americans to be driven back into the same condition in which they had always known them and in which they had always been able to control them.

While the drama of Reconstruction played out, whites bided their time, waiting for the North to simply tire of protecting Southern blacks and of trying to direct solutions to "Southern problems." Rather than assay any kind of cooperation with the black half of the population, Southern whites continued to quietly resist the black presence in positions of authority. Setting a framework for a white-dominated future society, the response of the majority of the South's white population began to evolve into an ever-tightening web of Jim Crow practices, a web that eventually spread like a shroud across the former Confederacy and its neighboring states. Long before the writing of actual laws, the customs that would harden into legal Jim Crow would have begun to permeate nearly every corner of Southern life. And these norms would prove highly successful in either segregating or entirely removing African-Americans from white Southern society.

An immediate fear of white Southerners sprang from the possibility that because of the Radical-dominated legislatures their children would eventually be forced to share classrooms with black children. But despite their Republican majorities, the Southern legislatures took pains to assure whites that education would not involve racial integration. Since the South had essentially been bankrupted by the war, much of the Reconstruction-era funding for education was supplied from Northern sources, both public and private. With integrated education still highly uncommon in the North, little impulse came even from that quarter for racially mixed education. For example, even the Peabody Fund, a Northern philanthropy that gave money to supplement Southern school districts' budgets, strongly opposed integration. Facing white intransigence from all quarters against integrated classrooms, black parents—most of whom understood that *any* education for their children was critically important—quietly accepted what crumbs came their way rather than push for the impossible. And those crumbs amounted to, at most, separate schools for blacks. Even Frederick Douglass conceded that education in segregated classrooms was better than no education at all—something he believed would become a reality if whites were pushed too far or too hard.

The schoolyard was only one of the arenas in which Jim Crow took permanent root and quietly began to entrench itself. Even though after 1867 the Black Codes were repealed by the Reconstruction legislatures, the greater share of what the Codes had set out to do remained to retard the lives of Southern blacks. Restaurants, theaters, and hotels all over the South engaged in a tidal wave of exclusion against blacks, with blacks' ability to pay being wholly irrelevant. It should, in fact, be emphasized that exclusion was based not on class, but on race: the degree of education or culture, the richness of clothing or importance of a man's position—all were immaterial to attitudes barring African-Americans from any activity or pursuit or involvement that even hinted that blacks might be held as the equal of whites.

In the lee of the war the South even began to develop its own internal—albeit unofficial—white army, a force designed to keep African-Americans securely under the control of Southern white society. In 1866, the prototype six-man group came into existence in Pulaski, Tennessee. It called itself the Ku Klux Klan, after *kuklos,* the Greek word for "circle." At first this parody of vigilantism amounted to little more than a social club for rambunctious ex-Confederate officers, mischief-makers presumably looking to replace the lost camaraderie of the late war. But the white robes and masks they affected on their midnight rides through the Tennessee countryside frightened blacks, who not unnaturally looked upon hollering whites astride charging steeds as something it was judicious to get as far away from as possible. Before long these Klansmen transformed themselves from pranksters into their very own "Invisible Empire of the South," purveyors of terrorism who aimed at suppressing—by violence up to and including murder—any black who offended white sensibilities and any white who defended black aspirations to achieve full citizenship. The point should be stressed that Klan lawlessness not only inhibited blacks from attempting to claim their rights—most importantly by keeping blacks away from the polls—but the organization's terror equally intimidated those whites whose sympathies lay on the wrong side of the color line. The Klan specialty soon became driving "carpetbaggers" back North and "scalawags" into retirement, the Klansmen's pointy hoods helping to shield these self-righteous miscreants' responsibility for their increasingly barbarous acts.

The former Confederacy's quickening surge against black political and social aspirations even under the Reconstruction governments did not pass without stirring unease in Washington. Nervous about the worsening situation, congressional Radicals responded with the three so-called Enforcement Acts of 1870–71, measures primarily designed to protect black voting rights. The first made it a crime to interfere with anyone's right to cast a ballot, such interference being, of course, one of the growing Klan's chief objectives. In effect, with this bill Congress attempted to ban the Ku Klux Klan and its copycat admirers—the Knights of the White Camellia, the Pale Faces, the White Brotherhood, the White League, the Society of the White Rose—by invoking the equal-protections requirements of the Fourteenth Amendment, a law that had so far little hindered Southern intransigence against black progress. Two additional bills added to the federal protections: the second Enforcement Act put the election of congressmen under the watch of federal officials, while the third outlawed Klan-like activities such as forming conspiracies against blacks and their allies, wearing headgear that hid one's identity, and threatening federal or state officials. Though these measures did succeed in breaking this first Klan, the efforts merely led conservative Southerners to find subtler means of harassing their victims.

Congress thus once again attempted to provide some kind of permanent racial justice in the postbellum South. In 1875 it passed the Civil Rights Act, the last such substantial help the federal government would extend to the nation's African-American citizens for nearly a century. In its fundamentals, the Civil Rights Act outlawed the humiliating Jim Crow practices that blacks were facing in ever-greater measure. The discrimination directed at them had reached a point where inns and restaurants had excluded all nonwhites from service, with few such establishments anywhere in the South any longer accepting black trade. Black congressman James T. Rapier of Alabama spoke passionately to the House of the need for the bill: "There is not an inn between Washington and Montgomery, a distance of more than a thousand miles, that will accommodate me to a bed or meal. Now, then, is there a man upon this floor who is so heartless, whose breast is so void of the better feelings, as to say this brutal custom needs no regulation? I hold that it does and that Congress is the body to regulate it."[3]

Congress predictably ran headlong into an impermeable wall of Southern resistance. To make the new civil rights law palatable, legislators had conspicuously omitted any mention of schooling. But the South bitterly resisted *any* black advancement. The *Raleigh Sentinel* editorialized that "if the principles of the Republicans succeed, the Negro will be forced upon ... [the white man's] wife, and his daughters, on the cars, steamboats, in public inns, at hotel tables, and in other places of entertainment." A Georgia representative spoke for the same constituency: "You cannot benefit the [Negro] by dragging the white race down to his degraded level." But with Civil War sacrifices still relatively fresh, Congress nonetheless remained convinced that the legislative branch had to assume responsibility for protecting the blacks the North had spent so much blood and treasure to free from enslavement.

Like the three great constitutional amendments to come out of the Civil War—the Thirteenth, which ended slavery; the Fourteenth, requiring equal treatment under the law; and Fifteenth, which "guaranteed" (with disastrous imperfection) the franchise to blacks—the Civil Rights Act would soon be circumvented by the combined forces of states' rights, white supremacy, and stark bigotry. The act was never commitedly applied in the South, where neither the federal government nor the flagging

---

[3] Russell, 75.

Reconstruction state governments enforced it with any rigor. In short, Southerners took its provisions to mean, at most, that segregated but "appropriate" facilities should be provided for African-Americans.

That "meaning" soon became moot. Eight years after it was passed, the Supreme Court ruled the Civil Rights Act unconstitutional on the grounds that the facilities it required to be made available to blacks were only those that were private in nature, not public, and were thus exempt from federal control. The court essentially told the South's blacks that they must look not to Washington but to their own state governments for whatever protections they thought they needed. Utterly unsurprisingly, this 1883 decision opened the floodgates to a sharp increase in the growth of Jim Crow.

After the 1875 passing of Congress's final Reconstruction-era law protecting African-Americans, the North's official commitment to their needs and security quickly began to collapse. Ulysses S. Grant, Johnson's successor in the executive mansion, conceded that the "whole public are tired of these . . . outbreaks in the South," referring not to Klan activities but to African-Americans' struggle for some measure of respect and the rights other Americans took for granted. The Republican Grant was no Lincoln in his vision for America, but he had at first been willing to at least allow federal power to be used to protect the lives and rights of former slaves. America, however, was inexorably moving to new causes, the growing nation ever more consumed with issues such as westward expansion, industrialization, and the accommodation of a tidal wave of European immigrants, with federal attention wandering ever faster away from the lives of what was by any measure the most tyrannized part of its population. The abolitionists whose fire and eloquence had done so much to lead to the Civil War and to the legal emancipation of African-Americans were gone. To Northerners the misery of blacks—the vast majority of whom were still far away in the South—had dwindled into a politically unsustainable concern.

The curtain on Reconstruction rang down in the weird wake of what was until then the most bizarre presidential election in American history. The two presidential candidates seeking to replace Grant in 1876 were Rutherford B. Hayes, a Republican and three-time Ohio governor, and the New York Democrat Samuel Tilden. Relative to how such things were measured at the time, Hayes was considered sympathetic to the increasingly desperate plight of African-Americans, particularly those in the South, while Tilden was, in terms of his regards for black civil rights, a typical Northern Democrat, which meant that the issue meant almost nothing to him.

The Reconstruction governments in the South had by 1876 found themselves extremely hard-pressed to retain power. In some of the Southern states the Democrats had, in fact, already regained control of their statehouses. The only force still providing any protection for African-Americans from the worst excesses of Southern bigotry was the federal government's now-dwindling oversight. Even the greater part of the force of federal troops that had protected blacks at polling places and tried to keep them from Klan barbarism had long since been removed by the Grant administration. But still blacks could make themselves heard at the polls, and Southern legislatures continued to include black members. The significance of the Hayes-Tilden race was that a Democratic administration in Washington would almost certainly mean the end of almost any federal protection for the South's African-Americans and herald the end of their remaining political strength.

Samuel Tilden won the popular vote on election day, achieving a majority of almost three hundred thousand votes out of the 8 million cast, and it also appeared he had cinched the decisive electoral vote. But a wrench was thrown into the works when vote fraud was alleged in Florida, Louisiana, South Carolina, and Oregon, and in the end Congress was required to decide whether Hayes or Tilden would move into Grant's about-to-be-vacated executive mansion.

So Congress appointed an electoral commission to work out a deal to resolve the impasse, a standoff that threatened to keep the presidency literally vacant. To assuage the protesting states' outrage at having their votes questioned and thus their honor supposedly impugned, the Republicans presented them with an offer they couldn't refuse. The Republicans promised to end the South's federally buttressed Reconstruction policies— and thus allow the Democrats to oust the remaining carpetbagger governments and at the same time be handed control of the South—*if* the Democrats would withdraw their opposition to Hayes's election. An agreement was reached on these terms.

Hayes duly took the oath of office in March 1877, meekly imploring the white South only that it not trample the rights of its black citizens, which amounted to leaving the foxes in control of the henhouse; a Tilden victory could hardly have been significantly worse for blacks. Thus twelve years after the Civil War ended, the Republicans—and thus the republic— in effect turned their collective back on African-Americans. African-Americans had helped the Republicans win three national elections, but the new Republicans, strengthened in their coalition with Southern Democrats, no longer needed any black help.

For African-Americans, the end of Reconstruction represented a catastrophe of incalculable magnitude. In the wake of Reconstruction's collapse, blacks, as a disfranchised class ever more trapped in economic peonage, found that only negligible barriers remained to block racism's spread: with blacks written out of the system, few white voices in either the South or the nation as a whole would speak forcefully for their civil rights. Reconstruction's failure added as well to the difficulty of instituting nationwide reform: with such a large segment of the American laboring population removed from the political system, the center of the nation's politics shifted even further to the right. And with a solidly reactionary Democratic political system entrenched in the South, progress in all areas of that region's public policy—not just racial—was brutally stymied.

Now the white South was once more free to deal with the black in its own way, just as it had been before 1861. The African-American was about to feel the built-up rage of ordinary whites who had watched relatively silently as Reconstruction had played out. A newly resurgent Democratic Party brought with it a white counterrevolution known as the Southern Redemption, a movement whose unapologetic and frankly stated goal was the permanent return of the black man as nearly as possible to his prewar status.

Rather than concentrating on black exclusion, the initial wave of Jim Crow measures that would eventually smother the South focused on the creation of separate facilities for them. Concerned that the federal government still might not stand by while blacks were driven completely out of Southern life, white Southerners chose to assiduously *separate* blacks from white society. Within little more than a generation after Reconstruction's end, this kind of racial segregation would almost completely characterize Southern and border-state life. To satisfy federal courts, Southerners built an overlay of "equality" into segregation, but it was rarely anything but a sham, a pretense that as long as the "same" was provided for both races, segregation would not offend constitutional law or the judges who said what that law was. This grand plan, essentially a preservation of the white South's antebellum way of life, spread like ground fog. It ran deepest through the old Confederate states, but seeped as well into the border states buffering them from the Yankees. And as it spread, segregation effectively *became* the law, even if actual Jim Crow legislation itself remained rare for a while longer yet.

Paradoxically, many blacks saw such segregation as an actual improvement over the exclusion they had been subjected to in the postbellum Black Codes; in fact, a considerable number of African-Americans regarded segregation as an almost positive state when compared to that kind of total separation from society. The preponderance of black protests was not at first spurred by segregation or discrimination, but instead by being faced with denial of any community services at all. The victims of racism generally understood they didn't have the strength to prevail against a white society buttressed with its legislatures and courts, institutions that had become the controlling agents of reaction. Even if a rare court decision came down in their favor, blacks tended to view such a victory as a mere "paper" success, knowing that in the isolation in which they were forced to live their lives no mere decree could protect them from determined white efforts to ensure their subjugation, efforts that often included violence. In a word, African-Americans simply did not possess the wherewithal to challenge white supremacy and the Jim Crow that came with it.

It wasn't, of course, apparent or understood at the time, but what the 1877 White House Compromise—the event that effectively ended the post–Civil War Reconstruction era—meant was that the South was going to be allowed to go its own way. Since whites controlled its economy, its police power, and its voice in the national legislature, its "own way" meant whatever whites wanted. And what white Southerners wanted most was as curtailed a state of citizenship as they could create for those men and women who had been their slaves. The white people of the South abhorred any notion of sharing the ballot, of sharing their social institutions or schools, of sharing their primacy by being with black creatures they held to be virtually another species. They were not only ready but eager to do whatever it took to keep African-Americans permanently and unmistakably in legal and social subjugation. They would use their economic power, their education, their ballot, and if necessary, their access to violence in legal police power and extralegal Ku Klux Klan power to achieve these ends.

It strongly bears emphasizing that discrimination against blacks by whites as well as segregation by whites of blacks continued apace in the North to a degree that ensured historic disgrace to that region and to America's loud and duplicitous self-proclamation of the ideals of liberty and democracy and the equality of man. In housing, in education, in the workplace, in the marketplace—everywhere in the North, black Americans were in this period treated with contempt, denied basic civil liberties, and subjected to lightning-fast, white-instigated violence.

But Jim Crow was a Southern phenomenon, the infrastructure white Southerners built to preserve, insofar as humanly possible, the old master/slave system. During the Jim Crow era, which is to say the roughly one hundred years between the end of the Civil War and the culmination of the civil rights revolution, only in the South did white superiority, and the Jim Crow that reflected and upheld it, overwhelmingly dominate the political and social fabric of an entire region. It became and remained *vital* for an entire century to the Southern white view of life over life's entire spectrum.

The differences between racial discrimination in North and South were manifold. In the South alone did white supremacy and white domination over blacks supersede all other public concerns, and then with an obviously far different tenor than it did in the North. In the postwar North, only during the abolition era—the two or three decades preceding the Civil War—did race subsume most other public and private concerns. In the North, the black man's right to a public voice, most vitally his right to vote, was not fundamentally questioned by the whole of surrounding white society, as it was in the South. In fact, the Reconstruction-era gains made by Southern blacks that spilled over into the North, especially in education, tended to last in the North, whereas they wouldn't in the South. What happened regarding race in the South represented a chasm separating the professed American ideal from the reality of the American experience as it was actually lived. In every place possible blacks were in the South segregated off from white society. Where it was not possible to segregate blacks from white society, then blacks would be excluded from almost every significant protection and right of American citizenship. This happened because white people, most pointedly white people with power, wanted it to happen. It happened because Northern white people gave up trying to stop it from happening, and it happened because the federal government and courts, which were composed virtually entirely of white people, also did not stop it from happening.

From the end of Reconstruction until the Supreme Court's *Plessy v. Ferguson* decision in 1896, Jim Crow spread like a pestilence. The virus settled in community after community, in county after county, in state after state, until its cells had taken over the entire body of the South. From a hazy and undocumented existence as simply "custom" until it was armored in the full force of statutory law, Jim Crow became what it meant to be Southern.

To escape life that bordered on reenslavement, many groups of desperate blacks ran away from the South. The largest such group were the famous Exodusters, composed mostly of displaced plantation workers fleeing forced peonage, who in 1879 headed for Kansas in search of what they expected would be free homesteads. Such would not be forthcoming. Wherever the black emigrants passed, they found not free land but rather the same kind of discrimination they were trying to leave behind. Even in undeveloped new territories whites made them pointedly unwelcome. Their attempt to found an all-black state in the Oklahoma panhandle was fended off, though they did manage to establish some two dozen towns made up entirely of African-Americans, settlements that were allowed to survive because they were completely separated from existing white communities. A few of these disappointed Exodusters eventually returned to the South and its familiarity, albeit to its severely limited opportunities as well. Others, though, headed even farther westward. Paradoxically, the further west blacks traveled, the worse was the bigotry they encountered. Californians had already instituted anti-Chinese statutes, laws easily and quickly transferable to the new black migrants seeking, as had the Chinese before them, a better life. By 1890, substantial numbers of blacks were moving to Northern cities then experiencing booming economies, though it would take another generation and a world war before the black stream northward was to become a flood.

Meanwhile, throughout the old South, Jim Crow dug in deeper every day. By the century's last decade, hardly a corner of life existed into which Jim Crow hadn't planted its talons, though the means and methods of segregation weren't yet spread evenly over all jurisdictions nor were they officially written in law. Some communities lagged behind others in their application of antiblack torments, often those places where blacks didn't form so high a proportion of the total population. Amazingly, a few white Southerners remained brave enough to question the need to segregate with such massive thoroughness. Of the latter, some were shrewd enough to realize that the path to complete segregation or exclusion of blacks might still force a federal reaction. Some whites questioned the unthinking marginalization of "respectable" blacks, meaning those educated African-Americans who comported themselves little differently from educated whites. What was more, no small concern on the part of some whites attached to the high cost of segregation, a financial burden especially felt in the requirement that any educational facilities be provided separately by race.

The Fifteenth Amendment's guarantee against the denial of the franchise on the grounds of color became a special target for Southern white supremacists. As long as African-Americans remained free to vote, Southern segregationists knew their goals stood in jeopardy. Through the 1880s blacks still managed to send a few representatives to Southern legislatures, but their doing so infuriated many whites, not least because it continued in contravention of widespread white-engineered election fraud meant to stop it. But polling places grew more dangerous for blacks every year. Violence, especially Klan terror, kept untold numbers of blacks from the polls, particularly those living in rural areas where African-American numerical strength was at its highest and therefore perceived by whites as the greatest threat to their iron grip. Yet terror didn't work fast enough or with sufficient thoroughness for whites bent on making elections white men's business. The white solution lay in creative disfranchisement, and not surprisingly, it was in Mississippi where legislators found the answer that would for almost seventy years satisfy white needs and white laws to keep the polls nearly free of black Americans.

In 1890, white politicians in Jackson sent a new and highly racially rigged constitution to Mississippi voters, which the latter speedily passed. The document nowhere specifically made elections a whites-only enterprise, its racism instead more subtle. First, the framers instituted a tax on voting, knowing even a nominal amount, say a dollar or two, would mean that, because many blacks were destitute, they would be unable to pay this "poll tax." Furthermore, the levy was cumulative, which meant unpaid taxes from prior years of "eligibility" had to be paid before a man was allowed to cast his ballot. (The measure, incidentally, disfranchised a good number of poor whites along with the blacks who were its intended target.) The new constitution also specifically aimed at disfranchising African-American men who had been convicted of crimes thought to be peculiarly "black"—fraud, arson, and theft—while ignoring rape, murder, and grand larceny, felonies allegedly more apt to be committed by whites.

In the second part of the package, and a measure of particularly clever political guile, Mississippi's reworked constitution also required that voters pass a literacy test before being allowed to cast a ballot in any election.

The Democratic politicians did not, of course, wish to entirely disfranchise ignorant whites, whose numbers were legion but whose votes were generally safe. So the registrar of voters in each polling place, a man guaranteed to be white, was empowered to say whether a given eligible voter's answers to questions on the literacy test—questions that usually pertained to the meaning of the state constitution—passed muster. White answers always did. Black answers almost never did. As it was dryly explained, "There was a general understanding that the interpretation of the constitution offered by an illiterate white man would be acceptable to the registrars; that of a Negro would not." Not a few whites evidently believed that even an educated black was incapable of understanding any part of the state constitution, one editorialist writing that "if every Negro in Mississippi was a graduate of Harvard . . . he would not be as fitted to exercise the rights of suffrage as the Anglo-Saxon farm laborer."

Not that slow-witted whites had to be overly concerned about getting the answers to the registrars' questions right. The revised constitution's provisions *also* included a "grandfather clause," a device guaranteeing any man the vote if his grandfather, father, or he himself had voted prior to 1867, which of course entirely excluded Mississippi's former slaves and sons of slaves.

When Mississippi's blacks appealed to the federal government to overturn this stunningly biased document, Washington turned a deaf ear. President Benjamin Harrison absolved himself of responsibility for black voting rights on the grounds that rules covering the franchise were a matter for each state to work out for itself. Unchecked by the federal government's lack of will in upholding the *intent* of the Fifteenth Amendment, the rest of the South followed Mississippi's lead as quickly as each state could get its own statutes or constitution rewritten. The damage done to black Southerners was staggering. For example, before the state of Louisiana changed its voting rules, 130,000 of its African-Americans had been qualified to vote. After the change, only a few more than 5,000 blacks in that state were allowed to register. The proportions were not largely different anywhere else in the South: from Virginia to Texas, the black Southerner was essentially written out of the electoral process and into a state of political powerlessness.

James K. Vardaman, a future Mississippi governor and one of the framers of his state's new constitution, as well as one of the most rancid-mouthed and long-lived racists in American history (he once remarked, publicly and indeed most likely hoping he would be quoted, that "the best way to control the nigger is to whip him when he does not obey without it") commented frankly on what his fellow whites had wrought. "There is no use to equivocate or lie about the matter," Vardaman said. "Mississippi's constitutional convention of 1890 was held for no other purpose than to eliminate the nigger from politics . . . let the world know it just as it is."

Though Mississippi was the groundbreaker in the disfranchisement of the black voter, the devices other states thought up to reduce the size of their African-American vote were equally creative. In 1882, South Carolina passed its so-called Eight-Box Ballot Act, a maneuver shortly thereafter emulated by Florida. The scheme was bald but effective. A voter's ballot was put in a given box—there were originally eight boxes and thus the name—with a candidate's name written on each box and each ballot; the voter was required to get the right ballot in the right box or else his ballot would be disqualified. For those who were illiterate—a disability from which the majority of blacks suffered—this maneuver could be tricky, especially when no help would ever be forthcoming from the white registrar overseeing the process. Voters couldn't even depend on being told by earlier voters where to find the right box for a black-favored candidate since the registrars kept moving the boxes around, as in the shell game this farce so tragically resembled.

Robbing the Southern black of his vote was not purely a Southern matter. The Supreme Court weighed in with its approval in an 1898 case known as *Williams v. Mississippi*. Here the justices supported these developments by declaring poll taxes and literacy requirements constitutional, their rationale hanging essentially on the hypocrisy of states' rights: in the opinion of the nation's chief interpreters of the law, these matters lay not in the province of the federal government to adjudicate, but rightfully within the power of each state. Many influential Northerners agreed with the tenor of the high court, their views bolstered by a flood of racist literature affirming the innate unworthiness of blacks. A white Alabamian remarked with a note of pride that "we now have the sympathy of thoughtful men in the North to an extent that never existed before."[4]

Segregation developed in an unusually diverse pattern in one major area of life. The providing of separate transportation facilities for each race brought with it costs and complexities that challenged even the most dedicated champions of Jim Crow. Attempts to segregate or exclude black customers on railroads and streetcars, the era's two major mass-transportation forms, brought both substantial legal reaction from embittered blacks and the first categorical legal authorization for Jim Crow. Most important, they also brought Homer Plessy to the Supreme Court.

Where whites could readily separate blacks out of most of the South's daily activities—eating, shopping, churchgoing—such segregation was particularly burdensome in the use of trains and other forms of transportation. The issue grew into a concern of considerable dimensions to race-conscious whites. Only on public transport did whites and blacks merge in perceived social equality, the state that so aroused white fears. Where whites confronted blacks as servants or as menials, close physical proximity was tolerated. But where the relationship was otherwise, whites felt mortally affronted, not to say threatened, when blacks came anywhere near their bodies.

Though sympathetic to white racial prejudices, the railroad companies found themselves in a quandary. Headquartered in the North and thus at a substantial remove from the Southern obsession with the minutiae of race separation, they weren't about to simply duplicate every facet of their service to satisfy white Southern bigotry, though their reasoning was far less moralistic than it was economic: running one set of trains for whites and another for blacks was obviously too expensive and too complicated. To meet white Southern demands that the races be transported so that whites and blacks were not in the immediate company of each other meant

---

[4] Levine, 114.

the employment of racially segregated carriages. And in 1881, Tennessee duly became the first state to require exactly that arrangement. A Tennessee statute forbade black and white passengers from sharing space on the same car, which meant obligating the railroad companies to instead provide blacks separate accommodations "equal" to those provided whites.

In the 1880s nonsleeping railroad cars consisted of two sorts: tobacco-free first-class carriages, the "parlor cars" on which women could travel in comfort and away from the worst male vulgarians, and second-class cars for everyone else, including men traveling alone, those who couldn't afford first-class fares, and tobacco smokers and tobacco chewers along with the paraphernalia, usually disgusting, necessary to support them. The atmosphere in the second category was as often as not squalid, what with the aisles running with tobacco spit and the general tone of conversation vulgar and loud. Moreover, the second-class seats were uncushioned. And the air reeked because these cars were almost always placed directly behind the engine, which meant far more of the smoke and cinders from the wood-fired burners oozed into the second-class cars than got back into the carriages hauling the better-off classes.

As white Southerners viewed the matter, there were two problems with all this. The first was that even though the great majority of first-class passengers were white—the main reason for this being that relatively few blacks could afford the higher first-class fares—a few African-Americans did nonetheless use first class. And those few blacks who did ride the parlor cars demanded, with perfect justice, that they be accommodated just as their pocketbooks allowed. Even though blacks in first-class cars were generally few in number, many white Southerners wanted *none* in "their" cars.

The difficulty in all this for the railroad companies was that only rarely were there enough first-class black passengers to fill an entire carriage so as to keep the better-off whites happy in all-white cars of their own. And the railroads bridled, understandably, at the prospect of being required to haul unfilled cars. The second problem involved the second-class cars, because even there blacks were not wanted. In fact, these carriages had long been derisively referred to as "nigger cars," and many whites of any class or condition disliked sharing them with blacks, white racists becoming particularly exercised at the prospect of white *women* finding themselves in inescapably close physical proximity to black *men*, something guaranteed to conjure fear of rape in the breast of the white Southern male. A visiting Englishman even reported having heard Jim Crow defended on the grounds of the "special aversion which . . . the negro male excites in the white woman."

Often station agents flatly refused to sell first-class tickets to blacks, their purpose being, of course, to keep carriages entirely white. And even when blacks had bought their tickets out of state (i.e., in the North), conductors still forcibly removed them. The upshot for the railroads was disruption in their services and outrage and lawsuits from the African-Americans whose rights were being denied. A few of the excluded blacks who sued actually won their cases, even a handful of those cases that were tried in Southern courts. In one such suit the railroad in defending its segregation practices said that even in the North common law allowed companies to segregate their cars "so as to avoid complaint and friction." The presiding judge—a former senator and obviously a man of rare courage—retorted that the railroad lost that right "when the money of the white man purchases luxurious accommodations amid elegant company, and the same amount of money purchases for a black man inferior quarters in a smoking car."[5]

Such was the state of affairs that had led the sovereign people of Tennessee to solve the problem by drawing on Jim Crow, now backed not with mere "custom" but with the full force of statutory law. Though the black members of Tennessee's two legislative branches attempted to stop the legislation, the new law required that "all railroad companies shall furnish separate cars, or portions of cars cut off by partition walls, which all colored passengers who pay first-class rates of fare may have the privilege to enter and occupy." The Tennessee legislators added a provision that separate cars must be kept "in good repair, with the same conveniences, and subject to the same rules governing other first-class

---

[5] Ayers, 141.

cars for preventing smoking and obscene language." Within a few years, legislators followed suit in Florida (their bill generously spelled out that "no white person shall be permitted to ride in a negro car or to insult or annoy any negro in such car"), Mississippi, Texas, the Carolinas, Virginia, and Louisiana. And the Louisiana statute led to the case that led to fully legal Jim Crow.

Drowned in a flood of Jim Crow—mostly still technically just customary, but the statutory kind was beginning to seep out of the South's legislative chambers—black Southerners were left virtually alone to face their torment as the end of the nineteenth century approached. The phrase that perhaps best articulates white America's regard for its 10 million blacks a century ago is *moral abandonment*. With the abolition of slavery, the American black had become, in the words of Russell Nye, "no longer a problem in morality, but a problem in politics." The concerns of Northern abolitionists had largely evaporated by the 1890s, and the entire nation seemed content to regard African-Americans precisely as Southern racists urged: as a hopelessly inferior underclass, and whose direction was best left to the South's lead.

And then came *Plessy*. The century closed with a decision that bestowed the blessing of the nation's highest court on Jim Crow. A case that had begun in Louisiana in 1892 took four years to snake its way along the serpentine legal road leading to the Supreme Court and ended in what can reasonably be judged the most catastrophic decision in American judicial history.

When the struggle began that would fix his name forever in American constitutional history, Homer Plessy was thirty years old. He was also thoroughly unextraordinary, at least to look at. Plessy, a shoemaker by trade, looked white. But he suffered from what in his time and place represented the great burden of having been descended from a black person, in his case one of his great-grandparents. Such singular descent in the racial jargon of that time made the young cobbler an "octoroon." This one-eighth part of black ancestry, despite his seven-eighths parts of

Caucasian descent, also made him in the judgment of the state of Louisiana a Negro.

But what was far from ordinary about Plessy was his willingness to cooperate in an attack on discrimination, which quality taken together with his literacy made him the perfect candidate to challenge the constitutional validity of Louisiana's Jim Crow laws that governed how blacks and whites would share the state's railroads. The challenge had been set up by a group of progressive New Orleanians calling themselves the Citizens Committee to Test the Constitutionality of the Separate Car Law. Plessy's volunteering to be the committee's guinea pig put the young shoemaker at no small risk to his safety, the risk dependent on, among other things, the lenience of the railroad conductor he was going to come up against to play out his role.

On June 7, 1892, Homer Plessy obtained a first-class ticket on the East Louisiana Railroad to take him from New Orleans to Covington, Louisiana, the committee having taken care to make sure the trip remained entirely within the state to avoid the interstate commerce implications that would have muddied the legal waters its experiment was about to purposely roil. The young cobbler boarded a "white" carriage, well aware, of course, of the new state statute that warned any passenger who entered "a coach or compartment to which he by race does not belong" was thereby violating the law, a law still objected to by the railroad because of its cost in extra cars. In consequence, the railroad, indirectly at least, was in reality supporting what the committee was doing, not because it gave a hoot about the moral injury to Plessy but because it wished to have the inconvenient (to itself) law invalidated in court. Plessy's committee handlers had made sure the conductor was informed ahead of time that their pink-skinned experimentee was in fact legally black. As planned, when the conductor came along after the train had started moving out of the station, he formally asked Plessy if he was "colored," and when the cobbler answered that he was indeed "colored," the conductor courteously told him he had to leave the car on the grounds that he wasn't white, to which demand Plessy courteously but firmly refused. The conductor, properly following the script, forcibly ejected the protesting passenger into the arms of the law. The now-miscreant Plessy was carted off to the New Orleans jail, there charged with violating a duly enacted state racial ordinance.

The next step in the admittedly put-up but nonetheless dead-serious tragicomedy was an appearance by Plessy before the bench of Judge John Howard Ferguson, whose name thereby inadvertently gained a measure of historical infamy for the chance of the young one-eighth-black man showing up in his courtroom on the morning after said black man had been arrested on the East Louisiana Railroad. This same Judge Ferguson had, ironically, already ruled in another case that the state's Separate Car Act was unconstitutional "on cars that traveled through several states," which he held as putting such instances in the province of interstate travel and thus beyond Louisiana law. But that was not to be his position with Plessy's situation. Plessy, or rather his well-prepared attorneys, argued that the arrest was illegal because the Separate Car Act violated their client's Thirteenth and Fourteenth Amendment rights. But Judge Ferguson ruled that Louisiana was indeed free to regulate in any way it wished railroad companies that were operating "entirely within its own borders." The court thereby found Homer Plessy guilty as charged.

When Plessy and his committee appealed the decision to the state supreme court, the justices upheld Judge Ferguson's ruling. Homer Plessy's case was then taken to the ultimate arbiter of the nation's law, the U.S. Supreme Court. In Washington, D.C., in 1896, eight justices—one had been excused for illness—thereby took up the increasingly momentous case of *Plessy v. Ferguson.*

The high court immediately dismissed Plessy's complaint that the Louisiana Separate Car Act violated the Thirteenth Amendment. That amendment, the court said, freed slaves *only,* and thus its provisions were immaterial to this case. The other amendment, the Fourteenth, and specifically its "equal protection" clause, became the pivot on which *Plessy v. Ferguson* would swing.

Of the eight justices deciding the litigation, seven ruled against Plessy, with the plaintiff thus, of course, losing. The majority based its decision not on what the amendment's "intent," or its "spirit," may or may not have been, but rather on the amendment's *specific* wording. The decision, in fact, seemed to have been precisely what the framers of the Fourteenth Amendment intended when they so cautiously wrote it three decades earlier. Those framers in 1869 did *not* write a color-blind constitutional amendment because they knew its implication would exceed what the nation would accept. The amendment they did write was one in which *judges* would say what was and what was not permissible in race-based discrimination. And those legislators had clearly not intended to prohibit segregation, though Congress had long and carefully considered such a prohibition. Congress instead specifically and purposely substituted "equal protection" for the far more radical concept of "no discrimination." To the legislators' lights, the constitution already allowed discrimination on many bases, including one that not only disfranchised women but also barred many other civil rights from being granted to and enjoyed by women. What the court thus held in 1896 was that the Constitution commanded *not* the abolition of racial distinctions, but instead specified equality of treatment, a command that obviously assumed that segregation and equality were not incompatible or mutually contradictory concepts. In short, the Fourteenth Amendment did not, so the justices confirmed, prohibit distinguishing between citizens on the basis of race.

Aside from the majority's central ruling on the impersonal constitutional merits of the case, the court appended to the decision (in shades of Chief Justice Taney four decades earlier) a statement on the moral rationale of the *Plessy* appeal, the justices' disdainful view of blacks coming through with blinding clarity. "We consider the underlying fallacy of the plaintiff's argument to consist," Justice Henry Brown wrote, "in the assumption that the forced separation of the two races stamps the colored race with a badge of inferiority. If this be so, it is not by reason of anything found in the act, but solely because the colored race chooses to put that construction upon it." Rarely if ever had official contempt for African-Americans been so plainly spoken by so high a court.

The *Plessy* case was, of course, tried in the frame of mind of its times, just as any part of the Constitution is written in the temper of its times. Theoretically outlawing express inequality between the races, the kind of inequality made manifest in the Black Codes that immediately followed the Civil War, so, too, was the amendment that decided *Plessy v. Ferguson* written as it was because to do otherwise would, for example, have logically meant that even marriage laws could not take race into account, an idea so radical in the nineteenth century as to be almost literally unthinkable. It would have meant education would have had to be integrated, which was then almost equally unthinkable. It would likely have endangered the peace of a still-healing nation in the wake of a great war because, *so it was then thought*, the South would never have peaceably submitted to a truly color-blind Constitution. But for that matter, such would likely have been equally the case with a large part of the still pathologically racially bigoted North.

The central reality of *Plessy* was that discrimination on Louisiana's trains would be legal under the following circumstances: namely, when the separate services and facilities offered black and white passengers by race were substantially *equal*. This soon-to-be famous "separate but equal" provision would quickly grow into the legal framework by which Jim Crow laws would for the next half century be written and enforced. Every Southern facility was after *Plessy* virtually free to follow the court's permission to discriminate. And every Southern state would legally justify Jim Crow on the basis of a decision made by seven men whose philosophies were, tragically and inescapably, squarely of their time.

As had been the case with the Founding Fathers vis-à-vis slavery a century earlier, these justices *could* have decided otherwise. They *could* have said the Constitution meant something other than what it did specifically and plainly say. Instead they chose, perhaps reasonably, perhaps not, to decide on the basis of the document's exact words. They *could* have foreseen that services and facilities for African-Americans neither would nor could ever in fact be equal. The court *could* have risked an outraged South by outlawing the principle of race-based discrimination. Instead, doing as they did, they left the aggrieved African-American to the tender mercies of Southern justice to say what was "equal" under the Fourteenth Amendment. Later judges, in the temper of their own times, would eventually rule differently on questions of inequality, but it took scores of court cases over a half century to end the kind of discrimination from which the plaintiff Homer Plessy sought redress. The court might have accomplished this at a stroke in 1896. And had it done so, it might have started another civil war. Or so it was feared.

One justice viewed matters differently from his seven colleagues. John Marshall Harlan seems, in retrospect, an unusual candidate for the near-sainthood his *Plessy* dissent gave him. Harlan was a Kentuckian, a former slave owner, and had denounced the Emancipation Proclamation and the Thirteenth Amendment at the time they were published. He did not believe that blacks were the equals of whites in any social or intellectual sense or in attainment. He did not believe that blacks should be granted social equality with whites. Given the society in which he lived and the state of achievement of most blacks, these views are, sadly, unsurprising. What *is* surprising is that Harlan, almost uniquely among the prominent jurists of 1896, understood the damage the high court's decision would do to the black man, to the black man's future, and to the future of American society. He had understood so well that thirteen years before *Plessy* he had also been the lone dissenter in the court's tragic invalidation of the Civil Rights Act of 1875.

"Our constitution is color-blind," he wrote in dissent in 1896, not technically correctly but certainly with laudable moral passion, "and neither knows nor tolerates class among its citizens. In respect of civil rights, all citizens are equal before the law. . . . In my opinion, the judgment this day rendered will, in time, prove to be quite as pernicious as the decision made by this tribunal in the Dred Scott case."

The *Plessy* decision did not create Jim Crow. Nor was it responsible for its spread across the South—that had happened in the thirty years before Homer Plessy had his day in court. But it legitimized Jim Crow in law. For another six decades the vast majority of the nation's blacks would be forced to endure this American nightmare. The *Plessy* decision struck an almost fatal blow to what was left of nineteenth-century black aspirations for equality and for assimilation into America's vaunted melting pot. As the twentieth century progressed, the disgracefulness of Jim Crow would be chipped away at by thousands of people, black and white, in and out of courts and statehouses and in acts of civil disobedience. Not a few of these persons would pay for their efforts with their lives. But the long night was still in its early hours as the new century approached. And the damage would be deep and the horrors many.

3

INTO THE NIGHT:
THE EARLY TWENTIETH CENTURY

eddy Roosevelt's proposal to Booker T. Washington one day in 1901 was almost more of a casual "Why don't you stay for dinner" to the last guest of his business day than it was an official invitation. But irrespective of its ad hoc nature, when the editor of the *Memphis Scimitar* heard about the most famous black man in America dining at the White House, his editorial called the president's gesture "the most damnable outrage ever." South Carolina's Senator Benjamin "Pitchfork" Tillman felt even more aggrieved. He predicted, or perhaps promised, that "the action of President Roosevelt in entertaining that nigger will necessitate our killing a thousand niggers in the South before they will learn their place again."

With the unique—though obviously not universally popular—access he had gained to the nation's president, Booker T. Washington was at the turn of the twentieth century as close to an unofficial "secretary of negro affairs" as America had. Washington's entire adult life had, in fact, been marked by a string of remarkable accomplishments, beginning extraordinarily early when at the age of twenty-five he founded what would become the world's most famous black teachers' college, Alabama's Tuskegee Institute. The son of a white man and a black slave mother, in his middle years he drew on his own upbringing to give glowing life to an international best-selling autobiography called *Up from Slavery*. And by the time of his White House dinner Washington had achieved not only the status of a black voice for much of white America but had become an idol to countless blacks reeling under the anguish of America's hypervirulent racism. But in a twist bordering on Greek tragedy, an enormously controversial speech he had delivered half a decade earlier was what became Washington's best-known legacy. In it this man of genius managed, in carefully measured words, to prop up white America's race prejudice and in the doing bestow an incalculable hurt on many of his fellow African-Americans.

The 1895 Cotton States and International Exposition in Atlanta had optimistically been meant by its organizers to be an exultation of the New South, a cheerful signal to the nation that the region's economic progress had finally made it the equal of the North. Unfortunately, the stain on this happy picture was the state of Southern blacks, racial segregation by this time having become the settled course of nearly every aspect of life in the white-controlled South. But the exposition's directors needed federal funds to pay for their extravaganza, and to help ensure they got the money they asked three prominent blacks—two bishops and Booker T. Washington—to appear with them before the House Appropriations Committee. With this presumed evidence of African-American inclusion in the exposition, Congress duly approved the funds, but also warily added a proviso that a substantial "Negro Building" be raised, an integral and important part of the fair and not just a "Negro department" stuck in a secluded corner of the Federal Building, as had originally been held sufficient by the exposition's planners. The directors accepted the congressional proviso and, for the fair's opening-day ceremonies, asked Washington to be one of the several speakers on the platform. The audience would, of course, be entirely white, as was normal at such a noteworthy occasion taking place in the heart of the Deep South.

In the Atlanta of 1895, it was indeed not in the least remarkable that so grand a ceremony would be held before a whites-only audience. In fact, the entire fair would be segregated, with blacks unwelcome in any of the pavilions except their own Negro Building. None of the refreshment vendors would be permitted to sell food to any African-American visitor or even so much as provide a black with a drink of water. But friendly spirits were meant to prevail on the opening day, and at the gala ceremony Washington would be given his chance to appear in a position of undisputed prominence before a good part of the cream of white Southern society.

Washington didn't disappoint. What the writer, educator, and presidential confidant said from the podium on opening day couldn't have pleased the white members of his audience more. In a speech remembered in history as the "Atlanta Compromise"—a poignantly derisive name later conferred on it by Washington's most prominent critic, fellow African-American W. E. B. DuBois—the idol of black America told his white listeners that he believed America's blacks would best be served by forsaking any thought of racial equality in the foreseeable future, substituting for such notions the more limited but, in his estimation, far more potentially fruitful goal of economic growth. Until blacks could bring economic success to the national table, Washington foresaw, the chances of whites granting them equal civil rights were nonexistent. "The wisest among my race understand that the agitation for questions of social equality is the extremest folly and that progress in the enjoyment of all the privileges that will come to us must be the result of severe and constant struggle rather than of artificial forcing." He added a phrase that, if memorable today mostly for its imagery, must have lain sweetly on the consciences of its white hearers in 1895. "In all things social we can be as separate as the fingers, yet one as the hand in all things essential to mutual progress." The short address was essentially a well-intentioned plea for blacks to work hard to earn white favor, and a promise to whites that they had nothing to fear but much to gain from the black half of the Southern population. But in terms of the South's racial impasse, Washington's advice represented a solution constructed wholly on white terms. Even then-President Grover Cleveland let it be known that he was "enthusiastic" about Washington's ideas, and the *Charleston News and Courier* remarked, in words notable for being comparatively noninsulting to the paper's black readers, "His [Washington's] skin is colored, but his head is sound and his heart is in the right place."

Almost immediately the black intelligentsia pointed out that Washington's remarks denoted little more than accommodation to Jim Crow as well as to the moral destruction of African-Americans betokened by the avalanche of Jim Crow treatment. Where in his "Compromise" Washington advised the Southern black man that he should put his future into "cultivating friendly relations with the southern white man," many blacks understood that the Southern white man had already *become* the sworn enemy of not only the black man but of black economic advancement, not to mention of black social progress.

The bitterest voice raised in opposition to Washington came from William Edward Burghardt DuBois, a militant and overwhelmingly eloquent advocate of every kind of equality for blacks. W. E. B. DuBois did agree with the part of Washington's speech that appealed for black self-help, but viscerally *disagreed* that black advancement should or could come in the framework of white supremacy or with any kind of expectation that Southern whites would even under duress help blacks to advance. DuBois charted his own equation to black headway in America: "By voting where we may vote, by persistent, unceasing agitation, by hammering at the truth, by sacrifice and work."

Yet Booker T. Washington had not spoken from naive wishfulness, but from a uniquely elevated understanding of the plight of the black Southerner. His speech had admittedly been a nod to accommodation, but one that recognized the facts of Southern life as they indisputably existed in 1895. Any realistic expectation of black civil rights in the South had died in the Compromise of 1877, in the growth of social Jim Crow, and now in the nationwide acceptance of the white Southerner's plea that the South—the white South—be left to deal with the Negro "problem" as it saw fit and as only it could supposedly "understand" that problem. Washington believed that the black man's efforts to gain equality with the white man were, if not actually suicidal, then at least self-defeating in his still largely uneducated and unassimilated state. To this dedicated educator, progress for Southern African-Americans lay in their own community, in using vocational training as a means of improvement, and in accumulating the capital that, Washington judged, would more effectively than any other force break down the walls barring black progress. At a time when blacks couldn't even get an antilynching bill passed in Congress, he sadly concluded that the path he outlined in Atlanta represented the only practical strategy by which African-Americans might better their place in the nation's life. Yet however admirable or reasonable his intentions may have been, Washington was mistaken. The record of white racism and discrimination against blacks would go from bad when he made his speech to far, far worse in the years that followed it.

In the whirlwind sown by the *Plessy* decision, a fanatical and increasingly statute-based Jim Crow spread across the South like an Old Testament plague. The Black Codes that had come in the immediate aftermath of the war would now be understood as having been but a feeble precursor of the white Southerner's resolve to turn into outcastes the 8 million bearers of the stigma of slavery who lived in the region's eleven states. As the encyclopedic roster of Jim Crow proscriptions reached its height, not a single facet—literally *not a single facet*—of Southern public life would exist in which the races were not divided by either law or ironclad custom. Where it was manageable and could be achieved, that divide meant simple segregation; where segregation was not possible, it meant complete exclusion of blacks from a given area of life. Having overcome the double-barreled threat of emancipation and Reconstruction, the white South now set the final bricks into its vision of a fitting and legitimate racial order.

After *Plessy*, it could reasonably be assumed by any knowledgeable person that the South would, without any further meddling, be legally and morally allowed to handle the region's race relations in whatever way it chose. The Supreme Court had already declared unconstitutional the Civil Rights Act of 1875 and that measure's protections against discrimination in public accommodations. Furthermore, it was equally clear by the turn of the century that Congress had no intention of compelling either non-segregated education or anything like universal education for black children; even in the North, the overwhelming majority of classrooms were populated wholly by whites or wholly by blacks, and it looked to stay that way. Near-total disfranchisement of blacks—meaning the virtual elimination of African-Americans from the South's politics and exclusion from the ballot and from the democratic process—was not going to be corrected by "guarantees" related to the Fifteenth Amendment, the Supreme Court having already let it be known that the region's exclusionary techniques— poll taxes, understanding clauses, and whites-only primaries and nominating conventions—would withstand any assault on their legality or constitutionality. When in 1915 the court did reverse itself and ruled some of these disbarments unconstitutional, Southern registrars and voting officials merely switched to well-established tools of intimidation to keep blacks from the polls. Less spectacular but more ubiquitous than actual physical terror, such methods included firing recalcitrant blacks or depriving them of the credit to obtain farm implements or destroying their property up to and including the burning of African-American homes. In the end, of course, there remained the almost always effective threat, and even delivery, of beatings and torture should a black ignore Jim Crow. All these measures, including lynching, the ultimate terror and the weapon of choice of the Ku Klux Klan, met with nearly universal official and public approval in the South—and most often, nearly universal official and public indifference in the North.

Legalized Jim Crow, the laws that set into stone an already existing way of life, infiltrated Southern life almost faster than could be comprehended. At first, the laws and statutes decreeing segregation in one form or another came either piecemeal or haphazardly, and it would be well into the young twentieth century before they would coalesce into an almost seamless whole. Often a community or government entity would institute some Jim Crow ordinance in the absence of any actual demonstrated need but when such official sanction would be thought to preclude any future situation where white sensibilities might be put at risk. And oddly, a few types of Jim Crow legislation weren't officially authorized in Southern communities until the system began to be seriously threatened in the late 1950s.

Besides the comprehensive drive to remove African-Americans from each community's political functioning, much of Jim Crow was enacted to forestall the possibility of a social breaching of the barriers that held back contacts between the races. Where members of the two races unavoidably met daily and informally—in common transportation carriers, on the streets, or in shops or places of business—whites strove to ensure that the caste rules separating whites and blacks were never and nowhere infringed, one of the purposes of which was to ensure blacks not be allowed for a moment to forget that they were in every way subordinate and inferior to whites. Importantly, this applied to *every* black man, woman, or child in relationship to *every* white man, woman, or child.

Historians have surmised a number of reasons why the South chose to "jurify" Jim Crow, which is to say to shift segregation from a de facto to a de jure system, to write discrimination into the law books rather than allow it to informally proceed simply by custom and extralegal coercion, the latter having been the principal arrangement for maintaining Jim Crow–like rules in the years following the end of slavery. As we've seen earlier, after the 1883 nullification of the 1875 Civil Rights Act and then the handing down of the *Plessy* decision in 1896, Southerners felt far less threatened by non-Southerners and thereby far less constrained by Northern opposition to their handling of the "Negro problem." But many whites in the South at the same time grew more physically fearful of blacks. Part of the reason was that by the turn of the century the majority of African-Americans no longer bore any personal experience of slavery, and as some younger and better-educated blacks began to press for greater opportunities, and even for equality, many whites considered such efforts a dangerous challenge to the sine qua non of their existence, which was, of course, the unequivocal supremacy of their race. In many of those minds, "custom" had become insufficient to guarantee this outcome, and accordingly it was time to make sure the African-American's place in the Southern order of things was spelled out, clearly and beyond challenge, in law.

This legalization of Jim Crow was further prompted because some Southern whites believed that some blacks were or should be to a degree acceptable, that educated or refined or well-to-do blacks should be exempted from *some* of the harsher rules that made the mass of African-Americans untouchables. Legalization of Jim Crow would end any such ideas. Fundamental to Jim Crow was the principle that any white person was superior to every black person, and conversely, that any black person was inferior to every white person. There could be no exceptions if the system was to retain its operating logic. White Southerners who flouted race rules would quickly find themselves labeled "nigger lovers," a status that would bring down the condemnation of the white community. And the same legal penalties that applied to blacks for violating Jim Crow applied equally—at least in theory and thus as a deterrent—to every white man and woman living within the operating jurisdiction of such rules.

The relatively "informal" segregation on trains and in streetcars—informal in that in some parts of the South it had never been codified or rigidly adhered to—could no longer be left to chance or to the actions of some town or community, which might find it unnecessary. Jim Crow had to be obligatory on every passenger train traveling through the South and on every streetcar (or later, bus) plying the streets of every Southern city. Not only could offending passengers be fined or jailed (or sometimes, merely kicked out or off), but the transportation official whose job it was to see that Jim Crow was obeyed could be assessed precisely the same penalty as the transgressing passenger.

Though the "separate but equal" formula in *Plessy* underlay the sweep of Jim Crow through the South, the "equal" half of the couplet never approached parity with the "separate" half. The reality of "equality" meant that the Negro part of everything would be indisputably and often grotesquely inferior to its white counterpart: black schools almost never achieved—and rarely even approached—equality with those for whites; black transportation facilities were famously and invariably shabbier than their white counterparts; when drinking fountains later became electrically cooled, a score of iconic photos showed the ice-water machines with For White Only signs hanging over them while under the For Colored Only placards stood ordinary and unquestionably nonelectrified appliances.

But bad as the foregoing was, think of the "separate" part of the couplet. Where a facility or service, a shop or place of amusement or café, couldn't be cut down the middle to keep the races from touching each other, then there was just none of that given thing for blacks. *Maybe* a café would sell a Negro something to eat out the back door, or a bowling alley might occasionally have a blacks-only night. But far more likely, blacks were just plain excluded. There was nothing "separate but equal" about the libraries from which blacks were barred entirely, nor was there anything "separate but equal" about the hotels that wouldn't allow blacks to pass a night in them, nor anything "separate but equal" about the gas stations that chose not to add an extra rest room in which African-Americans might relieve themselves. There was just exclusion, the quality that many blacks saw as their lot after the Civil War, and which they—at first, at least—understandably viewed with greater trepidation than mere segregation.

Little about Jim Crow was left to chance. Train and streetcar officials throughout the South were granted authentic police power for the sole purpose of overseeing and safeguarding Jim Crow. The conductor could arrest a train passenger in the South for sitting in the wrong seat and refusing to move, and the same held true on some streetcar lines. Not only did conductors have the authority to arrest offenders, they were also empowered with changing the Jim Crow arrangements on their particular form of public transport as the situation called for. Blacks sitting in "their" section could be made to move if the white section became filled to capacity and more "white" seats were thus required. Needless to say, the opposite—appropriating white seats to meet the needs of an overfilled black section—never happened. Only a very few cracks remained for exceptions to peep through. When, for example, a "mammy"—a white child's African-American nurse—accompanied her white charge, the woman was permitted to sit with that child in a white section, her unmistakably inferior servant's status allowing such situational dispensation.

Oddly, in some places blacks were required to sit at the *front* of the streetcar. One white remarked bluntly on the variant: "It isn't important which end of the car is given to the nigger. The main point is that he must sit where he is told."[1] The one universal principle of streetcar travel remained the absolute power enjoyed by the conductor to enforce or change the rules. And whenever the rules were changed, such change

---

[1] Litwack, 232.

inevitably accrued to the white passenger's comfort. Once when a black passenger complained about the arrangement, the conductor's less-than-grammatical retort neatly summed up the entire guiding philosophy behind Jim Crow: "The law was made to keep you in your place, not the white people."

Where streetcars were concerned, black sections differed little physically from white sections; they were, after all, merely the front and back of the same vehicle. But *Plessy's* "equal" requirement amounted to an altogether different situation regarding railroads. After the Supreme Court opened the floodgates to official Jim Crow, segregation in the South was usually maintained on trains with entirely separate cars assigned to the two races, the mixed-race second-class car now consigned to history. Furthermore, the one for African-Americans was never the equal of the one assigned to whites. Often the black car was the only smoking car, and though whites were theoretically barred from it, in practice they were generally allowed its use. As for black nonsmokers on such cars, they could put up with the situation or walk. The upholstery in the black coaches was rarely cleaned, the windows were often muddy, the floors were peppered with refuse that white conductors saw no need to have cleared. Conductors would use the black car for off-duty lounging, spreading across two seats in a way that would have been unthinkable conduct for railroad employees while in the white cars. When asked for help by a black passenger, white conductors would as often as not ignore such "impertinence." Well-dressed black passengers came to understand the special danger they faced: white passengers and railroad employees regarded such a display of black virtue as "uppity," as merely "darkies dressed up." W. E. B. DuBois wrote that "there is not in the world a more disgraceful denial of human brotherhood than the Jim Crow car of the southern United States." But the denial by whites of "human brotherhood" to blacks was precisely the point of the entire exercise. Making sure that the black occupied a place of inferiority and servility was what this miserable system was all about.

Jim Crow rarely stood still where innovation was concerned. Thus, shortly into the new century taxicabs were brought under the system's aegis. The first state to ban the use of integrated taxis was Mississippi, which in 1922 outlawed any "vehicle for hire" from allowing a white person and a black person to share it, excepting only when the white passenger was accompanied by a black servant; the Mississippi ordinance didn't address the situation in which a black person might be accompanied by a hypothetical white servant, likely viewing it as unthinkably moot. Before long, Jim Crow bans across the South would also prohibit white persons from entering taxis operated by black drivers and black persons from entering those driven by white cabbies.

In the early years of the twentieth century, opportunities remaining for black/white interaction in the South shrank almost literally every day. Even though most such chances for interaction had effectively been closed off by custom for decades, the Jim Crow laws making their (usually expeditious) way through Southern legislatures and council chambers in these years ensured any last windows of race mixing were eventually shut up tightly.

In jails and penitentiaries during the Jim Crow years, inmates were seldom imprisoned together: prisoners of different races were barred from sharing cells, from eating together, and if possible, from even being incarcerated in the same prison. Furthermore, white convicts couldn't be shackled with black convicts on the South's infamous chain gangs nor even till fields together on prison farms. The requirement that mental institutions separate the races could be as strict as the rules governing penal institutions. A North Carolina law passed in 1899 covered both the mentally ill and hopeless alcoholics in the state's asylums and provided that "the state hospital at Morgantown . . . and at Raleigh shall be exclusively for the accommodation of the white insane and inebriates of the state, and the hospital at Goldsboro shall be exclusively for the accommodation of the colored insane and inebriates of the state."

White libraries were as often as not closed entirely to blacks, the separate-but-equal rationale allowing a branch to be designated solely for black use. When a library did permit both races under the same roof, black patrons were generally assigned a room as far away from white patrons as possible. A 1901 Arkansas statute allowed blacks use of one room in the state library in Little Rock, a concession that at least recognized the

African-American thirst for knowledge, but a recognition that was by no means universal. In answer to a question as to why blacks weren't permitted to borrow books from the town library, one librarian responded simply but with perfect honesty, "Southern people do not believe in social equality."

The reader can be excused for wondering if in these years any corners of Southern public life were not controlled by Jim Crow. The answer is, very, very few—if any. The gusher of controls extended to ticket lines, some statutes even spelling out in mathematical detail how far distant the line for black ticket buyers had to be from the line for white ticket buyers. Officials passed out and stored schoolbooks by race, North Carolina and Florida even specifying that those used by black students had to be maintained separately from those used by whites. The lawmakers of Oklahoma decided that if a public telephone was handled by a Negro, it was no longer good enough (by which they really meant clean enough) for use by a white and promptly passed a law requiring the phone company to put up separate booths for black and white, each prominently marked with a handsomely lettered little sign informing potential users which was which.

Use of the public right of way became increasingly restricted for African-Americans after *Plessy*. Where blacks had since slave days been expected to step off the sidewalk to allow white persons to pass unimpeded—failure to do so could result in being murdered—some communities with the new century began to require blacks to keep off the sidewalks altogether when any white children were occupying any part of them. Much the same held for the roadway, where blacks could expect to be stopped by the police if they dared pass a white driver. So offensive to white sensibilities was a black driving an expensive car that even well-to-do African-Americans kept to older models so as not to give the dangerous impression of being above themselves.

The dead were as bound to Jim Crow as the living. A 1900 Mississippi act permitted the state's white Ladies' Auxiliary Cemetery Association to have black corpses dug up from "white" cemeteries and removed for reinterment in cemeteries "reserved" for blacks. One guesses the accommodation was meant to ensure that living persons wouldn't encounter others of the opposite race in cemeteries, but it is likely that sensitive Caucasians equally feared that the souls of their fellow whites would be offended at the specter of their bodies resting for eternity with those of blacks.

Nor was fornication exempt from Jim Crow, at least not the kind for which money was expected to change hands. Some jurisdictions duly legislated against integrated sex-for-hire: in 1900 New Orleans mandated white and black bordellos be located in different neighborhoods of the city. Nonetheless, many white men didn't hesitate to have sex with black women, relations that—with the men holding power or economic control over their "partners"—effectively amounted to rape.

Legislatures sometimes assigned harsher sentences to offenses they assumed would more likely be committed by African-Americans. For example, Missouri's politicians made chicken stealing a felony because of the stereotype of poultry theft as a black crime; the sentence was five years in the state penitentiary in lieu of a $200 fine, a sum few chicken thieves of any race would ever have been able to pay. As a result of these laws, before long a large number of African-American men were in prison, causing overcrowding in the region's penitentiaries. To relieve the congestion, some states decided to lease out prisoners, with corporations and individual employers thereby free to buy cheap convict labor. County and state officials didn't hesitate to use the prisoner-lease system to balance their own books and thereby keep taxes as low as possible. Corrupt officials could skim off their own profit, too, which tempted them to make false arrests of black men so they could rake in even more money.

White fear of blacks was virtually boundless, and curfews for adults thus became another Jim Crow harassment of African-Americans. In 1909, the commissioners of Mobile, Alabama, ordained that "all blacks must be at home or in bed at 10 P.M. Any of them caught wandering at large will be locked up. This action is due to an epidemic of hold-ups perpetrated by Negroes."

It went on and on. South Carolina's legislators in 1917 advocated appropriately intricate procedures to ensure that blacks were kept unoffendingly separate from white audience members at circuses, a form of entertainment especially beloved of both races when the twentieth century was young. Phrased in bureaucratic pomposity, the statute was typically precise: "Tent shows are to maintain separate entrances for different races. Any circus or other such traveling show exhibiting under canvas or out of doors for gain shall maintain two main entrances to such exhibition, and one shall be for white people and the other entrance shall be for colored people, and such main entrances shall be plainly marked 'For White People,' and the other entrance shall be marked 'For Colored People,' and all white persons attending such show or traveling exhibition other than those connected with the said show shall pass in and out of the entrance provided for white persons, and all colored persons attending such show or exhibition shall pass in and out of the entrance provided for colored persons. Any circus or other such traveling show exhibiting under canvas and failing to comply with the provisions of this section shall be deemed guilty of a misdemeanor and, upon conviction, shall be fined not more than $500. The sheriffs of the counties in which such circus or traveling show shall exhibit shall be charged with the duty of enforcing the provisions of this section." The cadences seem almost biblical.

The workplace became as thoroughly segregated as any other part of the Southern landscape. Whenever black and white toiled in the same office or shop or factory, every effort would be made to keep black workers away from white. In South Carolina, a law mandated that white textile workers labor in separate spaces from black employees, and that the two races further be required to use separate doors, separate pay windows, separate stairways and toilets and pathways. Where such separation was for some reason not possible, the solution was often simply to bar blacks altogether from employment—except, of course, in those jobs at which *only* blacks worked, which were the lowest, dirtiest, most backbreaking tasks and which were considered beneath even the most humble of white men.

In slave days, blacks worshiped with whites. They worshiped in a position of inferiority, of course, generally at the back of the church or in their own balcony. But at least the two races communed under the same roof with what was presumably their shared God, listening to the words of the same preacher, albeit invariably a *white* preacher. But in reaction to black emancipation, segregated religion quickly settled over the South as, frankly, was the case in the North. In fact, as with many aspects of social Jim Crow, segregated worship was nearly as widespread in the North as in the South, particularly among Protestant sects.

As a result, African-Americans found themselves by the late nineteenth century wholly unwelcome in white congregations, in some places legally barred from joining in worship. White interpreters of theology naturally tried to rationalize this religious discrimination, many pastors and priests simply declaring that segregation of the races—even inside God's own house—was the will of the Creator himself. It was instead, of course, the will of the white congregants that blacks not join them in worshiping the Almighty. Eventually, those churches that blacks established by and for themselves would become the most important social centers for African-Americans other than the family unit itself.

This titanic and obsessive effort on the part of white Southerners to separate the races created one predicament that was not always easy to master. The target of Jim Crow was obviously the black man, the Negro, the colored man, the slave, or descendant of the slave, the Americanized African. But exactly who was this being, and what specifically qualified him for these labels? Or, in a less usual way of putting the question, what *precisely* was it that kept a person from being regarded as white?

Through the slave era, America had no single, settled definition of what in social and legal terms constituted the "races." The category of "white" was fairly clear, though not *absolutely* so. A white person was generally held to be someone of European genetic stock. Full-blooded (which is to say unmixed) northern Europeans *were* unquestionably white, but southern Europeans weren't always quite so definitely white. In almost all senses, but particularly the social, the rule governing American society was "the whiter the better"—social attainments, political power, and wealth accrued in direct proportion to the indisputability of the whiteness of one's ancestry and physical features. Europeans who bore the darker skin tones of the Mediterranean, and who remained a comparatively small minority of the country's population until the nineteenth century, were often thought of as racially problematical, especially in terms of their intermarriage with fair-skinned northern Europeans, primarily meaning the Germanic, Anglo-Saxon, or Scandinavian people.

The category of "black" was considerably more complicated. In the antebellum South, *black* was nearly synonymous with *slave* for the straightforward reason that so few Southern blacks were legally free before the Civil War. *African* was a common term for blacks, though it was understood to generally exclude super-Saharan (Semitic or Arab Muslim) Africans. Black Africans were people whose skin was very dark and whose features were stereotypically "Negroid," and thus the Semitic Arabs of northern Africa didn't count as Africans in these terms, although, of course, sub-Saharan black Muslims did, as did the Christian blacks of Ethiopia, the two latter groups forming a tiny part of enslaved blacks in America. That said, virtually every statement in this paragraph had its exceptions, though the general drift of it suffices for the story of Southern Jim Crow.

Beginning with the earliest days of a black presence among the New World's European society, cohabitation (sexually, with or without marriage) between whites and blacks—what came in the late nineteenth century to be termed *miscegenation,* in Southern thinking "racially unsound unions"—created what was in fact a major new category of mankind. First called by the name *mulatto,* this creation from the mixing of white and black (or black and less black) genes eventually became the commonest kind of American "black." (Such were not, of course, the first persons of mixed white-black parentage in human history, but it *was* the first time this mixture became a key new social element within a major society.) Particularly after the cessation of any further mass importation of slaves, the American black had to a large degree metamorphosed into the American brown. Negroes in America began to make a new culture and a new sense of identity, one representing a blending of their various color-producing genes, their experiences on this continent, and their shared memories of the Africa from which they were torn by the slave trade.

Depending on an individual's own balance of white genes versus black genes, "black" Americans bore skins whose shade ranged from northern-European pink-white to sub-Saharan coal black. By the time slavery ended, a majority of American Negroes bore in their genetic makeup some degree of white, which is to say European, ancestry. Indeed, not more than a quarter of all African-Americans today are of unmixed African black ancestry. Of all the genes in those Americans who today call themselves black, somewhere between one-fifth and one-quarter were donated by European white people, as well as some further small percentage by American Indians and Asian groups. Conversely, of the total genes in Americans who today call themselves white, it is thought that about 1 percent come from black African ancestors.

The creation of this new American race began when the blacks first encountered the white indentured servants in the Chesapeake region of Virginia and Maryland. Important to understanding the story of Jim Crow is that from the first merging between the two groups, the results—their mulatto children—were socially shunned and often actively reviled by the majority white settlers and were almost invariably regarded as black persons irrespective of the lightness or darkness of their skin. When these mulatto children became adults and created new offspring with other mulattoes and with whites, the children of such unions further lightened the aggregate of black people. But as long as a person's physical black heritage—one's African roots—could be detected, either by his or her appearance or from general knowledge that he or she had been born of non-wholly-white parentage, that person was considered and treated as black. That was the beginning of America's almost-unique-in-the-world "one-drop" (i.e., one drop of "black" blood makes one wholly black) racial rule.

At first, the American colonies attempted to set official percentages, or quarterings, for determining who was and who was not a Negro. The upper South generally required a greater amount of African heritage to so label a person than did the colonies of the lower South. Virginia, for example, drew a color line in 1758 that specified a Negro as someone who had at least one black grandparent, with no other additional black genes (then called "blood") in the other grandparents. This "liberal" interpretation was important for black-appearing persons who coveted the considerable privileges conferred by Caucasian status. But, in point of fact, regardless of the law, if such a person in Virginia *appeared* colored to even the slightest degree, the wider community invariably treated the person as black.

When laws defining racial status were written in the colonies of the Deep South, *any* black genes—no matter how few—meant you *were* black. Caucasian appearance was irrelevant if public knowledge existed of one's black ancestry. If such a person's appearance was Caucasian, and assuming the black heritage was successfully hidden, that person could "pass" as white if he or she chose to do so. But such passing generally involved colossal sacrifices for the person affected. Principally it meant cutting oneself off from family and community and the security those resources brought. Furthermore, such people—meaning those aware of their African ancestry but deliberately passing to escape the social penalties black status brought in America—were constantly at risk of their legal racial classification being discovered. In not a few cases, people living as whites and entirely ignorant of their black heritage were "uncovered" and forced to assume legal status as Negroes.

The original justification for the one-drop rule reflected the monetary value of a slave. Logically, the child of a wholly white person and a wholly black person is half-white and half-black. But there was no such thing as half-a-white in Southern society, or for that matter, in any other segment of American society. Since almost all blacks in the South were slaves, most half-black children thus had one slave parent, that parent virtually always being the mother, with the white father often having been the black mother's rapist-owner. Such child was, ipso facto, valuable as property— as, in other words, another slave—and thus society acquiesced in this logic.

In rare cases, the owner-father may have felt some paternal empathy for his child, and as a matter of history, such illegitimate mulattoes were indeed often assigned preferable status as house slaves instead of being made to work as field hands. House servants gained many skills denied the less fortunate outdoors workers, particularly in gaining mastery of standard educated English as well as acquiring the manners and beliefs of their white owners. After emancipation, many such relatively favored ex-slaves settled in cities and became the nation's African-American elites. But in slavery, such mulatto offspring were almost never legitimized or made free, and only in instances too rare to be meaningful did such a child assume the same social status as his white father's other children—that child's own half brothers and sisters. In any case, throughout the Jim Crow era, appearance as the offspring of a black parent stamped one as the social and legal inferior of Caucasians.

In the early years of the Reconstruction era, black legislators and sympathetic and/or progressive white Republicans in the statehouses of the South overthrew the antimiscegenation laws that had made black/white marriages illegal. (These laws did, paradoxically, remain during those years on the books in Northern states, mostly for the reason that there were no black participants in Northern statehouses to overthrow them.) But as white Southerners regained political control as Reconstruction ended, they again saw to it that miscegenation was made illegal. As before the war, white men continued to father many illegitimate children of black mothers, often employing threats of violence if their sexual advances were rebuffed. Though blacks were no longer chattels after 1865, they were still valuable to Southern agriculture in their reconfigured serflike status, and so were their children, regardless of the father's color. The Southerner's postwar tendency to see all blacks as enemies helped ensure that mulattoes were never allowed to heighten their status to more closely match that of their white fathers. Under Jim Crow, mulattoes remained racially subject to the one-drop rule making them wholly and legally black irrespective of their white genes.

In the first decades of the twentieth century, most of the Southern states' legislatures legally adopted the one-drop rules to define what constituted being black. In 1910, Virginia switched from the single-grandparent measure to a one-sixteenth criterion, which meant even a single known African great-great-grandparent made a person black. But in 1930, Virginia's legislators again changed the law to codify a black person as anyone with "any Negro blood at all"—the one-drop measure. Louisiana had probably the least draconian law in this regard, defining blacks as people who *looked* black, a definition that would exclude many people who would in other Southern states be legally classified under the one-drop rule as black.

All over the South, whites grew increasingly frenzied that they themselves could actually be reclassified as black if an unknown black ancestor were to turn up in their family. Such fear of possessing "invisible black blood" was eminently realistic in a society in which white masters had raped black slaves at will, and whose descendants had slowly whitened with intermarriage with, first, mulattoes, then with whites. After 1920 the U.S. census bureau dropped the "mulatto" category, the government having concluded that at least three-quarters of all American Negroes bore white genes and thus officially specifying people as mulattoes no longer made much sense.

In the South and in the border states, law absolutely barred black-white miscegenation. Intermarriage, or even a sexual relationship outside marriage, was punishable as felonious behavior and resulted in serious prison time—as much as twenty years in Mississippi. But the white obsession with color and race mixing was pronounced nearly everywhere in America. In fact, by 1915 the one-drop-makes-you-a-Negro principle was upheld in every region of the country, and by midcentury twenty-nine states would have passed legislation prohibiting racial intermarriage and, in some instances, even nonmarital interracial sexual relations. Most such states forbade only the black-white union, but others—particularly those in the West—included all sorts of racial ordering in their proscriptions, barring American Indians, India Indians, Chinese, Malays, Mongolians, Hindus, and Creoles from marrying with some or all of the other groups.

There was, of course, one other kind of miscegenation. Logically, sexual contacts (and even marriage) between unmixed black Africans and persons with any lesser proportion of black African genes amounted to miscegenation as well—even though it was not generally thought of as such. But in fact this kind of miscegenation represented the greater share of mixing, since sexual or marital relations between persons with entirely white genes and those with entirely black genes was rare, the major reason obviously being that the latter category itself became increasingly rare in America.

The South's fixation with the mixing of the races had to do, at least superficially, with the "protection" of the white woman's "purity." And it *was* extremely rare in the South for the white partner in a (usually illegal) racially mixed relationship to be the female. Most white Southern men professed to believe that no white woman in her right mind, which is to say sane, *could* even mate with a Negro, such an act being more outrageous than murder itself. This delusion was nonsense, of course, but such vaunted and inviolate purity nonetheless provided the strongest psychological underpinning for the South's abhorrence of interracial sexual relations.

If you could accurately read the mind of a typical white Southerner during the Jim Crow era to inquire into the matter of racial bigotry, miscegenation would probably have been thought of as an almost interspecies phenomenon. Blacks were considered subhuman by most whites, simply not existing on the same plane as white Europeans. Whites thought blacks dirty, diseased, unable to reach white intellectual levels, with black males unable to control their "aggressive" and "brutalistic" sexual urges. That such creatures would and could bring down the white man in their undertow was the logic beyond any other for white antagonism to blacks and for white insistence on maintaining inviolate the barrier that Jim Crow represented. That the white man chose to overlook this "danger" every time he forced a black woman into sexual relations, and was furthermore generally allowed by Southern societal norms to get away with it, was the hypocritical hole in the system that is beyond explanation in rational terms.

If in all parts of their lives white people so strongly resisted contact with black people, it's not difficult to understand their rabid reaction to the thought of making their homes amongst those of African-Americans. This aspect of Jim Crow was as fraught in the North as it was in the South. In fact, San Francisco was the country's first city to pass a residential segregation ordinance, though its target was not African-Americans but instead the city's large Chinese immigrant population. A local judge quickly overturned the ban, ruling it a violation of the Fourteenth Amendment's equal protection clause as well as a violation of the provisions of a treaty between the United States and China.

In the antebellum South, residential segregation had been a comparatively insignificant part of the region's racial minuet. The overwhelming majority of blacks lived outside of the cities (as did, of course, the overwhelming majority of white Southerners), and the largest part by far of these rural blacks were slaves. Segregation on the plantations and smaller farm holdings of the South was in reality pretty much a nonissue: field hands lived in slave quarters, and house servants could at their owners' discretion live either in separate slave quarters or else be provided with beds in the workaday sections of the plantations' or farms' main houses. Broadly speaking, urban blacks lived according to whether they were free or slave. The latter were generally housed in servants' quarters of their owners' homes. Free blacks were rarely numerous enough to develop districts or ghettos of their own and tended to be dispersed fairly evenly throughout the towns, often ending up in alleys behind streets that were inhabited wholly by whites. These alleys were sometimes referred to as "nobody's alleys," too narrow to count in the municipal government's reckoning as streets and therefore left out of the provision of services and infrastructure normal to white areas. Rarely paved, the dirt-carpeted alleys turned to quagmires in the rainy season and, since garbage collection went begging for Southern black residences, were generally strewn with refuse throughout the entire year.

After the war Atlanta became home to one of the largest black populations in the South, a minority that represented some 40 percent of the city's total population by 1900. That year nearly half the babies born to Atlanta's African-American mothers died before their first birthday, the basic cause the abased conditions in which their parents lived. The commonest house for a black Atlanta family of the era consisted of a cramped one-story wooden shack divided into two or three rooms, the flimsy structure teetering on brick piles. These houses were generally unpainted, without plastering on ceilings and walls. The municipality supplied few such dwellings with running water or sewer lines, and the outhouses necessitated by the lack of plumbing usually served several dwellings. These conditions created a fertile environment for the spread of respiratory diseases, with tuberculosis and pneumonia running virtually unchecked. Furthermore, the lack of fresh running water meant stagnant water, and that invited waterborne diseases, with diarrhea, enteritis, dysentery, and childhood cholera generating much of the horrendous infant mortality. A further misery resulted from the typical siting of urban black housing: since many of any city's poor African-American neighborhoods were located in hollows, the drainage from the white districts on nearby higher ground poured into the black neighborhoods. Fetid pools formed, mosquitoes swarmed in them, and the inevitable malaria coming from these conditions struck African-Americans with an appalling virulence.

With emancipation, cities and towns drew in tens of thousands of former slaves with their greater opportunities for work. Blacks in increasing numbers then began to buy property, and residential race lines began to overlap, poor white neighborhoods often merging with black districts. Financially comfortable blacks increasingly bought homes in middle-class white neighborhoods, still being permitted by the law to do so even though such purchases often ended in white-generated violence perpetrated against the blacks and their property. Believing themselves threatened by black neighbors, whites began to pass local laws specifying precisely where African-Americans could live, which generally meant only in those streets where they already constituted a majority of the residents. Typically the rationale put forward for the new laws was to "ease" race relations, which of course meant "easing" white sensibilities.

Among the cities to legislate such residential Jim Crow were Louisville, Kentucky; Baltimore, Maryland; Richmond and Roanoke in Virginia; Winston-Salem, North Carolina; and Atlanta and Augusta in Georgia. Some towns excluded blacks entirely, while a few merely specified that African-Americans weren't allowed to work in them. Others barred blacks from as much as an overnight stay. A Virginia statute spelled out such discrimination in language that could serve as a model for all: "Whereas the preservation of public morals, public health, and public order in the cities and towns of this Commonwealth is endangered by the residence of white and colored peoples in close proximity to one another . . . the entire area . . . shall be divided into 'segregation districts.' "

Segregated-neighborhood ordinances came in several formats. One was designed on the Baltimore model as to how segregation should best be achieved: if a given block was primarily black, whites couldn't move in, and when a white home emptied on that block, only blacks could take up residence in it—and vice versa. This was the form Atlanta copied. Virginia's law was designed on another premise: it designated entire districts as either black or white and specified that each could be occupied by only one race after the borders were formally drawn, essentially ghettoizing the state's cities. These ordinances insisted that the stipulations apply equally to black and white, principally so as to pass constitutional muster.

For black districts to take on names like Niggertown and Darktown and Black Bottom was not uncommon. The latter name signaled that African-American neighborhoods tended to be located in flood-prone areas alongside riverbanks, places often neatly (and unmistakably) separated from white districts by railroad tracks. As towns became electrified, this new service commonly ended just where the black blocks and neighborhoods began. So too did paving on roads and sidewalks often fall short, as did gas and water services and telephone lines.

These residential segregation statutes finally came up against meaningful judicial review when in 1916 the Supreme Court agreed to decide the legality of Louisville's ordinance. As had been the case with the *Plessy* suit in 1896, so, too, was Louisville litigation's a collusive action, a put-up testing of the law, in this case by the NAACP. It took two years for the court to unanimously decide that Kentucky's statute was unconstitutional, a decision that, in effect, ended all the other residential segregation laws. The clear and obvious purpose of residential segregation ordinances—discrimination against unwanted blacks—was not, however, the principal basis on which the court struck it down. Instead, the justices said that the Fourteenth Amendment's "due process" issue meant, essentially, *property* rights issues. In other words, the right of the property owners to sell or dispose of their property to whomsoever they might choose had illegally been curtailed by Louisville's segregation ordinance. In so deciding, the court answered the terms of the NAACP's suit, even though to blacks the critical issue was not, of course, property rights but rather race discrimination.

Yet the Louisville case was indisputably important to civil justice for blacks. Though overtly basing its decision on property rights, the Supreme Court nonetheless seemed to be delivering fair warning to segregationists that there were limits to its acquiescence in Jim Crow. "This court," it said, "has held laws valid which separated the races on the basis of equal accommodations in public conveyances [*Plessy*], and courts of high authority have held enactments lawful which provide for separation in the public schools of white and colored pupils where equal privileges are given. . . . But in the view of the rights secured by the Fourteenth Amendment . . . such legislation must have its limitations, and cannot be sustained where the exercise of authority exceeds the constraints of the Constitution. *We think these limitations are exceeded in laws and ordinances of the character now before us.*"[2] (Emphasis added.)

Clearly, the members of the Supreme Court in 1917—as appropriate a year as any to represent the apogee of Jim Crow in America—were not yet ready to say segregation was wrong, its members certain the nation, particularly its Southern states, was not yet ready to be governed in its most tendentious and sensitive subject by a court, not even the highest. But at least the distant light of reason had now been shown, even if another half century of nonreason would have to pass before America would be substantially lit by that light.

Having lost a battle, white America was not, however, willing to concede the war. Where residential segregation was concerned, white politicians merely went back to the drawing board. New Orleans came up with a new ordinance that required anyone moving into an area to receive written consent of the people already living in the area, the city characterizing its bald racism as representing a "zoning ordinance" within the power of

---

[2] Kull, 140.

the city's policing authority. When the measure got to the Supreme Court, it was duly struck down on the precedent of the Louisville decision. An Oklahoma ordinance called for the use of military tactics to enforce residential segregation. The governor, William "Alfalfa Bill" Murray, declared martial law to give Oklahoma City time enough to set up racial boundaries within its municipal boundaries. That ploy, too, was quickly declared unconstitutional, this time by the state's own supreme court. The white supremacists needed to come up with something much cleverer, and resourceful as they were, they did.

The new gambit for residential Jim Crow was something called the "restrictive deed covenant," a stratagem that would enjoy a long and fertile life in virtually every sizable American city, both Northern and Southern. The earlier attempts to legislate segregation in cities might well have established, had they been successful, a true South African–style apartheid in America. Instead, restrictive deed covenants ended up creating a uniquely *American*-style apartheid, one that in some ways hobbled black freedom of action more than the South African variety ever would.

According to the dictionary, restrictive deed covenants are private contracts between property owners that bind the owners by specific restriction as to how they can legally dispose of their property. Under Jim Crow, these covenants were written by white property owners to restrain the contracting owners to sell their homes *only* to nonblack buyers (sometimes other minority groups were proscribed as well), the purpose clearly being to keep the neighborhood in which they lived entirely white or, in some cases, to "whiten" the district over time if some blacks were already there. All the parties to the covenant were free to bring suit for damages against anyone who violated the covenant. Some of the covenants ran for specific time periods—say fifty years, or ninety-nine years—while others ran in perpetuity, meaning until hell froze over.

This wasn't a new idea even in 1917. A quarter century earlier a group of California property owners had joined a covenant precluding them from ever selling their Ventura property to "a Chinaman or Chinamen." A federal court eventually overruled the deed on the basis of the Fourteenth Amendment's equal protection clause. But for white supremacists of any stripe, the scheme still seemed a likely one, and certainly worth trying somewhere else.

Sure enough, judges elsewhere did prove more sympathetic to these covenants, and the devices were legally upheld. In 1926, the NAACP managed to get a case—this one involving a Washington, D.C., covenant—all the way to the Supreme Court after having lost it at every prior stage of litigation. But the high court ruled, in effect, that such contracts did not fall under the Fourteenth Amendment's protections against inequality in the law on the basis that such restrictive covenants amounted instead to *private* agreements between individuals, and thus beyond government responsibility because the Fourteenth Amendment covered only the actions of *government* in perpetrating inequality. Remedy would therefore, it declared, have to be sought in state courts, from which quarter it would not, in fact, likely be forthcoming. Much as had happened with the spread of Jim Crow because of the *Plessy* decision, so, too, in the aftermath of this interpretation were now-legitimated restrictive covenants copied widely.

Some cities would actually see the majority of their housing stock come under the terms of restrictive covenants. In Chicago, for example, roughly 80 percent of all housing was bound by such restrictions, the major determinant in the nearly total ghettoization of African-Americans in the country's second-largest city. The irony of this wildly "successful" new form of Jim Crow was that it possibly rendered greater damage to blacks than if the courts had simply permitted statutory residential segregation—if, in other words, the Louisville decision had gone the other way. Whites jumped on restrictive covenants with a vengeance that made it almost impossible for blacks to escape the resulting ghettos in which they were to become virtually penned. It is unlikely that cities and states would have drawn racial boundaries nearly as restrictively or as tightly as the covenant-produced boundaries eventually became. The tragedy for America was that by the beginning of the Second World War more than 80 percent of urban African-Americans lived in rigidly segregated inner-city ghettos, districts carved into patterns of hypersegregation that remain to this day an ugly and seemingly permanent part of the nation's life.

While segregation ordinances and restrictive covenants represented the *legal* means by which whites kept African-Americans from living in their neighborhoods, in the early years of the century they weren't the only means—perhaps not even the primary tool—for enforcing this sector of Jim Crow. Instead, terror remained the white supremacist's weapon of first resort in preserving the rigid residential segregation that blanketed America for the ten decades following the Civil War.

In Chicago, the white remedy for blacks moving outside their own neighborhood was often a homemade bomb. The Chicago Commission on Race Relations reported on what happened to residences taken up by blacks, as well as to the offices of the white real estate dealers who sold or rented the properties: "From July 1, 1917, to March 1, 1921, the Negro housing problem was marked by fifty-eight bomb explosions. Two persons, both Negroes, were killed, a number of white and colored persons were injured. . . . With an average of one race bombing every twenty days for three years and eight months, the police and state's attorney's office succeeded in apprehending but two persons suspected of participation in these acts of lawlessness." The latter spoke to a large factor motivating white racism and violence, namely the assumption that such crimes would go unpunished and, often, even unnoted.

Few African-Americans living in the South hazarded their lives testing the boundaries of residential Jim Crow by actually taking up residence in areas forbidden to them, a risk that they knew would bring almost no help from any official quarter. For that matter, the risk to collaborative whites in renting or selling to blacks would have been fully as immediate and dire. In the North, better-off blacks attempting to settle in neighborhoods with housing superior to what they could find in ghettos would be subjected to picketing or even stoning. What followed from such realities was that in poorer areas of Northern cities, real estate agents often colluded in what was called blockbusting—the practice of selling blacks residences in white inner-city areas on the presumption that all the white occupants would simply flee as soon as they could sell, which would obviously result in abundant pickings for the agents.

In the South, this kind of blockbusting was almost unthinkable. An unlikely attempt at it would all but certainly have been stopped by terror, either Klan action or swift measures taken by the affected whites, meaning the bombing or burning out of the unwelcome would-be interlopers. Some all-white Southern towns gave unmistakably clear warning of what they thought of blacks attempting to live in their midst: they placed Burma Shave–style signs on the highways, all lined up in rows and warning blacks away with degrading doggerel and unmistakable hate: "Nigger if you can read / you'd better run. / If you can't read / you'd better run anyway."

The quarter century prior to World War I had seen white America relentlessly consign the nation's 10 million black citizens to the outermost reaches of the national conscience. The result was that by the early years of the twentieth century the forces responsible for it—white power, white supremacy, and Jim Crow—had returned the large majority of African-Americans to a status not unrecognizably different from that they had suffered as slaves, and left the country in a position where racism provided the dominant social undertone of American life. Nowhere nearly as much so as in the South did the emphasis on maintaining white supremacy ensure that almost every facet of black Americans' lives was entangled on a daily, never-ending basis in racial bias. The increasingly obvious answer to Southern blacks became escape, what became in effect a reprise of the cascade of fugitive slaves who had run away from captivity and the Black Codes half a century and more earlier—a less dangerous flight, perhaps, but no less urgent and no less profound.

When Europe fell into fratricidal war in 1914, what had been a seemingly bottomless supply of immigrants to America from that continent halted virtually overnight. The effect on the country's industrial economy was immediate: factories in the heavily industrialized North and West found themselves seriously, sometimes desperately, short of labor, particularly of the cheap and unskilled manpower that the untutored immigrants had provided.

Industry of necessity turned to a domestic labor pool that it had traditionally ignored. Southern blacks, largely undereducated to be sure, were nonetheless able and eager to work, fully capable of performing many of the factory jobs that would keep America's industrial economy humming along in high gear. All that had to be done to draw on this pool was to convince these African-Americans to travel to the North, as well as to provide the train fares to get them there. Accordingly, in the spring of 1915 hundreds of Northern companies dispatched labor agents southward to recruit this raw material. Echoing the agents were Northern black newspapers, such as the *Chicago Defender*, that portrayed the North as a "Promised Land," a refuge offering a way out of the black Southerner's economic and social misery.

The men and women who were the targets of these siren calls had historically been appreciated by Southerners for little more than one thing, their cheaply bought labor, a commodity that kept the costs of farmers (especially cotton farmers) far lower than if they had had to hire whites, even uneducated whites, to accomplish the same task. Working for minuscule wages as laborers or for minuscule profits as sharecroppers, in this first quarter of the twentieth century the South's black agricultural workers lived as bleakly and hopelessly as their forebears had as slaves. Considered subhuman by the whites who surrounded them, African-Americans nonetheless often outnumbered them, and little goodwill existed between the two races that could be expected to keep blacks in their Southern "homes." In short, few reasons existed why they shouldn't simply take the best offer to better themselves by leaving a South that despised them. Millions of African-Americans did just that, in fact sometimes whole communities, families packing up what little they had and, with far more hope than material resources, joining the exodus northward. The phenomenon resulted in the start of a monumental reordering of America's demography and, as a result, of its society, a realignment that would finally begin to change the destiny of America's African descendants. Few, though, could ever have guessed how vast the change would be, and how the migration would refactor America's racial equation.

Southern whites did not, of course, merely stand by and do nothing as their cheap labor pool "deserted" them. Some jurisdictions even tried, unsuccessfully as it turned out, to make such flight illegal—as if "their" blacks were mere land-bound serfs in fact as well as in effect. Some railroads refused to sell tickets to African-Americans asking for northward destinations. The commonest methods of trying to change black minds and halt this outmigration were, unsurprisingly, old-fashioned intimidation and fear-mongering. Even though Southern demagogues famously proclaimed "send 'em back to Africa," they rarely really meant it as more than anything but bluff: blacks had long been too important to Southern agriculture for such a scenario, and losing this commodity was the last thing most white Southern farmers wanted to have happen.

Within a year, the black flow northward had turned into a torrent, one that lasted until the end of the war in 1918. Nearly half a million African-Americans left in the war years for the North and West, all seeking the opportunities Jim Crow denied them in the South—higher wages, better lives, and spirits uncrushed (or at least, not *wholly* crushed) by white America's racism. One black man who had left his native Hattiesburg, Mississippi, for Chicago wrote a letter home that could have expressed the motivations of thousands of his fellow African-American journeyers: "I was promoted on the first of the month [and] I was made assistant to the head carpenter when he is out of the place; I take everything in charge and was raised to $95 a month. . . . I should have been here 20 years ago. I just begin to feel like a man."[3] When in the 1920s Congress permanently cranked down the flow of foreign immigration to a trickle, legions more of Southern blacks joined the trek northward until by the beginning of World War II a quarter of all African-Americans lived outside the South.

Given the nationwide white racism of the early twentieth century, blacks found social conditions in the North sometimes a mirror image of what they were fleeing in the South. Jim Crow, meaning the South's

[3] Levine, 145.

obsessional system of separating the races, was rarely found in the North, at least beyond the border states: blacks were not kept from the polls, and the South's pattern of race "etiquette" and its segregation ordinances were applied far more sparingly above the Mason and Dixon Line than they were below it. But many facets of Northern life involved a high degree of discrimination aimed at blacks, discrimination that was just as humiliating and often just as brutal as anything they had known in their former homes.

Where blacks had before the exodus been a small part of the general white-dominated population outside the South, Northern Jim Crow–like practices and policies had been, if not nonexistent, then at least muted compared to their openness in the South. Many of the blacks in Northern cities prior to World War I had been relatively highly educated, and Northern whites had established a modus vivendi with their stable African-American communities, a kind of truce that had for many years kept racial disharmony at a mere simmer. The terms of this arrangement were, of course, always white, and nowhere in the North had blacks been treated simply as ordinary Americans—not in the workplace, not in residential choices. But, compared to conditions for blacks in the South, Northern blacks had usually believed themselves fortunate.

The Great Migration radically altered those conditions. Before the war, indigenous blacks had almost always been born and raised in the North, but with the migration during and after World War I the proportion of Southern-born blacks living in the North increased dramatically: by 1930, they accounted for around 75 percent of New York's blacks, and upward of 90 percent of Detroit's. Sadly, if predictably, the blacks who surged into the North's cities changed white Northerners' perceptions of these communities' racial equations, leading whites to see what had before been a "stable" situation as now a "problem." Not only were the new black migrants dramatically less educated than those who had long lived in the North, they were also suddenly viewed as rivals for the low-paying jobs held by poorly educated whites and, even more dangerously, were sometimes suspect as potential strikebreakers. The result was vastly increased racial tension in the North, more discrimination and racism, and all too often racial disturbances leading to rioting and mass murder.

With these changes, the old equilibrium between white racism and black security disappeared in the North's cities. Blacks crowded ever more closely into substandard ghetto housing, while whites massively conspired to keep them there. The few blacks who attempted to move into white neighborhoods came up against all manner of violence, even as real estate agents connived in maintaining an absolute urban racial divide and banks denied home loans to financially qualified black families. Black neighborhoods found themselves hemmed in on all sides by whites refusing them expansion. The overcrowded conditions in African-American neighborhoods led to a catastrophic deterioration in living conditions, with single-family houses converted into multifamily apartments and boardinghouses, ever-more-shabby shelter from which white owners continued to extract exorbitant rents. Blacks were given little choice but to pay what was demanded, knowing there was nowhere else but the ghetto where they were welcome or even *allowed* to live.

Even many elements of the South's *social* Jim Crow established themselves firmly in the North. Just as the Great Migration upset the racial status quo in the North's cities regarding residential racism, it also worsened the social disbarments blocking African-American participation in many other areas of normal life.

Not all of the miseries of Jim Crow were to happen in the North, especially the so-called petty Jim Crow, characterized by, for example, the separate water fountains and segregated transportation. Yet only in a relatively few Northern jurisdictions were there laws protecting African-Americans from segregation in public services and accommodations. That meant that any restaurant owner *could* still refuse service to blacks, any hotelier *could* still refuse a bed to an African-American, any theater *could* refuse admission to blacks or require that they sit in a separate section. In other words, just like that which prevailed in the South.

And as they had in the South, so, too, did blacks in the North have to learn their limitations early on, venue by venue, service by service, hatred by hatred. Where an amusement park in Michigan might welcome African-Americans, a roller-skating rink in California might not. Where a cheap restaurant anywhere might serve blacks, expensive ones almost everywhere would not. Almost no recourse existed for those discriminated against because of the color of their skin—not to the courts nor to the police, not to anyone or anywhere. White Americans everywhere were free in those years—free to practice racism as they were free to reap the enormous benefits that were the birthright of their white skin.

What whites couldn't have foreseen, but what the blacks confined to those ghettos gradually came to appreciate, was the strength in their numbers. In their Northern ghettos African-Americans slowly acquired a political influence they hadn't known since Reconstruction. It would take time to learn how to use it, but they would one day force their collective voice to be heard and their collective anger to be felt. And, irony of ironies, even in the South the Great Migration left a salutary effect. Fear that the entire black population might desert and thus leave the region bereft of their cheap labor slowly began to force more pragmatic Southerners to begin to ameliorate some of the worst excesses of Jim Crow.

4

FULL-BLOWN JIM CROW:
BETWEEN THE WARS

During World War I hundreds of thousands of young black American men first tasted true freedom, the rights long enjoyed by their white countrymen, when their participation in that conflict revealed to them a world beyond the one in which Jim Crow governed human relations. When those same black troops came home from Europe, America's white supremacists, fearful of the consequences of those revelations, made it their priority to ensure that African-Americans understood that their place in the national hierarchy had in fact not in any way been changed by their contributions in the war. But as it turned out, the racists had good reason to be fearful. When the oppressed get a taste of freedom, the natural reaction is to want more of the same.

Since the nation's beginnings, the black presence in uniform has given African-Americans a measure of well-justified pride. But after the considerable black contribution in the Civil War—two hundred thousand African-Americans served in the Union army and blacks made up a quarter of the Federal navy's strength—the onrushing tide of Jim Crow and white supremacism would mean that *any* black presence in either the army or navy was unwelcome by whites, and as a result, such service was indeed eventually reduced to tokenism in the postbellum decades.

During the Indian Wars of the 1870s and 1880s, black enlistment was curtailed until a mere handful of segregated regiments remained, all of which were officered solely by whites. Nonetheless, blacks still constituted 13 percent of the enlisted men serving in these years, even though African-American units found themselves disproportionately stationed on the Western frontier, the reason less to do with logistical requirements than to ensure that they be posted as far away as possible from the Eastern and Southern states, regions of the country where their presence was immensely unpopular with whites. The army, of course, unquestionably needed its troops to serve in the West, but it speciously rationalized its patterns of black distribution with the scientific racism of the time suggesting that African-Americans adapted more readily than whites to the harsh conditions that were common to the Western frontier—not least to frontier diseases such as typhoid fever. What was more, the army generally outfitted the era's black troops with its inferior leftovers: poor horses, deteriorating equipment and supplies, and often inadequate and unhealthy rations. Black units operated in an entirely white-controlled world, one just as much infused as was civilian life with the racial bigotry characterizing the times. African-American troops—Indians, in apparent respect, called them "buffalo soldiers" after the massive animals they held to be sacred—were refused normal services by frontier townspeople, even in areas that they had just helped to secure from hostile Indians and where a measure of local gratitude might reasonably have been but wasn't forthcoming. Despite the hostility they faced, the postbellum black soldiers maintained the lowest desertion rates of any army units, and during the Indian Wars won 18 of the 370 Medals of Honor conferred by the army, including one for capturing Geronimo.

African-Americans were in this period virtually nonexistent at West Point and Annapolis, the nation's officer-training academies. At West Point, from its founding until 1936, only three blacks graduated from the four-year curriculum, one each in 1877, 1887, and 1889; twelve others were admitted during the same years, but eleven were dismissed for scholastic "deficiencies" and one by order of a court-martial. Henry Flipper, West Point's first African-American graduate, endured racism while a cadet just as bad as that experienced by his fellow blacks in civilian society. During his four years at the academy, Flipper was never—not even *once—*

spoken to by any of his fellow cadets, all of whom were white, being forced instead to endure a life of total social isolation. When he graduated in 1877, Flipper was assigned command of the black Tenth Cavalry on the Western frontier, but shortly afterward a court-martial convicted him on the extremely implausible charge of embezzlement of funds as well as of conduct unbecoming an officer. The army cashiered Flipper, and it took a century for the federal government to clear his name and posthumously grant an honorable discharge and, at long last, reburial in Arlington National Cemetery.

Another black academy cadet experienced even worse trauma. In 1880, Cadet Johnson Chestnut Whittaker was found, delirious and hog-tied, in his barracks bed, his ears cut off and his face drenched in his own blood. Amazingly, officers conjured that he had staged the dismemberment himself so as to gain "sympathy." The army court-martialed him for doing so, though the cadet himself swore that three masked fellow cadets had been the assailants, attackers who were never identified. Failing to rid itself of Whittaker with its kangaroo court, two years later the academy expelled him for examination "deficiencies."

At Annapolis, the historical record was at least as appalling as that which had dishonored West Point. Until four years after World War II ended, the Naval Academy had *never* graduated an African-American midshipman. Five were admitted, the first in 1872; of these, one was dismissed and four resigned, all on academic grounds. The five had been subjected to horrendous torment, far worse than the revolting but "normal" hazing white midshipmen endured. The navy justified the treatment meted out to the black midshipmen on the grounds of "meeting the best interests of general ship efficiency." It would be 1949 before Annapolis granted an African-American midshipman a diploma and a commission.

The presence of black representatives in Congress was the only reason for *any* academy appointments in the Reconstruction era—a total that can only be described as nearly meaningless. Conversely, the almost complete fall-off until after World War II reflected that the disfranchisement of blacks meant the end of African-American congressmen. The white senators and representatives who took over the few black Southern seats were hardly likely to appoint African-Americans to the service academies. White Northern legislators behaved toward blacks seeking appointments as cadets or midshipmen fully as shamefully as did their Southern colleagues.

After the turn of the twentieth century, the military further cut back on black enlistment, its drastic reductions trending in direct proportion to the spread of statutory Jim Crow throughout civilian society. By the time the United States entered the First World War, within its enlisted ranks the navy had permitted only two significant breaches in its policy of keeping blacks off its ships and out of this branch of service. One was engine-room duty as a coal stoker, and even that function was soon phased out as oil replaced coal in the fleet. The second was mess duty, which mostly meant acting as servants for officers in their private quarters; after the war the navy exchanged Filipinos for blacks in these roles, characterizing the former as more "tractable." Twenty-two black mess stewards were aboard the USS *Maine* when on the night of February 15, 1898, every one of them was killed in the ship's mysterious explosion, the spark that touched off the war between the United States and Spain; these dead African-Americans accounted for 9 percent of the deaths on the ill-starred battleship.

During the Spanish-American War, many blacks believed—or hoped—that the unambiguous patriotism they displayed, even in the face of the armed services' almost pathological racial bigotry, would earn them esteem from white America. In the main, they were wrong. To some degree their unarguably heroic fighting in Cuba had brought them the respect of the war's leading figure, Theodore Roosevelt, admiration that later translated into a measure of black influence in Roosevelt's White House. The African-American soldiers who had fought in Cuba and the Philippines had in fact garnered a tenth of the Medals of Honor conferred in the war, a reality that led one white soldier to reproach the army's racism by remarking, "They can drink out of our canteens," the implied sentiment being that they were *also* good enough to fight with. Some black newspapers—papers that were then, as they still are today, a feature of many of America's largest cities—called into question the propriety of blacks fighting side by side with the same Americans who routinely brutalized them at home, though most African-American soldiers had little time for such views despite the justice inherent in them. Yet the reality of the era was that white respect for black fighting men remained in short supply.

Six years after the Spanish-American War ended, a minor incident demonstrated just how quickly both white society and now-President Roosevelt were to believe the worst of blacks in uniform. When a brawl in Brownsville, Texas, involving black soldiers defending themselves from white-engendered abuse turned into a race riot, one leaving a white man dead and several others injured, Roosevelt unhesitatingly approved the court-martial's guilty verdicts of 167 blacks—most of whom had fought with him in his famous assault on Cuba's San Juan Hill. All were thrown out of the army without a trial and were disqualified from further government service, either civil or military. Six Medal of Honor winners were among those convicted. The affair rendered a telling appraisal of the government's treatment of any blacks foolish enough to assert their rights in altercations or disputes with whites.[1]

Within weeks after President Woodrow Wilson took the United States into the European war in the spring of 1917, contravening his campaign pledge that he would keep the United States out of the conflict, the army was faced with the dangerous reality that voluntary enlistments of white men would fail to attract the huge troop levies required for the European battlefields. Yet the draft plans initiated that year had at first barred the induction of any blacks whatsoever. In return for such contempt, African-Americans forcefully protested, shaming the government into reversing its position. Eventually a third of a million African-American servicemen were taken into active duty, with two hundred thousand of them experiencing overseas service, the great majority not in frontline units but in supply and labor battalions.

Many blacks openly questioned the justice of their fighting for the "freedom" of America's European allies when they themselves were any-

---

[1] It would be 1972 before the army reversed the Brownsville discharges and cleared these men's records by granting honorable discharges to all 167 of them.

thing but free at home. Making their moral resistance nakedly clear, some civilians displayed signs after the lynchings that were common to this period, starkly spelling out reality as they saw it: "This lynching was not made in Germany." In spite of the hypocrisy attached to black military participation when African-Americans were overwhelmed with the torments of Jim Crow, almost all African-American inductees nonetheless went when called and in uniform served with unimpeachable honor. Part of this conduct may well have been due to the appeal of W. E. B. DuBois, who urged blacks "to close our ranks shoulder to shoulder with our white fellow citizens." DuBois wrote that military service on the part of African-Americans would in the end result in "the right [for blacks] to vote, the right to work, and the right to live without insult." Many blacks likely believed such would indeed be their reward.

What young African-American men saw when they first confronted Britons and Frenchmen and Italians astonished the great majority of them who had never before encountered whites except as oppressors and overseers. For the first time, thousands of them realized that white people didn't *have* to be racist and consumed with hate directed at people with black skin, an awareness made apparent from the courtesy, even the unfeigned nonchalance, directed at them from the Europeans they encountered. European civilians openly expressed their gratitude to the black Americans for coming to help fight their war, and many white Allied soldiers, exhausted from three years of murderous confrontation with the Germans, were simply grateful for the support the African-American soldiers lent.

The comparative lack of racial awareness on the part of Europeans did not, however, go unnoticed or meet with any enthusiasm from the white Americans who led the still wholly segregated black units. The American commander in chief, General John "Blackjack" Pershing, informed his French counterparts that civilian and military courtesy should not be "overly extended" to black American troops, suggesting as well that Allied officers should not "commend them too highly," irrespective of the unimpeachable quality of their soldiering. The American army clearly had no intention of ameliorating the Jim Crow attitudes it had brought with it to Europe. A memo issued to French troops further amplified on Pershing's directives in respect of white America's race norms: "We must not commend too highly the black American troops, particularly in the presence of Americans . . . make a point of keeping the civilian population from spoiling the Negroes. Americans [the writer meant white Americans, of course] become greatly incensed at any public expression of intimacy between white women and black men." Black troops were even kept out of the postarmistice victory parade held in Paris, the intent to make sure the French government not be seen publicly honoring them, something American commanders believed would be interpreted as an insult to white American sensibilities. In spite of official white American attitudes on race, France did in fact honor 171 black Americans who had served alongside French soldiers, bestowing on each either the Croix de Guerre or the Legion of Honor.

In summary, the American military authorities scrupulously acquiesced to their nation's own domestic, primarily Southern, racial norms and behavior. The opportunity presented the army to curtail Jim Crow in its ranks was squandered, never even seriously considered. Even though the great majority of white Americans were overtly racially intolerant in these years, it is nonetheless likely that non-Southern troops would have met the novelty of serving alongside black troops with at least a measure of equanimity, especially if these men had frankly and without equivocation been *ordered* to do so. Instead, the white supremacism of most officers and the racist attitudes of Southern enlisted men were granted undisputed precedence in the army's racial behavior in World War I.

Over the months following the armistice, legions of African-American soldiers returned to the United States from Europe, many instilled with pride at having defended "liberty" abroad and justifiably expecting to partake of a portion of the same in their own country. But liberty was the last thing white America planned to bestow on these blacks, war-veteran status notwithstanding. In New Orleans a white official was reported to have told a group of veterans soon after their return, "You niggers were wondering how you were going to be treated after the war. Well, I'll tell you, you are going to be treated exactly like you were before the war; this is a white man's country, and we expect to rule it."[2] A brief look at the racial situation at that time in the nation's capital city lends credence to the truth of that warning.

In 1918, Washington, D.C., had more by elimination of competition than by design acquired the international status of seat of the most powerful government in the world. The old power centers—London, Paris, St. Petersburg, Berlin, Vienna—had with colossal stupidity wasted their power and vitality on a suicidal and largely pointless war, and the authority of the dead or damaged empires they represented had sunk or was sinking like stones dropped in the sea, though in London and Paris that truth still lay a bit beyond understanding. In reality, only America came out of the war whole and even energized, and its capital city was looked to anxiously by nations around the globe, all—or most anyway—eager to secure, as its president famously phrased it, a world "safe for democracy."

But few of the 125,000 African-Americans who lived in Washington, representing more than a quarter of the District's population, were aware of anything like a peaceful or democracy-loving community. Slavery had remained legal in the city until only a few years before the Civil War, and the franchise had been lost to all its residents in 1874, taken away by Congress mainly because of its relatively large African-American population. By the time the First World War was ending, Jim Crow had given the great majority of Washington's blacks a status not unrecognizably different from that they held when their brethren were toiling in slavery a stone's throw away across the Potomac.

White Washingtonians gave scant, if any, notice to an African-American's attainments or status, most caring not an iota whether blacks were criminals whose economic desperation forced them outside the law, or uneducated refugees fleeing rural destitution, or industrious barbers or grocers or druggists or undertakers who provided a social infrastructure for the black community, or even the highly educated and highly cultured leaders of the capital's African-American society: all were equally shut off from assimilation into the life lived by the city's whites. The well-to-do

---

[2] Appiah, 2028.

African-Americans aroused the particular indignation of the white working class who labored in an economic system that handed its drones the palliative of "superiority" over blacks. But all blacks shared the same boat insofar as white sensitivities were concerned: they were barred from virtually every facet of white Washington, from every white theater, from every white hotel, every white restaurant, from nearly every white institution of whatever description or use or quality.

Though the District held a few scattered areas where housing was as good or better than black housing anywhere else in the country—Le Droit Park, for example, formed a comparatively prosperous African-American neighborhood—residential Washington remained exhaustively segregated, with rigidly enforced housing covenants ensuring that racial housing patterns stayed that way. The core of the city's black slums were the "alley dwellings," ramshackle flats and houses built through a maze of some two hundred back alleys that had originally been designed to provide service entrances for white homes and businesses. These alleys formed ideal incubators of disease, part of the equation that resulted in a horrendously high death rate for babies born to African-American mothers as well as a correspondingly high crime rate for young, unemployed, uneducated, and desperate black men. The city's segregation depleted further the meager funds spent on schools that blacks were permitted to attend: the requirement that the District maintain two school systems wasted not only money that could have lessened these appalling conditions had the will to do so existed, but also furthered a system that reinforced white children in notions of their innate and God-given superiority and black children with corresponding notions of their innate and God-given inferiority.

The tragically flawed man who occupied the White House through both the war and the opening months of the twenties bore significant responsibility for perpetuating this state of affairs. Discussing Woodrow Wilson's role in governmental racism and the hardening of Jim Crow in both Washington and the nation at large makes for an awkward exercise in assessing a chief executive still regarded by many as a paragon whose vision of international security was thwarted by lesser and envious men. Wilson was a Southerner, a Virginian whose stewardship of Princeton University as its president included the unyielding maintenance of a completely white student body in sharp contradistinction to the racial liberalization then on the rise at America's other prominent Northern universities. His published prepresidential views that blacks represented "an ignorant and inferior race" and that black authority of any kind would always meet with "unalterable" white resistance provided an accurate foretaste of the kind of racial policies he would bring to the White House. Yet the enigma in this man is that Wilson wasn't a particularly vicious racist, but rather an intellectually convinced white supremacist who practiced the racial mores of his upbringing, of the state in which he was born and nurtured, and of the times in which he lived. That African-Americans voted for him in such large numbers spoke more to their lack of choice—Wilson's opponents, the "regular" Republican William Howard Taft and the "Bull Moose" Republican Theodore Roosevelt, seemed even less promising where racial issues were concerned—than it did to his likelihood of becoming any kind of authentic advocate for black Americans in general or for black civil rights in particular.

Irony abounded in Wilson's actions since his predecessors in their administrations *had* actually shown some slight sensitivity to black concerns. Theodore Roosevelt and William Howard Taft had appointed African-Americans to a number of meaningful, if not especially prominent, offices in the federal bureaucracy. For example, the registership of the Treasury had under these administrations become recognized as a black sinecure, as had a few customs and federal port collection posts. When Wilson was campaigning for the presidency in 1912, he openly courted black votes with his promise to continue such advances. Currying voting blocs certainly wasn't unknown in politics, but for blacks such pledges of equitable treatment were unusual indeed and must have been all but impossible to disregard. During the presidential campaign Wilson received a black delegation led by a prominent Methodist bishop. The candidate assured the group he would be as much the friend to African-Americans as had been the Democrat Grover Cleveland, hitherto considered by many blacks a relative model of balance in racial matters insofar as any balance in such matters existed at all in the two decades bracketing the turn of the twentieth century. For his pledges Wilson duly received more black votes than any Democratic presidential candidate before him.

What the new president brought to the White House, though, was not racial justice but instead Southern power and with it Southern racial mores, a force immediately felt in political decisions that were deeply damaging to what progress blacks in the District had, over crushingly long odds, been able to achieve.

Instead of an even or a fair hand in matters affecting the civil rights of the District's black federal employees, Wilson's first order of business was to painstakingly and exhaustively racially segregate the city's federal agencies—some of which had been integrated for fifty years—a move that resulted in weakening this exceptionally hard-won black presence in government. Wilson justified his actions by characterizing governmental segregation as "distinctly to the advantage of the colored people themselves," apparently meaning that he thought it would protect them from white animosity; he further explained these changes by asserting they were "in the interests of the colored people as exempting them from friction and criticism." That in actuality they created insuperable barriers to African-American advancement apparently didn't matter to the president. Moved by his equally racist wife's disgust at witnessing whites and blacks working side by side in the District's federal offices, an arrangement that had worked without serious incident during his predecessors' administrations, Wilson ordered the two races immediately separated wherever they came into physical contact with one another. The racist cabinet appointments he made, many of them fellow Southerners, zealously followed their boss's lead. Workstations, cafeterias, rest rooms—the entire workplace infrastructure of the government became subject to a Jim Crow as meticulous as anything seen in any backwater of the Deep South.

One of Wilson's most prominent cabinet officers was his son-in-law, Secretary of the Treasury William Gibbs McAdoo, who was, like the president, a Southerner. The malignity of the racist McAdoo's influence was particularly hurtful because his department controlled, through the Office of the Architect, the construction and maintenance of the nation's federal office buildings. Because these buildings housed dozens of governmental offices, departmental orders enforcing Jim Crow were widely and relatively easily enforced, even in Northern cities where such practices had not been common before Wilson's administration. McAdoo's Virginia-bred assistant treasury secretary personally ordered toilets in the Treasury Department be segregated by race, a demand that because of the connection with the Office of the Architect soon found itself being enforced in every federal office building in America, meaning that five thousand African-Americans in the District and ten thousand more around the country experienced in the most personal and humiliating way the racist thrust of Wilson's administration.

While the Wilson administration nurtured white supremacy in government, darker forces both organized and ad hoc were furthering the reach of Jim Crow elsewhere in American life. Racism's best-known and most-feared proponent had been born in the chaos of the just-ended Civil War, faded when much of its program was realized, and then, much like a virus that had lain dormant, gained life anew a generation later. Not quite dead even as the twenty-first century dawns, the Ku Klux Klan continues to agitate for white Anglo-Saxon Protestant supremacy just as it has since its beginnings, and today it remains perhaps the foremost symbol of systemized hate in America.

We've seen earlier how the Klan was spawned from defeated Southerners' need to keep former slaves under white control, its rationale largely fear of a black uprising in the chaotic aftermath of emancipation. Begun in 1867 by styling itself the "Invisible Empire of the South" and organizing around the principles of white supremacy and opposition to federal Reconstruction policies, Klan leaders invented an exhaustive canon of mumbo jumbo in which to clothe and legitimate their activities. As bizarre as anything else were the mysterious-sounding titles designating officers and members and specialist functions. Grand wizards, grand dragons, grand titans, and grand cyclops organized themselves into kleagles and klaverns and transported themselves around the countryside on horseback posses all the while covered with sheets and dunce caps and masks to hide their identities while terrorizing and sometimes murdering not only blacks but whites who befriended or spoke up for blacks or acted against what the Klan considered the white South's racial ideals. It was, in plain words, an out-and-out terrorist organization willing to perpetrate any outrage to hold blacks in as close to a state of complete social and economic debasement as possible. Though during Reconstruction the Congress and courts acknowledged the Klan's flouting of the law and passed laws and adjudicated against it to curtail its activities, the real reason for the organization's first demise was that it had accomplished what it had set out to do: it had helped to decisively reestablish white supremacy throughout much of the South, and no real need any longer existed to continue with the effort and expense of terror beyond keeping an eye peeled and a rope knotted for arrogant or insolent blacks who might be planning trouble.

At least, that's how Klan matters stood until 1915. The night before Thanksgiving in that year, the Klan awoke from its quiescence. The setting was Stone Mountain, outside Atlanta, Georgia. One William J. Simmons, "colonel," preacher, and professional promoter of fraternal organizations, revived the inert organization, the rebirth coinciding, almost to the day, with the release of D. W. Griffith's classic race-baiting film *The Birth of a Nation*. The movie carried a simplistically appealing but unmistakably white supremacist message that was praised even by President Wilson, who after screening Griffith's epic in the White House called it "history written in lightning"; joining the president at the screening had been the chief justice of the United States, Edward White, who was himself so taken with the melodramatic picture that he admitted with pride to once having been a member of the Klan. This kind of approval impelled many nativist-minded Americans to favorably and sentimentally regard the old but not forgotten Klan in a new and softly tinted light. The impetus this reassessment handed to Colonel Simmons was invaluable, as thousands enthusiastically rushed to join the organization at a time when denigration of the African-American had reached the point of national obsession. Taking as their symbol the tall crosses they set alight at initiation rites, Klansmen and their compliant Klanswomen viewed the burning tokens of Christianity as "glorifying the light of Jesus Christ," a savior they personally knew to despise as much as they did the notion of an "equal" black man.

The new Klan remained a localized phenomenon for four years, but in 1919 it began to attract serious nationwide notice, and a year after that it claimed one hundred thousand members. This time around, though, the Klan was not the same night-riding hordes of terrorists it had been in the years following the Civil War. Now it consisted of a cross section of middle- and lower-middle-class men—and unlike the first Klan, women, too, and in significant numbers—who aimed their flag-cloaked racial paranoia and hatred at not only African-Americans but at Roman Catholics and immigrants and, especially virulently, at Jews. Fueling its appeal and growth was the fear of loss of what its members regarded as "Americanism," a holy quality being defeated by the new internationalism and "cosmopolitanism" that they feared was dangerously weakening the moral fiber of the United States in the aftermath of the European war.

Furthermore, the new Klan was as much a Northern, especially a Midwestern and Western, phenomenon as a Southern one, a panregional, mass-membership organization that aimed at fascist-flavored political power and achieved it—especially successfully in Indiana (its headquarters state), Oregon, Maine, Texas, and Oklahoma. So mainstream an image did Simmons's brainchild achieve that it was allowed to march a hundred thousand of its members down Washington's Pennsylvania Avenue, legions of men and women baroquely costumed in their sheets and trademark headdresses. The Klan was seriously regarded at the time of the parade as the most popular organization in America, ranking ahead even of the Boy and Girl Scouts.

At its height in the midtwenties, the Ku Klux Klan claimed 4 million members (some sources have the number of authentic card-carrying members at half that, other sources more than double the number to almost 9 million), including its nearly half a million women, who were assembled into "ladies' auxiliaries." One of the factors fueling the organization's growth was the cash Klan organizers earned for recruiting every new member. At least five of its members were U.S. senators. Thousands more were ministers, from whose Protestant churches the wizards and dragons and titans drew immeasurable moral and financial support; the Klan even waived the $10 entrance fee to ministers who wished to sign up and don specially decorated clerical sheets. Many of these clergymen served as "kludd," or chaplain, of their local chapters, proudly invoking the name of Jesus Christ to uphold the organization's bigotry, lawlessness, and hubris. One of the Klan's anthems stated, "To arms . . . till the spoilers are defeated, till the Lord's work is completed." The Ku Klux Kreed stressed "pure Americanism" and declared that the "distinction" between the races was "decreed by the Creator."

Because the Klan had focused its hate on a wide variety of perceived enemies doesn't mean it had mellowed its antiblack views. Its leaders understood that it couldn't achieve a mass nationwide membership if it was solely associated with Negrophobia, but at its core it nonetheless always held the most dangerous enemy to be the black man. Thus its greatest energy always went into a nationwide endeavor to keep African-Americans politically powerless and, in the South, to ensure no dents were made in either the social or legal structures of Jim Crow. For example, Klansman Clifford Walker served as Georgia governor from 1923 to 1927, years during which in his official gubernatorial capacity he eagerly upheld the organization's black-directed terrorism. In the unlikely event that Governor Walker had weakened in his fervor, he would have been reminded that his predecessor, Thomas Hardwick, was driven from the governorship for daring to speak against—modestly, as it were—the Klan's less-than-democratic activities.

Georgia governors notwithstanding, Klan membership in its 1920s reincarnation was, as we've seen, considerably higher in the North than in the old Confederate states. In 1925, Michigan boasted more Klansmen—875,000—than any other state in the country, followed by New Jersey. Proportionate to population, Nebraska led the nation with its 352,000 members at this same time.

Astonishingly, in the late 1920s the reborn Klan would decline with stunning speed. Scandal among its leadership explained a part of its loss of popularity, though other organizations have survived corruption in high places. The most important cause of its slump was likely new statutes outlawing the wearing of masks in public, a prohibition that inflicted far more damage than had scandal: people seemed to be drawn to the thrills that came with the low-priced theatrics and secretive froufrou adopted by the Klan and weren't so interested when they couldn't scratch this itch. What was more, with the onset of the Depression the membership fee of $10 charged by the Klan became a highly dispensable luxury.

Suppurating like a gangrenous wound was the most terrible of all Jim Crow's infamies during the interwar years, the deplorably American phenomenon that was lynching. High in the nation's catalog of injuries done to African-Americans, the crimes of the lynchers—a cast, it should be said at the outset, that was immeasurably larger than those who simply did the killing—have covered America's common legacy in shame.

In modern terms, lynching means murder, by a mob large or small, of a man or a woman whom the members of the mob believe has committed a criminal act or a grave social wrong, which in the Jim Crow era most often meant a racial wrong. Occasionally, lynchings have served less as punishment for a specific transgression than as sport for the perpetrators' amusement or as a bolstering of the lynchers' sense of self-importance or self-righteousness. Dictionaries sometimes define the act more simply but less comprehensively, namely as execution in the absence of due process of law. The term is not, as is often thought, synonymous with hanging. Lynchings in their thousands have indeed been carried out by the rope, but they also have taken in shooting, burning, dragging the victim behind some kind of vehicle, knifing or razoring, pummeling, and other sundry and generalized savagery, occasionally including the literal tearing apart of a person. In the United States, the most common method has simply been to throw a rope over a tree branch and strangle the prey, though this latter mode of dispatch has often been combined with one or more of the other bodily tortures, routinely including for male victims genital mutilation and/or removal. In the kind of lynching that became a specialty of the Ku Klux Klan and which was widely applied where a black man had broken a rule of Jim Crow etiquette, the victim was simply shot to death, usually after having been kidnapped. Locals often said of the dead person after this kind of disappearance that the deceased had "moved."

Lynching—even of blacks—was never limited to the South. It was, however, *endemic* to the South, as it was not to any other section of the nation. Between 1882 and 1950 roughly five thousand men and women were lynched in the United States, and more than 85 percent of those crimes took place in the states of the former Confederacy or in the border states. African-Americans represented the great majority of the victims of what was, by definition, a participatory conspiracy. Lynching was for nearly a century Jim Crow's ultimate sanction.

The South's virtual free pass to lynch ranks among the most difficult issues in American history to comprehend or to explain. For decades, Southern senators and representatives in the U.S. Congress loudly and almost proudly defended the ritual that so grievously plagued and embarrassed their region. Men who would compare their Christian virtue with that of Christ's apostles never hesitated to filibuster into extinction any congressional effort to federally criminalize or even officially denounce this most noxious of hate crimes. Yet their defense of lynching under the guise of states' rights made the filibustering Southern senators fully as morally guilty of murder as the actual degenerates who dragged African-Americans from homes or businesses or jail cells and delivered them into the hands of mob-applauded death.

Until the 1880s lynching was neither primarily a Southern nor a white-on-black occurrence. The act was supposedly named for Colonel Charles Lynch, who during the Revolutionary War tried to set up a kind of private kangaroo court in which to sit in judgment on colonists suspected of loyalty to Britain. Lynch's court merely sentenced people to a flogging rather than death, but his name nevertheless came to be applied to extralegal execution, or "lynching." It can be rationalized that America's pre-independence system of courts and jails was in its infancy, meaning that law-abiding but largely unprotected colonists perhaps justifiably viewed extralegal punishment—even execution—as a necessary safeguard. But from the beginning, the practice was mainly directed at people whom society accounted as marginal or unworthy, categories into which African-

Americans seamlessly fit in almost every nonblack person's view. Slaves themselves were not, of course, often lynched because they were frankly too valuable to be so disposed of, the lash usually serving instead.

Directly after the Civil War, lynching would become most closely associated with the mob murder of rustlers in America's wild and still largely lawless West. But before long this kind of extralegal execution took an ominous turn. In its demonization of blacks, the South began to use lynching as a punishment for blacks who had probably actually committed some serious crime, at least "serious" as black misbehavior was then accounted. But eventually these brutal acts degenerated simply into a method to keep African-Americans in their "place," even to the extent of picking out the occasional sacrificial lamb whose killing, racists knew, would terrify other blacks and tend to even further docilize them. Though many Southerners were no doubt horrified by the racially motivated lynchings that darkened their region, pressure exerted by the Klan and other white supremacists kept all but a relative handful of opponents from challenging these tactics.

One overriding Southern taboo soon became associated with the region's white mania to keep the African-American population in social and psychological enslavement. That was the specter of rape committed by black men on white women, what one disgruntled observer of the time referred to as "the Foul Daughter of Reconstruction." No totem was holier to white Southerners than white Southern womanhood's sexual purity. And where that purity was befouled by a black man's lust—specifically, by his sexual organ—the white Southern male regarded the act as, unbelievable as it sounds today, worse even than murder. A white scholar characterized it as a black man's "biological imperative" to elevate his own offspring.[3] Any sexual contact—consensuality being entirely immaterial—of a white woman by a black man, let alone actual rape itself, was more than enough to ignite the Southern white man's frenzy. Remarkably, it was a woman who most starkly framed the white Southerner's obsession with the black man as a symbolic rape machine. At an 1897 meeting of the State Agricultural Society of Georgia, featured speaker Rebecca Felton

[3] Newby, *Jim Crow's Defense*, 48.

enlightened her audience with the view that "if it takes lynching to protect the [white] woman's dearest possession from drunken, ravening human beasts, then I say lynch a thousand a week."[4]

Though for decades white supremacists would defend lynching as a safeguard against unpunished rape of white women by black men, rape was not in reality the usual motivation for a lynching. Of the 3,811 African-American men lynched between 1889 and 1941, no more than 641—17 percent—had actually been accused of rape, either attempted or committed. Numerically, other offenses vastly outranked rape. Some of the imagined or real transgressions by African-Americans ending in lynching included attempts to sue a white employer, demanding to be allowed to vote, participating in union activities, exhibiting disrespect to a white or disputing a white, or simply for no reason that ever came to light—the latter perhaps a case of "sassing" or giving a white a "fresh" look (what was in the South sometimes called "reckless eyeballing") or, most shocking of all, simply for being in the wrong place at the wrong time when an "example" was thought by murderous whites to be needed to keep a black community in its "place." Furthermore, it wasn't only black *males* who were lynched. Many black women were murdered, too, including Mary Turner, who was killed by a mob in Georgia while nearly at the point of giving birth to her child, her killers hanging her and setting her body ablaze because she had threatened to disclose the names of the men who had earlier lynched her husband.

Of course the mania was self-induced and the lynchers were personally responsible for their mayhem, but the racial atmosphere of the time was so warped that murdering blacks became almost a socially acceptable tool for embedding white supremacy in the region's social fabric. It is particularly poignant, though, to recognize that little regard existed in the Southern white man's mind for *black* female chastity. Black women continued to be routinely raped, an act that has to morally include "consensual" white-male-on-black-female sexual relations where the woman had no realistic prospect of safely refusing such advances.

---

[4] Hale, 234.

Black men learned at an early age that the danger associated with white women was omnipresent and could never be taken lightly, and thus they avoided any contact with white women that could by any measure, reasonable or not, be construed as social equality or friendliness or sexually impelled. The merest brush against a woman's garment on a crowded streetcar could lead to a lynch mob and the "offender's" death, an example of the trivial but lethal mishaps that occurred many times in the Jim Crow years. A black man would immediately grovel with apologies and assurances of his own stupidity or worthlessness if he was accused of meeting the glance of a white woman or of "freshness" toward a white woman or of "sassing" a white woman. Knowing that failure to do so could result in the most brutal of deaths was usually more than enough inducement for such self-humiliation.

A part of the difficulty in comprehending the Southern lynching epidemic lay in the presence of the perfectly effective system the region employed to inflict *legal* lynchings, which was what judicial capital punishment often amounted to. Southerners had no legitimate reason to fear that Jim Crow-era courts might exonerate a black criminal, least of all a rapist. In fact, many of the executions ordered by judges after convictions by all-white juries—no black jurors served at the time anywhere in the South—pretty much equaled state-sponsored murder. Blacks were found guilty upon mere accusation, with no substantive evidence offered, no adequate counsel granted, and no real attempt on the part of the courts to provide evenhanded justice. Such judicial lynchings occurred when the *lack* of guilt was, at least in retrospect, as clear as water. For those genuinely guilty blacks accused of rape or murder of a white, the chances of exoneration were close to nonexistent. All of which leads to the conclusion that lynching can most often be seen more as sport or bloodlust than as any true concern on the part of the perpetrators that they were making sure a criminal didn't get away with his crime.

The actual spectacle of a lynching could be mind-boggling. Even so, what should have made spectators sick evidently rarely did. Lynchings became a kind of circus, the victim himself (or herself) the star attraction. Women and children were as much a part of the audience as the most hard-bitten men, and viewings of such proceedings by children were considered salubrious, a part of the elementary life experience of a certain class of youth. The real lesson being learned was not one related to crime control, but of control over the great and dangerous mass of what many adults considered the South's animal-like Negroes.

In his 1929 book, *Black America,*[5] Scott Nearing described some of the most depraved lynchings on record, giving scorching testament to white America's depravity toward African-Americans. The story he told of Henry Lowry can stand here for the thousands of African-American men and women who lethally raised the hackles of potential lynchers.

Henry Lowry was in no way remarkable, but rather a man whom everyone agreed was neither a troublemaker nor a person who challenged the Jim Crow code that in 1921 saturated the South's civic life. He was forty years old that year, rated by his neighbors, Nearing said, as an "honest, hardworking, and inoffensive Negro." Together with his wife and six-year-old daughter, Henry Lowry lived on the farm of O. T. Craig, a prosperous planter in Arkansas's Mississippi County. He was what thousands of black Arkansans were in 1921, a sharecropper.

Sharecropping has over the last century attained a patina of nostalgia that it little deserves. The system worked fairly uniformly in Henry Lowry's surrounds. The sharecroppers, overwhelmingly African-American by race, would contract with farmers, overwhelmingly white by race, the latter owning land that they rented out by the "parcel." The contract gave the cropper little other than the right to cultivate the land he had rented. The owner generally provided the cropper his necessary farming tools as well as the requisite seed and fertilizer. The tenant's share of whatever crop he harvested generally fell somewhere between a quarter and a half of the total, the exact percentage having been spelled out in the contract between himself and the landowner. The sharecropper did not actually *own* any of the crop, even though he and his family—which most often included children—had done all the work in producing it.

The landowner sold the cropper's harvest and paid the tenant out of

[5] Nearing, 198ff.

the proceedings after he had deducted whatever goods he had put out—seed, fertilizer, food, any cash loans—all the accounting for which debts was entirely in the landowner's hands, and any questioning of which by the usually illiterate cropper was generally looked upon with dangerous infuriation by the landlord. Many croppers took it for granted that they were being cheated every year, but were unable to do much about it. Nor did the cropper have anything to say about the price received by the farmer. Some farmers were comparatively forthcoming and honest in their dealings with the tenants, while others weren't. In any event, the sharecropper often ended up owing more than his share of the cash received by the farmer, keeping him—the sharecropper—in perpetual indebtedness, unable to leave, but liable to being thrown off the land whenever he did something the farmer didn't like or for whatever other reason the farmer might conjure up. Living cashless, electricityless, medicineless, doctorless lives, many croppers were old by the time they turned forty.

The system became synonymous with black poverty of near medieval proportions, effectively enserfing generations of rural blacks (who before World War II still represented far more of the South's great majority of African-Americans than did city or town dwellers). Their ambition stifled by the rampant inequities of sharecropperdom, most blacks remained bereft of land ownership, dependent on the will—good or ill—of the white farmers in whose temper and graces their lives hung in the balance. After World War I, more and more blacks wanted out of the formula. Perhaps Henry Lowry hoped for such an escape for himself and his family. But in the last weeks of 1921, Mr. Lowry still lived within the boundaries of these barren circumstances.

Mr. Craig, the landowner, was, together with his sons, the guardian of those boundaries. The well-to-do family controlled life in their part of Arkansas, calling the political shots and seeing to it that the economic and social realities of white versus black never changed by so much as a hair's breadth. The reasons for it aren't known, but that particular year Henry Lowry had confronted Craig to demand a settling of the crop share. Some said there was talk of Mr. Craig moving, and Lowry may have been worried he would never get any money at all. *Any* confrontation between white and black was potentially lethal to the black party, but when the confrontation was initiated by the black man, trouble—*serious* trouble—was almost a sure bet.

Just before Christmas, Henry Lowry went up to Mr. Craig's house. The cropper asked for his "settlement," a fair request given the work he'd put into the land Mr. Craig owned. During the talk between farmer and tenant, one of the Craig sons—Richard, who had a reputation around town as a "bad man"—came out on the porch and smacked Henry Lowry a good lick, which was neither an unusual nor even an especially remarkable thing for a white man to do to an importuning Negro. Richard told Lowry he'd just have to wait before the family would do anything about indemnifying any of their sharecroppers.

On Christmas Day, Lowry went back to the Craig house. The cook saw the black man approach and went into the dining room where the holiday meal was being served and told the family that the black man had returned. When the elder Mr. Craig came out on the porch, Lowry repeated his request for a settlement. Craig then hit Lowry with a stick of wood. A moment later Craig's son came running out to the porch and, just as Lowry was retreating, shot the sharecropper. For reasons one can only guess at, Henry Lowry had brought his own gun with him, and he fired back, not only killing the elder Craig, but also hitting and mortally wounding the son's wife as well, the latter evidently having wandered out to the porch to see what was going on.

Knowing his life was forfeit if he was apprehended, Lowry bolted the state and got as far as El Paso, Texas, before being captured and arrested. The local police turned him over to a pair of Arkansas deputies who had arrived expressly to take him back to their own jurisdiction. But the train carrying Lowry and the deputies only made it as far as Sardis, Mississippi, before running into what was, in that time and place, almost the inevitable. In the little town, half a dozen cars full of grim-faced men were waiting at the local Illinois Central station, where they made the town marshal halt the train and forced the deputies to deliver up their prisoner. Immediately upon the train's stopping, a pack of white men boarded it to find Henry Lowry handcuffed between the two deputies. The mob ordered the officers to release their man to them. Understanding it meant their own lives if they refused, both complied. As the pair of officers watched, the white vigilantes and the black man strode off the train, the captive Henry Lowry enclosed by a circle of guns.

The headline on the following afternoon's *Memphis News Scimitar* left no doubt as to the organized nature of the events to come: "Lowry Lynchers Announce Program; Negro to Pay Mob's Penalty for Crime." Not that the lynchers-to-be actions foretold by the newspaper headline bestirred the local law to intervene. The pending punishment of Henry Lowry at the hands of impassioned lawbreakers was neither extraordinary nor something that many small Southern police forces in the 1920s would take any great measures to foil. The same day's *Memphis Press* amplified on the schedule of events: "Lowry Nears Tree on Which It Is Planned to Hang Him; Taken Thru Memphis Today." Appended to the story was a road map for the curious along with additional information: "While five of their number detoured around Memphis in a closed automobile with Henry Lowry, negro murderer, who is to be lynched at Modena, Ark., tonight, other alleged members of the mob which took him from officers at Sardis, Miss., early this morning, came to Memphis and dined at the Hotel Peabody today." Anticipation of their evening's work evidently called for a decent meal in the city's finest dining room.

The agonies meted out to Henry Lowry that evening were somewhat more elaborate than the treatment dealt to most lynch mob victims. But they didn't differ in their result, the same end that had awaited thousands of black men accused of crimes against white society. Lowry was said to have died, so the *Memphis Press* reported the next day, "by inches." The doomed man was first bound with chains to a massive log. The participants then piled leaves around his feet and, after pouring gasoline over this fuel, lit them. As the leaves flared up and Henry Lowry began to slowly roast, men and women gaily threw more dry tinder on the fire, the conflagration growing until its flames reached the victim's belly. Lowry did not cry out, either in pain or for mercy, though witnesses said he was clearly conscious. Lowry tried to pick up the hot ashes and put them in his mouth, his motive surely an attempt to hasten his own end. Finally someone threw gasoline over the doomed sharecropper's entire body, the flames quickly taking the life out of Henry Lowry and consuming his body so that little was left except for a pile of bony ashes.

As the crowd—said to have exceeded five hundred persons, with more than a few women scattered among the swarm—looked at the pile of embers that had replaced the man Henry Lowry, the killings of O. T. Craig and his daughter-in-law had been, by the terms of mob justice, neatly avenged. It had been done openly and without fear on the part of the participants that they would ever be called to account for their actions. The location and time of the bloodletting had been widely disseminated to the public, yet the law enforcement authorities of the state of Arkansas at no time appeared in Modena to try to halt the proceedings that had been so carefully planned and meticulously executed.

Voices had been raised to protest lynching for decades before Henry Lowry died, but almost all had been black voices and thus disregarded. One of the earliest and most passionate had been that of Ida Wells-Barnett. When as a twenty-five-year-old schoolteacher Wells-Barnett had been brave enough to sue a railroad company for throwing her off a train because she refused to sit in a Jim Crow car, she won $500 in damages from a circuit court for the injustice. But when in 1877 the Tennessee Supreme Court overturned the award, a sense of rage filled the educator with the resolve to make her career one of righting such wrongs. Wells-Barnett soon switched from teaching to journalism, becoming editor of two weekly church newspapers in Memphis, becoming a crusader for civil rights. Her editorials demanding racial justice cried out loudly and at great peril to her own safety.

Wells-Barnett's real immersion into the fires of racism came in the aftermath of a mob seizure of three black Memphis businessmen, all of whom were lynched. The men's "crime" had been to succeed in their grocery business at the expense of a competing white grocer. Assaulted by a gang of white thugs, the African-American men defended themselves with guns. This self-defense especially enraged the attackers and led to the lynching. Acting in self-defense, getting above themselves, amounted to a capital crime for Southern blacks.

Wells-Barnett was a friend of one of the slain men, the grocer Thomas Moss. She wrote of him that "a finer, cleaner man than he never walked the streets of Memphis. He was well liked, a favorite with everybody, yet he was murdered with no more consideration than if he had been a dog, because he as a man defended his property from attack." The journalist expressed her outrage in print, denouncing the lynching with the white-hot anger of the convert and the eloquence of a writer of uncommon skill. The words shocked Memphis, especially the city's complacent white citizens, who had never before seen a Memphian, black or white, register such fury against the "traditions" of Jim Crow. Wells-Barnett made it plain that her words were directed not just at these murders but at every other lynching as well.

Characterizing the slayings as "an excuse to get rid of Negroes who were acquiring wealth and property and thus keep the race terrorized and 'keep the nigger down,' " Wells-Barnett addressed those who believed that lynched men were rapists by writing words that got to the heart of the most taboo theme in Southern society. "In numerous instances where colored men have been lynched on the charge of rape, it was positively known at the time of the lynching and indisputably proven after the victim's death that the relationship sustained between the man and the woman was voluntary and clandestine, and that in no court of law could even the charge of assault have been successfully maintained."

No African-American person, neither man nor woman, could publicly voice such truths in Memphis. A mob attacked her newspapers' offices, and had she been caught, she would likely have suffered the same end as the three lynched men. Instead, the fiery journalist escaped Memphis and fled northward. Black papers in Chicago and New York soon began printing her articles detailing the injustices being perpetrated against black Americans, and especially in her antilynching writing, her voice became a respected clarion against the horrors of racism.

Partly because Wells-Barnett's eloquent writing brought to America's notice the truths of lynching for the first time, the nation's greatest African-American hero, Frederick Douglass, linked his prestige to her campaign. Their goal, and that of crusaders both black and white who followed them, was to get legislation enacted that would make lynching a federal crime so as to override the local law enforcement agencies that ignored such barbarism. The organization Wells-Barnett and Douglass helped to found, the National Association for the Advancement of Colored People, made this specific legislation its principal goal.

Yet no white American leader—certainly never the nation's chief executive—would join the NAACP in supporting such an antilynching bill, either because of personal indifference or, in the case of politicians, fear of forfeiting the Southern vote. When legislators did manage to get a bill to the Senate floor, Southern senators would invariably filibuster it to death, publicly justifying their stance on the spurious altar of states' rights but privately pleased that Congress wasn't able to further black advancement even to the small degree of declaring lynching a federal crime, which would, of course, have allowed the federal government to prosecute lynchers when a state refused to do so. John Rankin, the arch-segregationist congressman from Mississippi, crudely suggested one antilynching proposal be retitled "a bill to encourage rape," an outcome, he said, that would be the only result of its enactment. Southerners subscribing to Rankin's views warned as a single voice that black men would interpret an antilynching measure as an invitation to rape white women and, more generally, as license to press for social equality.

In the 1930s the NAACP was joined by the American Civil Liberties Union in a united front aimed at ending lynching, which had become an international embarrassment to the United States. Though such crimes had dramatically decreased since the turn of the century—partly because of the increasing revulsion against them in the South—lynchings still regularly occurred, the practice tacitly approved by Southern law enforcement, and legislators refused to vote against the practice.

Though influential Southern voices of racial moderation were limited in number, a few well-known Southerners did lend their energies and prestige to the war against racism. One of the most influential was Jessie Daniel Ames, whose Association of Southern Women for the Prevention of Lynching, founded in 1930, sought to make clear the true basis of lynching and how the practice besmirched any claim the South asserted to civil decency, especially to the kind of declaration made by South Carolina's Senator Ed Smith that lynching was necessary to ensure the "sanctity of our firesides and the virtue of our women." In truth, as late as 1939, 64 percent of white Southerners said they believed lynching was justified in cases of sexual assault, sentiments eagerly put forward in Congress by their elected representatives. Jessie Daniel Ames's association responded that lynching was a perversion rather than a defense of white womanhood. Yet even Ames, a voice of relative reason, stood against the NAACP's efforts to get federal antilynching legislation passed, her grounds essentially based on states' rights.

Throughout the 1930s the NAACP continued to press for a national antilynching bill. Its efforts were bolstered when in November 1933 Senators Edward Costogan of Colorado and Robert Wagner of New York sponsored a measure to hold criminally responsible those who permitted lynching to take place—which meant the law enforcement officials who ignored it. Knowing that the actual lynchers would be almost impossible to arrest in the South, the new approach would allow the federal government to pursue state and local officials who failed to actively pursue suspected lynchers. Though famous and prestigious Americans—among them Pearl Buck, Sherwood Anderson, and Thomas Benton—spoke passionately for the bill, the opposition to it came, as expected, from Southern congressmen, the regional bloc's strategy to defeat the measure being delay. The Senate's filibuster finally killed it. Josiah Bailey, senator from North Carolina, said, "This bill is not going to pass. . . . We will be here all summer. . . . We will speak night and day." Bailey and like-minded Southern legislators—which meant every Southern and border-state lawmaker—proceeded in the summer of 1938 to do exactly that. Senator Wagner tried to invoke cloture to bring the measure to a vote, but his effort failed to gain the required two-thirds vote.

Still the debate went on, but in February 1939 the sponsors gave up when they accepted the impossibility of getting around the Southern filibusterers. The NAACP tried desperately to keep the undertaking alive but could do nothing. The Congress of the United States could not pass such an act. Though the American people had by this debate been made aware as never before as to the seriousness of the problem, the stain on the nation's legislature was not so amenable to correction. During the Jim Crow decades when lynchings occurred with metronome-like regularity, the American people would never see the practice officially condemned in their national legislature.

In the last years of her life, Ida Wells-Barnett put her by now famous pen to work on one more kind of assault against black Americans both Northern and Southern. Yet another peril on the all-too-often-lethal road African-Americans negotiated every day of their lives was the undifferentiated urban lynching called a race riot, an onslaught in which hordes of maniacal white Americans took up racial violence where the lynch mob had left off. The individual victims of these riots weren't usually suspected of or charged with any particular act—other, of course, than that of bearing a black skin.

The goal of race rioting was typically twofold. First, the white participants—primarily young, working-class males—appeared to actually enjoy these occasions, as though they were a kind of sporting event, a combined chase and slaughter aimed at African-Americans. Second, the white leaders of the riots and the men who led the leaders regarded the terror generated by a race riot as fair warning to blacks to never forget or overstep their place in the American social order.

The relatively small early riots—for example, those in Washington, D.C., in 1898, New Orleans in 1900, and Atlanta in 1906 (the latter leaving twenty-five African-Americans dead and more than a thousand homeless)—were but precursors of the catastrophes that would come with the First World War. In 1917, the twentieth century's genuinely warlike race riots began in a city ripe for a racial explosion. East St. Louis, Illinois, was a classically inferior "second city" and a town then being increasingly viewed as a "threatening" black suburb to the wealthy metropolis lying directly across the Mississippi River in Missouri. Many of the mores and racial and social attitudes of this border region were in fact far more Southern in character than they were Northern, and racial tensions in the East

St. Louis of World War I had been on high simmer ever since blacks had begun to arrive from the South in significant number a few years earlier. The town was a physically unattractive and intellectually infertile, white, working-class town before African-Americans were drawn to the community by its low-wage jobs. By the first month of the American involvement in the European war, white animosity had reached the point where the local unions were demanding that the black presence in East St. Louis actually be limited by law.

As with most such race riots before and since, here, too, a rumor touched off the deadly storm. When word began to spread around East St. Louis that a black man had shot a white shopkeeper, mob psychology overcame the law-abiding instincts of many of the town's whites. At the riot's apogee, three thousand white men attacked the black community as though a biblical plague, burning homes and churches, looting stores, and killing helpless individuals whose only fault was to get in the way of the throng of mindlessly enraged thugs. Whites mowed down scores of blacks as the latter ran from their homes, among the victims a child who was shot, then snatched by a marauder and thrown back into its burning home to perish in the flames. By the time the rioters' energies were spent, more than a hundred black residents of East St. Louis lay dead.

The end of the European war brought a heightened level of racial strife to much of the United States. War experiences had altered many of the tens of thousands of black soldiers and sailors returning from active duty, making them less passive than the undeveloped youths they had been before their military service. Before leaving Europe, their commanding general rendered tribute to the black soldiers: "You officers and soldiers . . . stand second to none in the record you have made since your arrival in France. . . . The American public has every reason to be proud of that record." Though the accolade was deeply deserved, such faith in the decency of the American public was seriously miscalculated. Instead of gratitude for their war contributions, white Americans rewarded African-Americans with more than two dozen race riots in 1919 alone. In twenty-five cities, some of the same black soldiers who had marched down New York's Fifth Avenue in a victory parade would that lethal year be warding off white marauders intent on killing as many blacks as they could get their hands on. For the blood of African-Americans mauled and murdered in the midmonths of 1919, those days came to be known as the Red Summer, with riots lacerating the country from Knoxville to Omaha to Washington to Chicago. The last—the convulsion in Chicago—was the deadliest of all the rampages of that violent summer.

The sinking of Chicago into racial flames didn't happen because of an imagined rape, the commonest kindling lighting these urban fires. This particular explosion was instead the product of long-brewing racial malice on the part of whites who were themselves economically oppressed and who aimed their frustration at blacks who were also struggling to better their straitened lives. Chicago's racial animosity came from a tangle of jealousies and animosities emanating from two main sources: first, whites and blacks contending with each other for limited jobs—chiefly the union jobs that spelled a dependable income—and second, the same two groups competing for the city's cheap housing. As for the latter, the city's black population had more than doubled—to over one hundred thousand—in the ten years prior to the riot, which most pointedly meant that African-Americans had to either suffocate in their constricted South Side "black belt" or else expand into what were then white neighborhoods. In 1919, the second option represented as sure a road to racial strife as existed in any large American city.

Regardless of the root causes, Jim Crow set off the conflagration. The working-class poor of Chicago possessed but a single free escape from the sweltering heat that pressed down on it every summer, and that was the great lake that lent the city the reason for its founding. But the 29th Street Beach was divided by race, with the separation fully as ironclad as if Chicago were part of the Deep South rather than of the theoretically racially liberated upper Midwest. The spark was innocuous: a seventeen-year-old African-American boy named Eugene Williams swam—or perhaps merely drifted, purposely or not—across the racial dividing line that stretched into the lake, a barrier unmarked but one known to all who used the beach. As the youth swam toward the shore, a group of hostile whites began to stone him. One of the blows was mortal, and Eugene Williams died before he could reach or be rescued to the safety of his "own" beach. The police who arrived made no attempt to arrest any of the stone-throwers. Fighting broke out between blacks on one side and whites on the other, the latter group joined by the police officers. From where the hostilities started at the 29th Street Beach, like a forest fire they quickly jumped to the surrounding streets of the inner city.

Assisted by the indiscriminate spread of racial rumors, the rioting that followed lasted a day short of two weeks. Despite the presence of the state militia beginning on the fourth day (after scores of deaths and injuries had already been sustained), for that thirteen-day period much of central Chicago went without effective police protection. Battalions of youths of both colors guarded their own neighborhoods against invaders. In the end, twenty-three blacks and fifteen whites died. The damage left more than a thousand families, mostly black, without homes. Even President Wilson, the man whose attitude toward African-Americans contributed in no small measure to white notions of their own racial supremacy, for once accurately castigated whites as being the "aggressors" in the strife.

From this era of brutal racial warfare, the today almost-forgotten Tulsa riot of 1921 remains perhaps the most terrible of all. In none of the other riots did the agencies of white government treat a city's entire black population with such shamefulness, and nowhere else did the circumstances of the conflagration so resemble an old-world pogrom. This happened not in a Russian shtetl, but in the heart of a thriving African-American community that lay directly in the shadow of Tulsa's modern downtown. That in a city so far from the Deep South's racial nightmare, one oriented toward the Western frontier and where it seemed there would have been enough prosperity to raise all of its citizens, that such a paroxysm of racially based hate and terror and murder could have happened in Tulsa seemed then and still seems little understandable.

Yet for all its prosperity, the thirty-five-square-block precinct of Tulsa called Greenwood unequivocally constituted a ghetto, if such is defined as a city within a city populated solely by people of a single color, or ethnicity. But if *ghetto* implies material impoverishment, then such was not the case with Greenwood. In fact, much of what happened there in 1921 was caused by white resentment of the shining accomplishments of the city's African-American community as a result of its own hard efforts. The black neighborhood of Tulsa, Oklahoma, existed because the white people of Tulsa refused to allow the city's black people to live amongst them, yet the residents of Greenwood had succeeded despite their disadvantage.

Greenwood lay beyond the Frisco Railroad tracks, the frontier that separated race from race in the prairie metropolis. The thirty-five blocks of the African-American neighborhood were home to some of the hardest-working and most-prosperous Tulsans of any color, people proud of what they had wrought and who had every right to that pride in light of what they endured every day from white-on-black bigotry. Businesses lined the neighborhood's mile-long and eponymous main street, ranging from hotels to barbershops, from doctors' offices to poolrooms, and all efficiently serving the community's fifteen thousand people. Among the most prestigious men on Greenwood Avenue was Dr. A. C. Jackson, called by one of the founders of the Mayo Clinic the "most able Negro surgeon in America." A matter of no little satisfaction to the residents was that Booker T. Washington had referred to Greenwood Avenue as the nation's "Black Wall Street."

With tragic irony, Greenwood had made itself far too successful for whites who believed blacks belonged in slums. The hustle of the black neighborhood's streets—of its businesses and schools and movie theaters—instilled no pride in white Tulsans, but only a bitter, vengeful, and jealous hatred of what they thought of as "niggers getting ahead of themselves." The Ku Klux Klan had established an ominous presence in the city, to the point where the terror organization considered itself to be the city's real law. Since the turn of the century, several of Tulsa's blacks had been snatched off the streets for trumped-up reasons and subsequently lynched by white supremacists, while since the war's end three years before whites had entertained themselves by joining "whipping parties," wherein a defenseless black would be beaten for the whites' amusement while serving as an object lesson in the realities of white power. Having gotten to be too much for Tulsa's whites, Greenwood had in 1921 become ripe to be taken down a few notches.

Every race riot needs a spark to set off the powder keg of pent-up furor. As had happened so many times elsewhere, here, too, in Tulsa the spark was the rumor that a black man had "assaulted" a white woman. In this case, the white woman was a Miss Sarah Page, elevator operator and recently separated wife of a man in Kansas City whom she had deserted two months earlier. The local sheriff later commented that if the charges alleged in her husband's divorce proceedings were true, then "she is a notorious character."

Dick Rowland was the black man in the equation. A young carrier of messages around the city, on the morning the riot started he had stepped into a large downtown building to use its toilet, one of the few available in the city center to a man of his color. Since the facilities were on the top floor, he rang for the elevator, which was being run by Sarah Page. When Page descended to the ground floor to answer the call button, from the open-barred cage she saw Rowland waiting to board. Racial "etiquette" meant that blacks could be treated like freight, and ordinary courtesy would not, therefore, be required. When Rowland stepped in, Page yanked up on the starter, causing her passenger to lurch. Attempting to break his fall, the young man reached out to grab something. The something was Sarah Page. She screamed, a yell that quickly attracted a knot of people trying to make out the cause of the commotion. Page immediately claimed Rowland had tried to assault her, which in the sex-speak of the time meant he had tried to rape her. Though Rowland was, inexplicably, not immediately held, the sheriff arrested him the next day, but with little enthusiasm in light of what he had in the meantime learned of the accuser's less-than-sterling reputation.

Given the explosive nature of the charges lodged against Rowland, the editors of the *Tulsa Tribune* couldn't wait to get the story in headlines, headlines designed to sell a lot of papers. And with its routine references to "Little Africa" and "Niggertown" in its stories on the city's black community, little question existed as to which side of the city's racial crevasse the paper stood. In its article on the elevator "rape," Sarah Page was melodramatically referred to as "an orphan who works as an elevator operator to pay her way through business college." Within hours of the *Tribune's* coming off the press, talk had already spread around Tulsa of lynching the "rapist" Dick Rowland.

When members of Greenwood's black community got news of the dangerous charges, a number of its leaders decided to try to intervene to stop any lynching. About two dozen African-American men quickly gathered at the courthouse, where the sheriff talked them into returning to Greenwood so as not to raise white anger at this black show of solidarity. When one white man saw a black man holding a weapon, he thundered at him, "Nigger, what you doing with that pistol?" The answer—"I'm going to use it if I need to"—was, unfortunately, as foolhardy as it was brave. When the white man sprang to grab his own gun, the weapon went off, touching off the tempest that would soon bear down on Greenwood.

After the black leaders retreated to Greenwood, throngs of whites—the crowd around the courthouse had by now grown to perhaps ten thousand—began to scour the city's gun shops for weapons. Scouring turned to looting, and after pillaging every downtown weapons store, the mob turned as if as a single man toward Tulsa's African-American district.

Meanwhile, the city's police chief was urgently calling the governor to request National Guard troops be sent immediately by special trains, this even as Greenwood began to be swamped by a flood of armed marauders. Greenwood's agony would last through the night and into the following morning. As though it were Gettysburg, black men positioned themselves to defend each building and each block, Greenwood's guardians desperately trying to save their homes and businesses and community. But these African-American men soon found themselves under massive attack, even being strafed by the machine gun of an airplane buzzing over the district's residential streets. The whites attacking Greenwood far outnumbered the community's defenders. Enraged whites shot at any black person they saw, woman or girl, man or boy, it made little difference. Blacks trying to escape burning buildings were shot, sometimes even being thrown back into the flames of their homes. Black corpses were tied to car bumpers and dragged through the city. White rioters turned back fire trucks, and those few police officers who arrived on the scene acted more as rioters themselves than as law enforcement officials. Uncounted numbers of black corpses were later found dumped in the Arkansas River, where they floated downstream under the blistering Oklahoma sun, rotting carcasses missed only by grieving families and friends.

All told, twenty-five thousand whites had rampaged through Greenwood, supremely defiant of the law and determined simply to kill as many African-Americans as possible; many of these rioters were Klansmen. Estimates from research conducted almost seven decades later by the Tulsa Race Riot Commission indicated that some three hundred Tulsans died, perhaps 90 percent of them black; the precise number is unknowable because of the sheer disruption the riot caused to Greenwood and its people. Property damage was also staggering: twelve hundred buildings were burned, many of them looted before being set ablaze; black Tulsans afterward saw white people in the city's streets wearing familiar clothing and jewelry. Tulsa's African-Americans were never reimbursed on their insurance claims, the companies refusing to pay because of antiriot clauses in the policies. Nor did the city of Tulsa ever pay a penny to a single black citizen.

It is unsurprising that all facets of the white establishment blamed the events entirely on the city's black residents. Newspaper headlines over the following days reflected such blame: "Black Agitators Blamed for Riots." "Blood Shed in Race War Will Cleanse Tulsa." "Negro Section Abolished by City's Order." When the National Guard did finally arrive as rioting was in full swing and Tulsa's own police forces were doing nothing to stop it, the soldiers solely focused on rounding up as many blacks as possible, after which they penned them in large holding areas located at some distance from the Greenwood district. These troops often drew blood with their bayonets—the blood of the people who *in theory* were under their protection. About half of the city's black population—some six thousand people—were effectively imprisoned while their community was being destroyed.

The destruction dealt Tulsa's black population was incalculable. Not only lives were lost, but a hard-won community was thrown to the wind. In the aftermath of this mortal storm the city's lawmakers did what they could to make sure no Greenwood—no African-American district—

would spring up again. While hypocritically extending civic sympathy to the "law-abiding Negroes who became victims of the action and bad advice of some of the lawless leaders," the city planned to turn what had been Greenwood into a new industrial and transportation center, and only a court ruling in the end prevented such a travesty. But white civic leaders still made sure no money was available to rebuild what had been lost, even going so far as to refuse charity that had been sent from all across America and which the donors meant as a help in getting Tulsa's black community put back together again. For a long and cold winter following Tulsa's pogrom, nearly a thousand blacks lived in tents on the city's outskirts.

Dick Rowland was released from jail two weeks after the riot. Sarah Page left town after recanting her "charges" against Mr. Rowland.

5

HOW WHITE AMERICA
RATIONALIZED JIM CROW

Occupying every shade of the intellectual spectrum from cultured liberal to lunatic reactionary, the men and women who justified, rationalized, defended, and sustained Jim Crow agreed on few things beyond their shared belief in the inferiority of blacks. In this they came together on one overarching principle: the certainty that white human beings were innately superior to human beings of black African descent. The expressions of this conviction varied drastically, from at one end a sort of charitable and courtly paternalism that declined from kindheartedness only when the black man attempted to get above his "proper" place, to at the other a venomous conviction that blacks represented a low and dangerous subspecies who, inexplicably, possessed the iniquitous ability to interbreed with whites. A hatred of blacks furthered by religion, science, and history extended right across the wide American landscape, but as we've seen in this book, nowhere during the Jim Crow era were white supremacist beliefs upheld with greater energy and fervor than in the South. Historian Ulrich Phillips wrote in 1928 that Southern whites "have a common resolve indomitably maintained [that the South] shall be and remain a white man's country. The consciousness of . . . these premises, whether expressed with the frenzy of a demagogue or maintained with a patrician's quietude, is the cardinal test of a southerner and the central theme of southern history."[1]

[1] Newby, *Jim Crow's Defense*, 4.

Beliefs are not genetic. One isn't born with them. Racism, to name one belief, is an entirely environmental phenomenon taught to those who don't have it by those who do. During the Jim Crow years racism was sometimes taught from the floor of the U.S. Senate. In the post–World War I era, J. Thomas Heflin of Alabama had become one of the most powerful legislators in America. He was also one of the most racially inflammatory men ever to occupy a Senate seat.

In 1929, Senator Heflin read a newspaper account of white parents who were begging New York's Governor Franklin Roosevelt and New York City's Mayor James Walker to prevent the marriage of their daughter to a black man. In a letter to reporter Sam Reading of Philadelphia's National News Service, Heflin wrote that reading the piece had left him with "a feeling of sadness and indignation" at the specter of a "humiliated and grief-stricken" white mother and father bereft of any legal means of preventing such a union, and equally unable to hide their "tearstained faces and humiliation" in the newspaper photo that accompanied the story. Heflin wondered what had become of the "brave knights of the white race who once boasted of their proud Caucasian lineage [and who for generations had] stood guard" on the "great divide" between the races, the "dead line" between black and white. The senator affirmed his conviction that the real villain of the piece was the "Roman-Tammany" regime of Al Smith, the former New York governor and the Democratic candidate who in 1928 had lost the presidential election, a man whose candidacy fellow Democrat Heflin had found "impossible to support."

After reading a copy of his letter to his fellow legislators from the Senate floor, the Alabama lawmaker continued with a few additional remarks. "Mr. President, I cry out against [racial intermarriage] in New York, in Alabama, in every state of the Union. I tell you . . . it leads to troublesome things. When Negroes in other states read about some Negro marrying a white girl up in New York under Tammany rule, it puts the devil in them . . . you have a Negro buck going out and waylaying a white girl on the way home from school in the rural districts of my state or some other state.

"I have in mind now a picture of the beautiful, bright girl in the mountains of north Alabama a few years ago coming home from school, stopping on the roadside in April, the spring of the year, gathering wildflowers, and a Negro man leaped out from behind a tree, caught this girl, choked her into unconsciousness, dragged her into the woods, assaulted her, and left her for dead on the roadside. The father of the girl and his neighbors pursued that Negro, they caught him, and lynched him, and I approved that act.

"Talk to me about being patient, holding your temper, and observing law in a case like that. A father with his heartstrings torn out, with his darling daughter assaulted, disgraced, and almost dead, came up on the black brute who committed the crime. Of course he would kill him, and he ought to have killed him.

"That is the way we feel about it. Whenever a Negro crosses this dead line between the white and the Negro races and lays his black hand on a white woman, he deserves to die. That is the way we feel about it, and we are not the only ones who feel that way. The senator from Idaho [William Borah] once said in this chamber, 'You Southerners are not the only ones who lynch Negroes for rape. We in the Northern states lynch them just as quickly as you do when they commit that crime against a white woman,' and that is true. It is the *call of the blood.*"

Not a single senator moved to censure Heflin's remarks.

The forces that informed Americans' racial prejudices during the Jim Crow era were deeply observed almost everywhere, North and South, and thus nowhere were they easily escapable. Before the civil rights revolution caused a wave of white empathy to arise in the 1950s, the American social and intellectual mosaic lay buried under a blanket of racism that by its omnipresence gave whites a near seamless certainty of their superiority over blacks. In every generation and in every combination of whites—parent and child, pastor and parishioner, teacher and student—the principles of racism and of white supremacism were almost effortlessly passed from the elder to the younger, from the formed mind to the unformed. Few places existed where one could hide from or be spared this face of American life. Intellectual authorities both scientific and historical supported the superiority of white and inferiority of black. Most significantly, the relationship between man and God, likely the ultimate bond, was saturated in the rhetoric of racial separation. These realities represented the greatest tragedy of the European experience in the Western Hemisphere, an experience that from its earliest days gave itself over to a fetishlike obsession with white cultural supremacy.

Religion stood as the most potent rationale white Americans possessed in affirming their ascendancy over the colored races, with both clergy and laity poring over Scripture for the better part of four centuries in search of and believing to have found support for this view. The scientist finding inequality between races through inerrant "proof" or the historian professing how the relative ranking of one race of men to another has "always been historically so" have paled beside the preacher falsely acting as the spiritual agent of God and His word. For three and a half centuries spiritual conduits fed and nurtured white Americans' certainty that, in racial matters, God was on their side. Tragically, well into the mid–twentieth century mainstream religions would assert the superiority of whiteness, long after reputable historians and scientists had assigned such notions the obloquy that they deserved.

Whites in the very young America nearly universally considered non-whites "savages," a line of thinking that pervaded every section of the country. Paradoxically, some of the slaves captured in and imported from Africa had been Christians. Yet rather than acknowledge that reality, which would have morally conflicted with the white view that all blacks were fit for nothing but slavery, the white American dismissed Africans as incapable of any belief system except "paganism," particularly condemning African ancestor worship, the latter having in reality represented a spiritual respect system not altogether different from Christian reverence for saints or for the cherished dead. The mature civilizations that had arisen in black Africa with their centuries-old codes of ethics meant nothing to slave traders, slave transporters, or slave buyers, whose captives were regarded not as sentient humans but merchandise solely useful as a means to an economic end.

Until the turn of the eighteenth century, the attitude of most white religious sects in America was to keep blacks away from "their" churches. A handful of congregations allowed such persons in back pews or in balconies, but almost never did white denominations accept blacks as fully equal. Sharing their worship services with creatures of whom the vast majority represented white people's owned chattels obviously tended to create untenable moral misgivings among whites. But it was relatively easy for Europeans, who were already dubious about the black man's common humanity with whites, to write Africans out of their religious observations, a course taken up with enthusiasm by white clergymen and congregations both Northern and Southern. Since the white policy was simply to exclude blacks from participation in their spiritual rites, African-Americans—at least those who weren't slaves and were thus able to control some part of their own destiny—devised their own exclusively black churches. Unsurprisingly, most of what blacks created were virtually liturgical carbon copies of the existing white Protestant churches, sects that then represented the overwhelming majority of organized religion in America.

If in the North black-controlled congregations were sometimes grudgingly tolerated, in the antebellum South such churches were either restricted or totally suppressed under state statutes on the rationale that they imperiled white interests, which is to say they were thought to be breeding grounds for black insurrection against whites. The first independent black congregation in America was the First African Baptist Church, set up in Savannah, Georgia, in 1778; its members were unceasingly harassed by slave patrols, its services broken up, and its congregants jailed. Probably as provoking to whites as insurrectionary fears was the specter of blacks communing independently with the same God to whom they themselves prayed, setting up threatening notions of social equality that ran directly against the ideology of white supremacy. Most troublesome of all, whites even feared that a slave's Christianization might somehow lead to his claim to freedom, which could open up all sorts of theologically based mischief. The economic masters of the antebellum South—primarily the planters who owned most of the slaves—believed that instructing their chattels in religion was tantamount to jeopardizing their own property rights. One writer neatly summed up this position: "Talk to a planter about the soul of a Negro, and he'll be apt to tell you that the body of one Negro may be worth twenty pounds, but the souls of a hundred of them would not yield him one farthing."[2]

Despite white opposition, by the turn of the nineteenth century successful independent black churches were getting off the ground—though it was, at first, Northern ground. In 1787 black Philadelphians established the Free African Society, an offshoot of the city's white Methodist denomination, whose members had made clear their lack of welcome to African-Americans. Out of similar efforts came the African Protestant Episcopal Church and the African Methodist Episcopal Church, both of which were set up entirely independent of Philadelphia's white churches. In 1816 these congregations met in conference and declared themselves a denomination unto themselves, henceforth to be called the African Methodist Episcopal Church. By the time legal Jim Crow ended in the 1960s, the independent black denominations—the Methodist offshoots, three black Baptist groups, and the black Church of God in Christ—would represent about 95 percent of the black Christians in the United States, with the remainder dispersed among smaller black churches, white Protestant denominations, and the Roman Catholic Church. It was estimated in 1969 that one-tenth of one percent of all black Protestants in America have ever actually worshiped in the company of whites—a number made out to be about eight thousand African-Americans in all.[3]

The question remains as to why black people in America ever wanted to adopt a theological configuration that had so obviously been riddled with racism and whose white communicants so clearly did not want to communicate, even in the theological sense, with black people. The answer lies in the reality that most blacks in antebellum America were slaves, and

---

[2] Lincoln, 42.
[3] Miller in Sternsher, 106.

as their generations passed with fewer and fewer memories of whatever philosophies they or their ancestors had known and practiced in Africa, knowledge of which their owners and their owners' governments had taken great pains to eradicate from slave life, their sole option was to participate, insofar as they were allowed, in the Christianity that entirely surrounded them. But what they did feel free to do was to transform much of the white racist Christian practices into forms more congenial to their own oppressed circumstances.

Congregating away from their owners and overseers, African-Americans expressed both their oppression and their hopes in the deeply felt and loudly voiced emotionalism of song and message that became the hallmarks of black Christianity in America. Free from a white intermediary, African-Americans found a style of Christianity that recognized and soothed their agony in the present while promising glory in a life to come. It also importantly replaced some of the social institutions that had been lost to them in their diaspora. As historian Eric Lincoln put it, these churches became for the African-American "government, social club, secret order, espionage system, political party, and impetus to freedom and revolution."[4]

Though Protestantism in the New World has discriminated against African-Americans since the one first encountered the other, the historical record of America's churches in race relations is not unrelievedly malevolent. Throughout American history countless clergymen and lay members of white congregations reached out in friendship across the country's treacherous racial divide. A few Protestant denominations, principally located in the North and including Congregationalists, Presbyterians, and Quakers, offered blacks at the least a formal welcome. But all were, even in the North, small minorities, and virtually none below the Mason and Dixon Line were willing to risk white retaliation by demonstrating any true ecumenism.

Roman Catholic and Jewish dogma were never as specifically racist as that of most of the Protestant sects, but in practice Catholicism and

---

[4] Lincoln, 72.

Judaism did not welcome blacks. As late as 1950, St. Mary's Catholic Church in Piscataway, Maryland, refused entrance to nonwhite members except through a side door leading to segregated pews. The official spokesman of the chancery of the archdiocese in Washington, D.C., helpfully explained that the side door was "practically the same" as the front door. Notably, Southern parochial schools did not pursue any kind of integration, likely grateful for the convenient justification that to do so would be to violate state law everywhere in the South and the border states. Catholic religious communities were not much more welcoming of African-Americans than were Catholic schools. One applicant to a convent was told by the sisters that they "would pray to the Holy Spirit" to guide her somewhere else. At a parochial school in Chicago the sisters "dared not talk about religious vocations for girls lest a colored girl should perhaps be attracted to their own order."[5]

Latin American Catholics found the American church's racism hard to stomach. When a dark-complexioned Panamanian was at prayer in a Washington church pew, a priest quietly approached and handed him a slip of paper on which was written the address of the local Negro Catholic church; the priest whispered to the visitor that special churches existed for his kind, and the priest was sure the foreigner would be more comfortable there.[6] Roman Catholic and Jewish clerics only comparatively rarely spoke out with any vigor against Jim Crow, seeming to accept that to get along with the rest of society they were forced to go along with that society's majoritarian attitudes, and neither priest nor rabbi was often willing to incur local wrath by identifying with the spiritual needs of African-Americans. (If any African Jews, i.e., Ethiopian Falashas, experienced slavery in the United States, their numbers were minuscule. By the end of the Jim Crow era, some forty-four thousand Falashas lived in this country.)

During the Jim Crow epoch, organized religion rarely found itself

---

[5] Griffin, 36.
[6] Stetson Kennedy, 199.

ahead of prevailing social thinking on any issue, least of all the racial questions that occupied almost all Americans and that so deeply held the attention of the great majority of Southerners. Even where religious leaders spoke out for compassion toward blacks, notably by condemning lynching and the countless other forms of hatred and intolerance directed at African-Americans, through World War II the South's white churches emphatically rejected any policy or degree of toleration that might suggest actual social equality between the races. The preacher Theodore Bratton pronounced in the early years of the century that most blacks were "still children intellectually" and "little short of the savage morally,"[7] a view that would find little opposition among the Southern white population. Even the white rationalizing belief that blacks preferred to worship with other blacks just as whites so favored for themselves was rarely tested in the Jim Crow South with a white invitation for blacks to join them in exalting their (theoretically) common deity. With few exceptions, Southern Protestants defended segregation as strongly in the mid–twentieth century as they had slavery in the mid-nineteenth. As it remained quiet about race riots, and as it did the same in questions of lynching, so, too, did the voice of the Southern church remain silent about the primal Christian command to love one's neighbor, a precept ascribed to the founder of Christianity and one that presumably was not restricted to a particular skin color.

Fundamentally, American Protestantism before the civil rights revolution stood foursquare, shoulder to shoulder, and homily to homily as a defender of white supremacy. So long as the dominance of the white race could be defended in religious terms—God made it this way after all, the preacher says so, it *has* to be the truth, so blacks really *are* lesser beings— then no other kind of moral suasion or humanistic impulse could overcome such a psychological shield. Whether the churches' message on race was couched in gentle patronization or in fiery demagoguery, the message was at bottom that blacks were irremediably inferior and whites possessed a literally God-given right to construct society on that premise.

[7] Newby, *Development of Segregationist Thought*, 89.

Though the Christian churches provided the most powerful and prestigious bulwark upholding Jim Crow, white supremacism found plentiful and powerful support in doctrines other than religious. Science and the academy stood for decades at the forefront of support for America's racist attitudes and views. During the Jim Crow era academic scientists "proved" black inferiority, supplying the credulous with plausible-sounding doctrines, most tellingly by pointing out the economically and educationally degraded state of so many African-Americans. The poor blacks of America—masses of sharecroppers, of servants, of poverty-stricken city dwellers—was all the "proof" most whites needed to accept the bona fides of racist historians. The truth that uneducated blacks differed not at all from uneducated whites in their illiteracy and that prosperous blacks equaled prosperous whites in their prosperousness failed to register where a white mind-set had already been unalterably congealed.

Unsurprisingly, history eagerly joined the pseudoscience of the day in rationalizing racism. Historians unctuously explained that American whites had sprung from two millennia of European civilization, whereas blacks were viewed as arriving on American shores straight out of the jungle and paganism. This rendering partly derived from the Eurocentric notion that because African culture was different from that of Europe, it was, ipso facto, inferior. Such interpretations as that the tropical life of Africa was too primitive to have inspired either inventiveness or artistic enterprise seemed eminently plausible when presented in respectable history books with luxurious leather bindings and when universally taught to the exclusion of any other interpretation of history or of historical forces.

What this supposedly "scientific" approach resulted in was a conviction shared by most Americans—Northern as well as Southern—that blacks achieved their fullest potential when engaged in simple tasks, as field laborers or servants. The "scientists" and "intellectuals" who expounded such views might well have personally abhorred the image of white-on-black violence—the lyncher, the mob, the Klansman—and they might have been wounded if their bias was negatively remarked upon. But it was, of course, such justifications for the racism of the day that acted as spiritual succor to those who did actually kill and maim in the cause of white supremacy.

The pseudoscience of eugenics, a popular enterprise in America through a large part of the nineteenth century, persuaded many whites that blacks had gone as high as they could go on the ladder of civilization, that there was plainly no way to breed greater capability into the race. All sorts of studies of human head capacity and cranial thickness and brain weight were cooked up into an ingenious-sounding soup to support such claptrap. Robert Bennett Bean in *The Races of Man* provides an example of this eugenics approach to racism: "The neuromuscular mechanism in the Black Race is less controlled, and when the nerve impulses, not so finely graded as in the White Race, reach the mimetic muscles, the latter are set into sudden, strong contractions of a primitive type. The bulky lips are pulled upward and outward, the large white teeth are exposed in contrast with the black face, and instead of a graded smile or laugh we notice the broad grin characteristic of the Black Race."[8] Combined with the ubiquitous writings of racist-minded historians and the racial dicta springing from Sunday morning's pulpit, it would be hard to understand how the mass of the white American people could have believed otherwise about the veracity of their innate superiority.

In discussing such defenders of American racism, the author Thomas Dixon merits special mention. A college roommate of Woodrow Wilson's, Dixon concocted a particularly malignant formula by which he posited black inferiority. Described as a man whose obsession with race was unrivaled until trumped by Adolf Hitler, Dixon's lasting contribution to American culture came in 1905 with his novel *The Clansman: A Historical Romance of the Ku Klux Klan.* Ten years after it was published, the book was turned into the first truly sophisticated motion picture, a movie still in use today by the Ku Klux Klan as a recruiting inducement.

Retitled *The Birth of a Nation* after having been shown as *The Clansman* for the first month of its release, director David Wark Griffith's film was

---

[8] Newby, *Development of Segregationist Thought*, 43 (footnote).

extraordinary on two counts. First, its production values were the highest yet seen (and not for many years surpassed) and its technical innovations startling, attributes that on viewing today still manage to astonish the viewer. But *The Birth of a Nation* was equally astonishing for its unrelenting portrayal of African-Americans as mentally and sexually depraved, creatures who upon their emancipation desired only to destroy the "poor bruised heart" of the South. Griffith meticulously translated Dixon's "clan" into a meritorious fraternity striving to save the South from the anarchy of black rule, heroic white men united in common defense of their Christian birthright. The black legislators from whom the white Southerner is being saved are represented as lazy, idiotic, shoeless megalomaniacs whose sole interest is passing laws to allow intermarriage between black and white.

In educating the nation about the "Negro question," Dixon spoke passionately for Southern white supremacism. He excoriated the North for the cordial treatment it rendered to Booker T. Washington, calling it "the most loathsome and disgusting worship of a Negro." And he knew the power of invoking black male sexuality and the bugaboo of miscegenation, writing that "if a man really believes in equality, let him prove it by giving his daughter to a negro in marriage"—the South's habitual formula that presupposed the symbolic daughter had no choice as to whom she would be "given" in marriage.

In his book Dixon told his story of the postbellum South wherein the put-upon whites miraculously formed the brave Ku Klux Klan to protect its womenfolk from marauding freedmen and its future from the depredations of carpetbaggers, scalawags, and especially, the black stooges whom they placed in power over whites. Griffith transferred the novel to the screen with skillfulness until then unknown in the young medium; one of the film's stars, Lillian Gish, breathlessly remarked that he "gave us the grammar of filmmaking." In step with the times, Griffith used white actors in blackface in the major African-American roles, employing real blacks only in minor parts.

The NAACP tried and failed to have what it called "the meanest vilification of the Negro race" banned, and riots erupted in cities over the film's defamatory portrayal of blacks. The film went on to enormous (white) acclaim, costing the viewer an unprecedented $2 to see, which meant that its then-staggering $110,000 cost was quickly earned back. The entire textual thread of reviling and stereotyping African-Americans was so historically inaccurate that today *The Birth of a Nation* is regarded with the same contempt as the novel upon which it was based. But the havoc it created on its release was real: the deadliest legacy of *The Birth of a Nation* was the impetus it gave to the men who re-created the Ku Klux Klan as a far more powerful weapon of terror than the one Dixon had employed his pen to exalt.

The Etiquette of Jim Crow

Jim Crow came in two formats. The first, the legal structure, represented statutory law in the overtly white-supremacist states, namely the old Confederacy and the border states. In this guise, police and the courts enforced the acts of lawmakers, who represented every kind of jurisdiction from municipal and county administrations to school districts and state legislatures. If, for example, an African-American sat down in a "white" seat on a bus, in many jurisdictions a "deputized" bus driver could legally hold the offending passenger until a policeman arrived to take the lawbreaker into custody. If a black man entered a "white" restaurant, the owner's call to the police would result in an on-the-spot arrest, one that was entirely supported by the law. A black child attempting to register at a "white" school, never mind the improbability of such an effort, would quickly find his or her racial disbarment from attending the school upheld by a court of law. A black woman caught using a "white" drinking fountain would be arrested for violating a statute specifically prohibiting persons of her race from using such a facility. In all these cases, the lawbreaker was liable to whatever penalty the statutes imposed, ranging from small fines to terms of imprisonment.

But Jim Crow existed in countless aspects prohibited not in statutory law but instead by uncodified but agonizingly real customs and mores.

Before the Civil War, most Jim Crow–like restrictions on blacks were in fact customary rather than statutory. This was largely because most African-Americans rather than being commingled with whites in civil society were enslaved and thus came most directly under the control of owners. "Laws" regulating the behavior of blacks were made and enforced by their owners, with civil or police authorities rarely entering into the relationship except in instances of extreme abuse inflicted by masters on slaves. As a result, legislatures and other official bodies in antebellum America created few specifically segregatory statutes.

The white-imposed customs and mores of racism came to be called the "etiquette" of Jim Crow. This body of protocol did not constitute etiquette in the sense of normal manners and courtesies exchanged between individuals. The rigidly enforced etiquette of racism was in reality a contradiction in terms, a style of black-toward-white deference whose rules a black American ignored or violated at peril to his or her life. Whites, of course, often meticulously returned such deference with their own self-assured courtesy, but the difference was that they didn't *have* to play their part in this caricature of normal etiquette, and it was almost never for *them* a matter of life and death that they do so.

Slave-era etiquette of interracial relations did not end with the Civil War. If anything, it calcified. Over the additional one hundred years that racism held much of America in thrall, the etiquette of Jim Crow became an unbendingly enforced system of social control, a strict mode of life throughout the South, its tenets observed by white and black just as strictly as if it were written in the constitutions and statute books of these white supremacist states.

Much of the etiquette of Jim Crow did superficially relate to the normal meaning of etiquette, to the simple common courtesies exchanged between ordinary people. The falsity of Jim Crow etiquette was in its one-sidedness—and in the depth of coercion applied to enforce such conventions. Though the purpose was to ensure that black people proffered obeisance to white people and thereby marked their relative inferiority, the matter was not a one-way street. Whites were in ordinary circumstances fully expected to observe their part in the Jim Crow minuet.

Whites could not flout expectations—to eat privately with a black, a matter restricted by etiquette rather than statute, was as dangerous to a white person's reputation as it was to a black person's physical safety. What was more, not a few whites even got themselves lynched for important lapses in race etiquette. Yet, at bottom, the etiquette of race represented an obligatory ritual to keep whites in mind of their first-class rank and blacks of their second-class standing. This etiquette was not written law, but violations could be and were tried in court, although generally under euphemistic charges: a failure to show due respect to a white was elevated to unspecified "criminal" mischief. Infractions of the etiquette of race were often on effective legal par with violations of statutory Jim Crow. The obligation to cleave to race etiquette was reason enough, according to one Southern black, "to at least pretend you respect white folks when you know they will get you killed for disrespecting them."[9]

By the mid–twentieth century, Jim Crow in the Byzantine mix of its statutory aspect combined with a complex body of racial etiquette had come to control practically every public or semipublic facet of the lives of African-Americans in the South. No less dangerous than breaches of statute, lapses in race etiquette resulted in many of the criminal assaults that beset black American life: the so-called back talk or sassing that whites were taught from earliest childhood not to tolerate from blacks, the "crime" of blacks getting above themselves whether with a too new or too fancy car or a suit of too fine a cut, or—deadliest of all for the transgressor— an inadvertent or casual or misplaced indication of a black man's interest in a white female.

Race etiquette was, under most circumstances, viewed by white Southerners not as malicious or malevolent or without positive value. Absent these communally accepted rules designed to maintain blacks in a friction-free association with whites, whites couldn't conceive of a workable society—at least not a social order underlain by the all-important code of white supremacy. Race etiquette, though, was unlike the normal codes of behavior that enable persons of different social classes to react to one another

[9] Stetson Kennedy, 206.

within an acceptable framework. Instead, the conventions of Jim Crow provided that the highest-class black, the most-educated black, the black learned in his profession of law or medicine or academia was required to respond to *any* white person of *any* social class as his *superior*. And, it bears repeating, for him not to do so represented a potentially life-threatening breach of the Southern social order, one for which many African-Americans in fact found themselves the objects of lynch mob fury.

Moreover, race etiquette subtly varied from place to place in the South as, for example, in where blacks were allowed to shop, or to what degree blacks were permitted to share sidewalks with whites. Though African-Americans learned the race etiquette of their own community almost by osmosis from birth, moving to another location with different rules could cause deadly problems for them. A black man unacquainted with local rules might well find himself the subject of a beating by the police if his locally incorrect actions were interpreted by whites as either insolence or indifference to his "proper" place. And avoiding situations where race etiquette was required or opting out of its strictures was next to impossible for Southern blacks—in small communities where the races were often nearly equal in proportion, interaction between black and white was necessary to any semblance of normal commercial life.

The protocol of race in the Jim Crow states extended to areas where it would seem logically idiotic to employ color as a factor. Yet, for example, blacks were expected to defer to white sensibilities of racial justice on the highway, even in lieu of the normal rules of the road. As was their lot everywhere in the South, African-Americans experienced no more anonymity on the road as drivers than they did on the sidewalk as pedestrians. Since the onset of the automobile age whites expected a black in a car to be a chauffeur for white people. Blacks themselves owning cars was never illegal in the South, but in many places and at many times it created peril for a black to consume to so conspicuous a degree. When African-Americans did begin to routinely own their own automobiles, many blacks of means in small towns and rural areas avoided expensive cars, which could easily and dangerously arouse white envy.

Not only was it wise for blacks to downplay their success in being able to own a car, but race etiquette actually governed their driving. One requirement was to sometimes illogically cede the right-of-way to a white driver—or even to a black driver who was chauffeuring white passengers. At many four-way-stop intersections in the South, the right-of-way was determined not by who reached the intersection first, but rather by the race of the drivers. When confronting a white driver who was female, a black male driver in the South could and sometimes did face a life-or-death decision. Compounding the difficulty facing African-Americans was the lack of universality of any of these conventions. In some places whites did maintain normal driving rules. But in others, Jim Crow was more important than highway safety. To the African-American, much of the danger lay in not knowing which applied in an unfamiliar setting.

To black sensibilities, some of the most galling conventions of Southern race etiquette were the rules governing white treatment of African-Americans in their own homes and the parallel procedures blacks were expected to follow in white homes. To some degree, class set the procedures in this area, with professional blacks occasionally accorded courtesies denied to, for example, black domestic servants. But not always: the lower the class of the white, commonly the more insistent would be demands that any and all blacks debase themselves to the most stringent extent of Jim Crow.

Under all but extraordinary circumstances, blacks in the rural and small-town South entered white homes through the back door. They were invariably denied access to the living room in even the most modest dwelling. Social calls by lower-class blacks to any white home were all but taboo, most whites contending that there could be no conceivable reason for such a visit. To avoid humiliation, many middle-class blacks refused to visit a white home even on business, knowing that the owner might demand he or she enter by the back door. Sufferance might sporadically be cranked up a notch if, for example, there was a side door between the front and back doors, one through which a respectable black—a schoolteacher for example—might be shown a degree of respect by a more socially secure white homeowner. Often professional African-Americans refused to visit a white home unless a clear understanding had been arrived at beforehand that they would be welcomed through the front door. A Birmingham school supervisor commented on the situation in the early 1940s: "I always try to avoid going to a white man's home. Any business that I have with him I try to do at his office. . . . It happens that they invite you to their homes once in a while. . . . If they do that, they will expect you to come in the front door. It is the rule that Negroes . . . are expected to go to a white man's back door. . . . Most of the Negroes who would not relish going to the back door would probably not go to the house at all unless they could not get around it."[10]

The other side of the coin was just as full of consequences and grounds for even greater resentment on the part of African-Americans. Blacks could generally avoid ever going into white homes to deflect the attendant humiliations, but whites coming into the homes of blacks were not as easy for the latter to prevent. Callers such as repairmen, utility men, bill collectors, and salesmen were not only sometimes unavoidable, but such people generally represented the lower types of white society, men, and sometimes women, who subjected blacks to every Jim Crow indignity possible, even—perhaps especially—in their own homes.

Often entering without even a knock at the door, Southern whites who invaded the privacy of blacks were bitterly resented. White officials would refuse to remove their hat once indoors, something that was in the Jim Crow years extremely offensive. In the last decades of Jim Crow, whites well understood that blacks wanted hats to be removed before the wearer entered their home, but such a gesture remained to white sensibilities a taboo sign of equality. Another gesture Southern whites refused was to *sit* while in a black home, believing it would also be seen as a mark of equality forbidden under the canon of white supremacy.

Once in a black home, whites on official business as often as not addressed the occupants by either their first names or the labels *boy, auntie, nigger,* in one of the most egregiously offensive of the Jim Crow rituals. To many white officials, it made no difference whether the homeowner was a physician or a field hand—Jim Crow was based on *color,* not status.

[10] Johnson, 131.

Southern police officers were especially notorious in refusing deference in any black home. African-Americans had little recourse but to accept whatever disrespect was directed at them by law enforcement officials. Police held the authority to arrest "troublemakers," "uppity" blacks, blacks who "got above themselves," and many Southern police officers didn't hesitate to routinely wield their power as they saw fit, including in the most brutal manner at their disposal.

In the etiquette of racism, another facet often ranked highest in the hurt it caused its victim: the denial of even the simplest titles of courtesy to African-Americans. Throughout the Jim Crow century, white Southern custom withheld from any black person the spoken or written titles of *Mr.*, *Mrs.*, or *Miss.* No Southern newspaper preceded the name of a black person with any of these seemingly routine designations. No matter the importance, the skills, the honors, or the fame of an African-American, well into the 1950s no newspaper editor so styled a black person's name. Instead, African-Americans would first be identified in a news story by their full names, it being considered a mark of respect to a black if subsequent mentions of his name in the story were the last name alone. In the great majority of cases, subsequent references would be by *first* name alone, and as *white* men were invariably identified as *Mr.* So-and-So, the contrast was stark and unavoidable. An exception would sometimes be found in columns with titles like *News of Interest to Colored Persons*, a feature found in many Southern white newspapers. Because whites weren't expected to read these sections, the black correspondents who wrote them were permitted to include normal titles of respect, titles editors assumed whites wouldn't notice or would condescendingly find amusing.

The Jim Crow code for whites addressing blacks in person was even more humiliating than the conventions of the press. The greatest courtesy a black could reasonably expect from a white was to be addressed by his or her first name. The alternative to this familiarity was a good deal worse. Men under the age of gray hair were, if their name was unknown, routinely addressed as "boy." Older men were "uncle." A young black woman was "gal," an older woman "auntie." Very young black children were "pickaninnies," a contemptuous term derived from the Spanish *pequeño*, or "little." Whites routinely called out for the attention of blacks with the anonymous "you there." At any time and any place, and regardless of rank or distinctions or station in life, black Southerners were subject to being called "nigger" by white Southerners. When used as a common noun, *nigger* was sometimes softened into *nigra* by more charitable whites. But as a habitual command address employed by a white person with any semblance of authority when bidding an unknown or anonymous black man, woman, or child, it remained simply and bluntly "nigger." (In the 1920s the poet Carl Sandburg suggested that African-Americans should indeed officially be referred to as "niggers," his unbigoted but bizarre intent to rob the term of its "sting.")

Letters addressed in the Jim Crow South to African-Americans did not if the recipients were known to be black include the usual *Mr.* or *Mrs.* *Dear* and *Sir* or *Madam* were also omitted from the salutations in such letters, department stores and credit agencies and utility companies keeping careful records of the race of their customers so as not to accidentally include this mark of respect for nonwhites. Such letters generally started out with, for example, simply "John" or "Mary."

A few special titles were "reserved" for African-Americans. Whites of any claim to breeding could not under most circumstances refer to highly educated blacks as "gal" or "nigger." So substitutes for white titles of respect were devised. Many such designations were exaggerated versions of white titles, this pointed amplification keeping them from being taken too seriously by whites. Under Jim Crow, a male black schoolteacher became "professor"—the white mark of a member of a university faculty, the black mark of anyone instructing in anything from poker to philosophy.

The Jim Crow principle regarding African-Americans addressing whites was, not unexpectedly, just as inflexible as its mirror image. According to strictest Jim Crow etiquette, every white man from the richest county landowner to the meanest hardscrabble farmer was addressed by blacks as "sir." Some exceptions were made, as with roughly coequal job-holders at the lower rungs of the employment ladder, who called each other by first names. But if white strangers were within hearing distance, many whites bridled at being addressed by their first name, the reason being that the white was likely to lose status with his peers if known to be on a first-name basis with a black. As for blacks, rather than use terms of respect to persons they considered inferior to themselves, many would just walk up to a white person and start talking with no greeting whatsoever. When in Jim Crow days police departments were totally white, blacks especially resented the universal contempt shown by police toward all African-Americans, officers almost always using their authority to demand deference from blacks. An African-American, regardless of his economic or educational status, who failed to address a police officer with due deference became an obvious target for police reprisals.

In almost everything they would do during almost every day of their life, black Americans in the Jim Crow South were forced to negotiate the minefield of race etiquette. The regimen wasn't always a literal matter of life or death, but it *could* be. Black *men* were especially well advised to remain on high alert—cautious in addressing police officers and overseers and petty officials, in driving their cars on roads controlled by whites, in achieving a successful crop or business or child so as not to make some white person jealous enough to do violence. And, most importantly by far, a black man had to ensure beyond any question that his interactions with white women remained devoid of any sign of intimacy, of friendliness, or—to be as safe as possible—even of simple notice of her existence.

The etiquette of Jim Crow maintained a cardinal rule: *Whites first.* Forgetting it or ignoring it almost always brought trouble—and it sometimes brought tragedy.

6

THE WAR YEARS

harles Richard Drew was a student at McGill University in Montreal when he found that he was smitten with the mysteries of blood. He wanted to unravel the mystery of how this extremely perishable fluid might be kept usable for a longer time when extracted from the human body—long enough so it could save lives. The dilemma, he knew, was that within a few days of being drawn, blood deteriorated, becoming, in effect, rotten and, if medically transfused, liable to kill whomever it was injected into. Charles Drew made it his mission to figure out how to make the stuff storable so it could be employed as and when needed.

While working at New York's Presbyterian Hospital in the late 1930s, the young doctor finally hit on the solution. He found that if he took the solid cells out of the liquid blood, what was left—a fluid called plasma—remained wholesome for a long period and, most importantly, could serve in place of "whole" blood during lifesaving transfusions. As an experiment, Drew set up what he called a blood bank at Presbyterian. Shortly afterward the war started in Europe, and he received a cablegram from Dr. John Beattie of London's Royal College of Surgeons. The British physician asked Drew if he could immediately send five thousand ampoules of the plasma for injured British soldiers in dire need of transfusions. Drew put together what he called his Blood Transfusion Association to ship the plasma, saving many lives with the blood banking that was then established in Britain. A year later, Drew asked the American Red Cross to establish a similar program in the United States, which the organization agreed to do.

At this point a problem arose. Someone in the War Department suddenly thought of the possibility that white people might get transfused with blood donated by black people, and this public-spirited bureaucrat formally warned that it was therefore "inadvisable to collect and mix Negro and Caucasian blood." The Red Cross took the admonition with due seriousness and quickly directed that any non-Caucasian blood be banked separately and not be transfused into white people and, just to be safe, ordered that no blood from black people be accepted for the U.S. program, either domestically or overseas. Justifying the practice, the organization explained that it was bound by its congressional charter to perform in accord with the demands of the armed services—which had, in fact, already ordered that blood be banked according to the needs of racial separation. When asked about all this at a press conference, the army's surgeon general said he knew of no reason why this policy should be changed, even though he admitted that he also knew blood contained no physical differences related to race. Dr. Drew protested the Red Cross decision, rationally and temperately explaining that the "blood of individual human beings may differ by groupings, but there is absolutely no scientific basis to indicate any differences by race." The bureaucracy nonetheless clung to prejudice, knowing that many white Americans could never be convinced of the truth of the matter. Segregated blood banking stood. And even when blood from African-Americans *was* later accepted, it was still stored separately from blood from whites and was not transfused into whites. Only four years *after* the end of the war would the U.S. armed services reverse their policy of segregating blood by the race of its donor.

Dr. Drew was killed in an automobile accident in 1950, when he was only forty-five years old. Eight months after the accident the American Red Cross finally removed racial distinctions from its own blood donor program, and at last, *all* of America's banked blood flowed together, as Charles Drew knew it should. The poignancy of this tale lies in that the blood of Dr. Drew himself would not have been acceptable for transfusions into any of the hundreds of thousands of American soldiers, seamen, or airmen injured in World War II. Not any of the *white* ones, that is, since Charles Richard Drew was an African-American. Six years before his death, the NAACP had for his phenomenal contribution to mankind bestowed on the physician its highest honor, the Spingarn Medal.

Toward the end of the same war in which Charles Drew contributed so mightily, a Swedish citizen named Gunnar Myrdal published to both vast acclaim and caustic criticism a book that opened the door on the ultimate evil in American life. The book, called *An American Dilemma*, was not published in Sweden, but in New York, the author having been commissioned by the prestigious Carnegie Corporation to survey race relations in the United States. Brought out in 1944 by Harper & Brothers, one of the nation's oldest and most distinguished publishing houses, what so astonished readers in this revolutionary work was its cogent and unshrinking attack on America's racial tyranny even while the United States was consumed in a war to oppose racial tyranny being perpetrated by Germany on Jews, Slavs, Gypsies, and anyone else below the exalted rank of pure Aryan. The book said much, very much, that Americans had never heard before, and that many of them hadn't ever wanted to hear.

Across fifteen hundred pages of exceptionally small print, Myrdal applied a literary scalpel to the wound of American racism. Though the book's subtitle was *The Negro Problem and Modern Democracy*, the Swedish sociologist made clear that the race *problem* wasn't a "Negro" problem but was instead the *white* American's problem—that it was caused by whites, perpetuated by whites, and would have to be ended, or at least ameliorated, by changes in how whites treated and viewed blacks. It was whites, in the book's telling indictment, who had created the attitudes and conditions that were directly and immediately responsible for the many vicissitudes borne by African-Americans—poor education, insuperable barriers to social acceptance, victimization by violence, substandard housing, discrimination in the workplace, maltreatment from the police and the justice system. *An American Dilemma* logically saw that when blacks gained in these areas, so would white convictions regarding black inferiority prove less and less sustainable. And ultimately, so at odds with what he called the American Creed was the nation's racism that Myrdal anticipated a time when the country would, if for no other reason than to maintain its standing in the world, plainly *have* to change in regards to race.

As the country had approached another international war in the fading years of the Great Depression, the majority of African-Americans found themselves living lives not fundamentally different from those their great-grandparents had lived in the immediate post–Civil War period. Most blacks remained firmly tied to the land as nonowning laborers, and most still lived in the old Confederacy, where hope for an improved future was, as it had always been, dimmer than in any other part of America. African-Americans as a class were far more illiterate than white Americans, far poorer, much less healthy and therefore forced to look ahead to appreciably shorter life spans than whites, their labor was physically harder than that done by whites, black women were far likelier to work outside the home than were white women, and most blacks remained essentially voteless— only 5 percent of African-Americans in the South of voting age did vote— almost always because they were forcibly kept from the polls or stayed away because they knew the danger inherent in even attempting to register or to vote. Conditions for blacks in the North were still admittedly appalling, but at least Northern blacks often could count the law on their side, and black disfranchisement in the North remained sporadic rather than systematic.

But what was happening to Americans and to the world when *An American Dilemma* appeared would finally begin to break the back of Jim Crow, not to mention contributing to breaking the cultural grip of the Western, Christian, colonial-inspired racism that infected huge expanses of the planet. At the same time that the worldwide war would present continents full of colonialized people of color with their first prospects of independence, it would also open for America's blacks a window on a vastly extended vista of inclusion in their own nation. But at the beginning of the 1940s the window still seemed tightly shut, and prying it open would prove neither easy nor quick, and it wouldn't be accomplished without a great deal more pain.

As had been the case a generation earlier, again in the century's second global war the military would serve as a critically important catalyst for change in America's struggle with race. The difference would be that from this new war substantive change *would* finally emerge. Woodrow Wilson had committed the nation to help make a world "safe for democracy" when hundreds of thousands of proud and invigorated black troops returned from Europe in 1918, but the administration and the government expected those men to resume their second-class status in American society, expected that those African-Americans would not be allowed to present a just bill to a racially unjust nation. And with only negligible exceptions, that was exactly what had happened. Most of those soldiers and sailors went back to their Southern homes and to the same torment of Jim Crow that had always been their lot. A few had returned to or resettled in the North, but there, too, employers and unions denied them jobs, real estate agents and politicians confined them to ghettos, and vast numbers of whites treated them with deep-rooted racial antagonism and generally did their utmost to keep them from the riches that America had given to so many others. Hoping for the goodwill of white America after serving in a war that had changed much of the world, instead black Americans got the back of its hand.

Between the end of the first war and the onset of the second, a new and far more assertive stamp of black leadership and civil rights organization had come forward, individuals and groups determined to press long-overdue demands on America's vaunted but profoundly dishonest national promise of equal rights for all. The National Association for the Advancement of Colored People, the National Urban League, and the National Negro Congress represented three of the principal bodies seeking justice for blacks in this period. Charles Houston, a lawyer who served as the special counsel to the NAACP, emerged as one of the most eloquent of those who appealed directly to the federal government for fair treatment of African-Americans, and when in 1937 he met with Franklin Roosevelt, the African-American attorney asked the president to issue an executive order banning racial discrimination in the military services, specifically "to give Negro citizens the same right to serve their country as any other citizen, and on the same basis." The NAACP later devised its "Double-V" campaign to popularize the issue, with one *V* standing for victory over the Axis, the other for victory over American racism. William Hastie, another African-American lawyer, was appointed as a civilian aide to the secretary of war to deal with military race issues. Hastie publicly criticized the army for adopting "the traditional mores of the South . . . as the basis of policy and practice affecting the Negro soldier" and urged the administration to require racial integration throughout the military. Indeed many blacks believed at the beginning of World War II that the homefront battle against racism was fully as important, if not more so, than that against the Axis, a stance pointedly challenging the overwhelming white endorsement of segregation in both civilian and military life. Though African-Americans as a whole remained a long way from the cohesiveness that would in another generation play a critical role in civil rights gains, determined men and women, civilian and military, black and white (especially judges in this latter group), had by Pearl Harbor begun to dislodge Jim Crow from its position of unassailability.

On one major domestic front, these efforts garnered a significant success. In 1941 labor leader and civil rights activist A. Philip Randolph organized what he hoped would be a massive protest march of thousands of African-Americans on Washington's Lincoln Memorial. Trying to both appease Randolph and head off the embarrassment such a spectacle would bring to his administration, Roosevelt unenthusiastically signed Executive Order 8802, banning racial discrimination in defense and government hiring and, to put some enforcement bite in the order, establishing the Federal Employment Commission. Though not directly affecting the status of blacks in the armed services, the president's action did persuade Randolph to cancel the march. More importantly, it brought the century's first meaningful labor advance for blacks.

With the opportunity another world war provided, Randolph and his fellow leaders continued to view the armed forces as the most obvious place to press for real and immediate change. African-Americans almost universally regarded the Jim Crow that permeated the military as one of the greatest humiliations of American life. Every branch of the services had long clothed itself in the principles of white supremacy—in recruiting, in training, in assignments, in promotions. America's military structure acceded not just to the racial bigotries of white Northerners, but it wholly and unapologetically accommodated Southern-style Jim Crow, while officially regarding blacks as difficult to train as well as socially inassimilable in the virtually all-white world of the nation's defense establishment. As liberal as Franklin Roosevelt's policies were by the standards of his presidential years, after Pearl Harbor finally pulled the United States into the war he nonetheless saw as his first duty the need to win the war rather than to try to correct the nation's social ills, most particularly the racism that counted as by far its deepest and most intractable evil. Tragically, he didn't see ending racism as even a secondary priority, nor was his administration seen to firmly include racial justice *anywhere* on its list of national priorities.

In fairness to Roosevelt, partisan politics largely shaped the president's options on racial affairs. The president believed that in this area his hands were effectively tied by the South's senators and representatives: if he were to press a social agenda that thwarted their regional interests, legislators from the old Confederacy, men perfectly ready to put their white supremacism ahead of the critical interests of a nation planning and preparing for world war, could and would block the White House's most urgent defense needs.

But in seeking equality of treatment for blacks already in the services and for those ready to enlist, civil rights leaders showed they could play the game as hard as Southern lawmakers. The *Pittsburgh Courier*, one of the country's most influential African-American newspapers, organized the Committee for Negro Participation in the National Defense Program, a body aimed at pushing the administration toward opening the services to black enlistment. With lobbying from this and similar groups, a bill managed to get through Congress requiring that in the selection and training of servicemen "no discrimination against any person on account of race or color" would be permitted. But because the measure lacked policing authority, the services essentially made an end run around it, instead establishing racially separate draft calls to make certain that draftees could be accounted for by race and that blacks could thereby be dealt with entirely separately. Most importantly, discrimination and segregation were not officially looked upon as incompatible concepts, thus the services' practice of keeping men separated by color not legally equating to impermissible discrimination. The upshot was that Jim Crow retained control of the military and that black enlistment remained low because many young African-Americans were plainly unwilling to serve in a segregated fighting force.

With the revised draft law now including African-Americans—though as virtually a separate species of draftee—thousands of young black men would in fact be called up. But an unanticipated consequence of African-American enlistment was the effect on *Northern* blacks of joining a social structure as rigidly segregated as any Southern community, creating unforeseen—or at least, unavoidable in the times—harm. Being introduced to Southern-style Jim Crow for the first time in their life, Northern African-American enlistees came face-to-face with more vitriolic social racism than most had ever experienced in civilian life. As the military established new bases throughout the country to meet the war's vastly expanded needs, Jim Crow symbiotically came as part of these facilities, the federally mandated military racism actually introducing segregation in places where it hadn't before existed in rigid or statutory terms.

Many blacks refused to be inducted into this Jim Crow environment, even though refusing induction because of racial discrimination did not confer conscientious objector status and was a felony. Thirty-six-year-old Winfred William Lynn was one such African-American resister who learned the consequences of such refusal. In September 1942 the New York City gardener was ordered by his draft board to report for induction, but when he read his notice informing him that "your quota for this call is the first 90 white men and the first 50 Negro men who are in Class

I-A," Lynn refused to report. He explained in a letter to his draft board that he was "ready to serve in any unit of the armed forces of my country which is not segregated by race," but wouldn't go if his race *were* taken into account. His stand constituted a felony, and a federal grand jury duly indicted him for draft evasion. Arguing that the army's procedures for inducting African-Americans under a quota system violated the Selective Service Act's prohibition against racial discrimination, Lynn continued to refuse to answer his draft call. When a federal judge ruled that Lynn would have to enter the service *before* the case could be decided on its merits, he reluctantly acceded. But after his induction, a court declared that the Selective Service Act forbade not segregation but *discrimination*, and that the military could segregate as it wished without the practice being construed as discrimination. The only requirement on the army's part, according to the verdict, was that all whites had to be treated like all other whites and all blacks treated like all other blacks, which vouchsafed the services' version of Jim Crow from being accounted as impermissible racial injustice. The U.S. Supreme Court twice refused to review the case, the second time on the grounds that because Lynn had already been shipped to the South Pacific, he couldn't be produced in a courtroom where a judge could order his release from the service in the eventuality that he won his appeal.

Ending such judicial travesties appeared to many impossible when the administration's highest leaders themselves seemed intent on perpetuating racism. The president addressed black leaders with relatively soothing generalities about the need for "fairness," but they resulted in few specific orders to his subordinates to carry out measures aimed at racial equity. Critical to even toning down Jim Crow was the man in charge of the army, Henry L. Stimson. Having already once served as secretary of war (under William Howard Taft), he had most recently been Herbert Hoover's secretary of state, and Roosevelt had retained the experienced New York lawyer in his cabinet, again as war secretary. Raised as a strict Calvinist, the traditionalist Stimson believed that an army in wartime or, for that matter, at any other time was the not the right place to correct social "problems." In any case, Stimson viewed the problem—the nation's racism—as "insoluble." Protesting that he himself was "sensitive to the individual tragedy which went with [segregation] to the colored man himself," he nonetheless counseled the president not to place "too much responsibility on a race that was not showing initiative in battle." How a race that was not allowed to participate in battle could be accused of not showing battle initiative remains a historical mystery, but the sentiment stood fully in accord with popular, however stereotyped, attitudes about the service-worthiness of black units in general and black soldiers in particular. Stimson's views were, in fact, well within prevailing white public opinion of the day. His statement about "foolish leaders of the colored race" seeking "at bottom social equality" was predicated on his conclusion that such equality was out of the question "because of the impossibility of race mixture by marriage"—the words merely a clumsy refrain of one of the principal supports upholding white America's race attitudes in the Jim Crow era.

As important as Stimson's thinking was that of General George C. Marshall, particularly among the uniformed leaders who were defying Congress's relatively liberal directives regarding the handling of blacks in the military. A strict observer and defender of military regulations, the army's aloof but widely admired chief of staff—he had been sworn into the position on September 1, 1939, the day World War II began in Europe—believed that at least overt discrimination against blacks should not be tolerated. Conversely, the native Virginian insisted, like Stimson, that the army was no place for social experimentation, which meant it was no place to change accepted national patterns on the treatment of blacks, which was to say accepted national majoritarian views, which were *unquestionably* overtly discriminatory. In keeping with Roosevelt's stand, Marshall held that fighting Germany and Japan should dominate every ounce of the nation's attention, and that any effort to resolve the nation's "vexing racial problems" must not be permitted to jeopardize military discipline and morale.

In retrospect, it is understandable that accomplishing the phenomenal undertaking of a two-front world war did seem to require commanding every ounce of America's physical and moral energy. But even if ameliorating racism had held a high place in the administration's or the military's priorities, it did not hold a high priority for white Americans. In response to Hastie's pleas to bring racial justice to the services, Marshall commented harshly but in perfect tune with the times that "the War Department cannot ignore the social relationships between negroes and whites which have been established by the American people through custom and habit."[1] During World War II no groundswell ever arose among whites to correct the racial inequities against blacks, neither for those African-Americans in uniform nor for those who suffered in the far wider forum of civilian life. Racism remained concretely entrenched among white Americans both Southern and otherwise, and the many kinds of discrimination African-Americans endured during World War II barely reached the notice, let alone the concern, of the overwhelming majority of the country's white population. Instead, simply winning the war consumed the full attention of both government and people, and in truth, the conflict commanded virtually the unanimous backing of the population—the last of America's wars to date to do so.

And in this framework Jim Crow proceeded apace. Despite the unavoidable irony in the prevalent belief that America was fighting to defeat the most racist state in history, it left undisturbed the racism in its own backyard. "Postponing" reform in the services, the government's leading voices pleaded that the social relationship between blacks and whites had been established "by custom," and that experiments to solve social problems were "fraught with danger to efficiency, discipline, and morale." Some professed to believe that attempts at wide-scale mixing of the races would end in revolution even while the United States was fighting a worldwide war. The adjutant general wrote that "the Army is not a sociological laboratory. . . . Experiments to meet the wishes and demands of the champions of every race and creed for the solution of their problems are a danger to efficiency, discipline, and morale and would result in ultimate defeat."[2]

Though the government had agreed to allow blacks to be drafted or voluntarily enlist in proportion to their percentage in the general popu-

---

[1] Smith, 26.
[2] MacGregor, ch. 2, p. 4.

lation, permitting them to serve in integrated combat units remained almost totally out of the question. Even creating all-black units specifically for combat duty was considered a luxury that the military couldn't afford during the national emergency. Because of the generally lower educational levels of America's blacks, a painful reality that bolstered the expectation that African-Americans would not be able to adequately absorb training, military planners decreed that individual blacks would perforce amount to inferior troops and, in the aggregate, to inferior combat units, whether on the ground, in the air, or at sea. The Army General Classification Test that was introduced in March 1941 appeared to justify the decision. Measured only by educational achievement instead of by innate intelligence, blacks placed disproportionately low relative to whites. But more than three-quarters of the African-American inductees who failed the test came from the South and the border states, the origins of only one-quarter of white inductees. In absolute numbers, a higher proportion of blacks than of whites did score in the lower categories but, unlike whites, were treated as a single group rather than as individuals, a methodology that resulted in the squandering of the talents and potential contributions of thousands of educated blacks. As a result, no one in a position of authority was about to advise energy be "wasted" on forming blacks into regular fighting units, based on a high probability that such effort would not justify the expense.

Blacks in their segregated units further suffered, at the very least psychologically, because of the paucity of black officers to command such units. (In these years the officer-producing service academies admitted virtually no blacks.) In the first year of war only one-third of one percent of blacks entered the service as officers. But even when the percentage began to slowly rise as the war progressed, white commanders continued to insist that the segregated African-American units be commanded by whites, their reasoning being that even educated blacks couldn't effectively lead and, what was more, that blacks themselves preferred white officers. Army practice further forbade black officers to outrank or to command white officers even in black units. It was also held to be "unnecessarily" expensive to create appropriate living quarters and clubs for the few black officers, who because of the military's Jim Crow would not be allowed in many white facilities. In sum, black officers were so hedged in by white supremacist beliefs and practices that they weren't regarded as "real" officers by whites or, sometimes, even by blacks. And attitudes from the top seeped down through the ranks: Secretary Stimson wrote in 1940 that "leadership is not imbedded in the Negro race yet and to try to make commissioned officers to lead the men into battle—colored men—is only to work disaster to both." Though Stimson was later to try to improve conditions, he added, "I hope for Heaven's sake they won't mix the white and the colored troops together in the same units for then we shall certainly have trouble."[3]

Still other difficulties stood in the way of racial evenhandedness. Black units were often difficult, sometimes even impossible, to deploy or base. Local governments in the United States resisted posts or bases with black units, and local commanders often objected to their presence. During these years white racism was by no means restricted to the United States, making foreign postings equally problematic. Panamanian officials flatly told the army that black soldiers would not be welcome on that nation's territory. Elsewhere in Latin America, Chile and Venezuela would echo Panama's sentiments. As for the Atlantic theater, Iceland, Greenland, and Labrador were specifically and unequivocally unwelcoming to blacks. The administration rarely objected to these attitudes, holding to the logic that race difficulties shouldn't be added to already overburdened commanders' concerns.

What African-American soldiers largely became in World War II were laborers in uniform. There were exceptions, important ones, where blacks were allowed to fight and where many distinguished themselves in combat units. But basically the black experience in World War II was pretty much a repeat of the African-American experience in World War I. Most black soldiers were denied admission to specialty training and found themselves relegated to unskilled labor details in segregated units, outfits commanded mostly by white officers. The vast majority of the hundreds of thousands of blacks who voluntarily enlisted or were drafted into the army went into

McGuire, 32.

the Quartermaster Corps, the Corps of Engineers, and the Transportation Corps. There they functioned as stevedores, as casual laborers, as servants, ditchdiggers, and latrine cleaners, as truck drivers and permanent KP detailees. Of the nearly 1 million blacks who served in uniform in World War II, only 15 percent received combat assignments. Yet serving in noncombat units did not mean such troops remained away from danger. As an example, the Red Ball Express drivers, black truck drivers who supplied frontline troops after the invasion of the European continent, faced perils fully as real as those confronting infantrymen or aircrewmen even though the Express operated well behind the front lines. Driving trucks at night with only a slit of light allowed from the headlamps on runs that typically lasted thirty-six sleepless hours over roundtrips averaging more than five hundred miles between the Normandy ports and the advancing Allied armies, all the while loaded with extra gasoline and ammunition for self-defense, was a regimen that killed many of the Red Ball drivers.

Undeniable advances did come for African-Americans in uniform, some clearly a result of embarrassing (to the establishment as well as to the country's reputation) litigation compelling such gains. The most famous occurred in 1942 when the Army Air Corps established its first black flying unit. The famed Tuskegee Airmen were set up as the Ninety-ninth Pursuit Squadron under the command of Colonel Benjamin O. Davis Jr., the first black West Point graduate since Reconstruction and son of the sole African-American flag-rank officer in World War II, Brigadier General Benjamin O. Davis Sr. (The elder Davis was in 1940, after forty-two years in the army, promoted from lieutenant colonel to brigadier general in a move designed to boost political support for the Democrats; his wartime role would be to oversee black-white troop relations, spending much of the war in Britain as Eisenhower's black adviser.) The NAACP had, with logic and justice, criticized the segregated unit on the grounds that black fliers could never get the flight training that was the equal of what white fliers could acquire, if for no other reason than that they were restricted from flying in and out of many air bases, an impediment not faced by whites. But fair-minded Army officials nonetheless fought to keep the black unit, contending that a segregated squadron was better than none and that it would eventually lead to widespread integrated aviation training.

Even when twenty-five hundred blacks were eventually accepted as army pilot trainees, many ended up performing menial tasks on the air bases to which they were assigned—and grouped and quartered, of course, in segregated units. It was almost impossible to shatter the assumption by the bulk of the white military leadership that these blacks would not be able to perform to the standards of white fliers, and because Jim Crow meant they couldn't be incorporated into the general units, they therefore often ended up as laborers. The point was that even blacks with superior educations would not be effectively utilized because, firstly, they could not be put into white units, and secondly, the military believed (with a certain logic) it couldn't run an effective war with separate white and black first-line combat units. Even in a nation fighting for its life in a multifront worldwide war, one in which almost every conceivable resource was needed for victory, the United States refused to set aside its racism by effectively deploying the skills and talents, not to mention the overwhelming desire to participate, of the black 10 percent of the American people. The ultimate paradox lay in the reality that while thousands of blacks participated in the war (particularly the air war), providing valuable service both to the military and to the allied cause, none was universally seen as truly fit to do so in the company of white servicemen.

Of all the shocks facing black servicemen and servicewomen in World War II, one of the worst for many was the Jim Crow discrimination that permeated and surrounded their training bases in the United States. Jim Crow–style discrimination was by no means confined to the South, black service members experiencing overt racial discrimination in military towns in every section of the country. But the South housed a disproportionate percentage of military bases through the war years, and throughout the region the humiliations of racial discrimination were brought to a high and sometimes deadly degree of malignancy. Blacks native to the South at least understood the dangers of Jim Crow and usually knew how to avoid white racial wrath, notwithstanding that some discovered what was permissible in one part of the South brought serious and sometimes vicious retribution in another. But what often touched off the most brutal incidents of white-inspired racial terror were instances where Northern blacks were unaware of the fine points of Southern racial etiquette and the kinds of black actions or behavior that could trigger white violence.

That a service member was wearing the uniform of his or her country meant absolutely nothing to most white Southerners in their meticulous wartime maintenance of Jim Crow in all its myriad particulars. Furthermore, the reality that blacks were expected to risk their lives in helping defeat racist Nazism was equally immaterial to the region's Jim Crow. African-Americans in uniform were routinely denied many of the comforts and off-duty amusements provided their white compatriots in Southern military towns in the war. The famous United Service Organizations clubs provide a sad example: unless an all-black club was established in a given town, the USO simply remained unavailable to African-American soldiers and sailors. In the South, blacks in uniform were forced to drink from "colored" drinking fountains, were refused the use of white rest rooms, were denied food or drink at white cafés, were confined to the back of the buses. When Lieutenant Jackie Robinson refused to sit in the rear of a bus at his Texas base, he was arrested and court-martialed for his action. Though Robinson was acquitted of the charge, the verdict did nothing to change the Texas law that forced this black officer and future sports hero to be humiliated in his own country—and while serving that country under arms.

A black soldier in Durham, North Carolina, wasn't as fortunate as Robinson. When Private Booker T. Spicely was ordered by the driver to move to the rear of a city bus, he did so, but not without angering the white operator: the driver shot Spicely dead for this "impertinence." In October 1944 in Dublin, Georgia, police chief Mitchell Bohannon shot and killed a black soldier named Willie L. Davis, Bohannon receiving not even a reprimand after he said he fired on the young African-American for making a disturbance at a local roadhouse. In Elizabethtown, Kentucky, three black Wacs didn't leave the bus station's white waiting room quickly enough to satisfy a pair of the town's police officers. After shouting, "Down here when we tell niggers to move, they move," the officers clubbed the women, mauled them, dragged them across the street to the jail, and threw them in a cell. When the women finally got back to their base, their commanding officer upbraided them for violating the state's Jim Crow laws. The South could be—and not infrequently *was*—as dangerous for blacks in uniform as were the real war's front lines in Europe or the Pacific.

Officer candidate schools were among the few settings in which the military attempted substantial racial integration. Even so, great pressure was exerted on the War Department by whites in Southern communities adjacent to OCS bases, locals who wanted to end the integrated training that they regarded as "mongrelization." The president of Georgia's White Supremacy League complained to the army that the requirement that young white officer candidates at Fort Benning share sleeping quarters and dining halls with black candidates represented "the most damnable outrage that was ever perpetrated on the youth of the South." The War Department meekly responded that physical separation of the races was not always possible because of "the small number of Negroes involved."

Only at the very end of the war did the army begin to substantially ameliorate its racist treatment of black soldiers. A few months before the war ended in Europe, it finally undertook to allow black soldiers to volunteer for racially mixed combat units. Transferred in from the service units—catering, truck driving, quartermastering—the black volunteers fought as capably as did their white fellow soldiers. The experiment put a persuasive dent in the army's longtime justification for restricting black soldiers from reaching their full potential as frontline fighters.

If in the army African-Americans gained at least some limited headway in correcting racial injustice, the same would not hold for the other service branches. The Marine Corps and the Coast Guard shared an almost equally abysmal record in their racial practices. But the navy, if for no reason other than its relative size and importance, merits particular historical scorn for its wartime racism.

Though in the Civil War the navy found that racially mixed crews could advantageously serve aboard its ships, the postbellum calcification of American society into separate white and black nations effectively ended any further prospect of an integrated seaborne service. If whites could not or would not live side by side with blacks in civilian life, the navy reasoned that such intransigence was even more certain within the confines of a ship. Where in America's later wars a place could be found for segregated all-black units in the land-based army, naval leaders refused all but a token berth for blacks. And with the post-*Plessy* national legal consensus validating the separation of Americans by race, the navy's answer was to simply exclude African-Americans from any role except as officers' manservants, what the black press derisively labeled "seagoing bellhops." For more than half a century, this dismal reality fairly represented the racial landscape of the U.S. navy.

By the time of the attack on Pearl Harbor, 5,026 blacks were in the navy, a little more than 2 percent of its ranks. There were no black officers whatsoever (two blacks had been admitted to Annapolis in the late 1930s, but both resigned before graduation; Wesley A. Brown of New York, the next, the *very* next, black to be admitted to the academy began his studies in June 1945, and thus did not, of course, serve as an officer in World War II), and every black was a member of the Stewards' Branch, a billet blacks shared with Filipinos, who were likewise restricted to this one duty. A few chief petty officers were included among these enlisted ratings, but their uniforms and insignia were distinct from those of the rest of the navy, and because they were rated outside the navy's general service, stewards could not exercise any authority over regular enlisted men, including even those below them in nominal rank.

Though these stewards didn't do the cooking, a function fulfilled by white ratings, they served officers in their dining rooms, cleaned officers' quarters and cared for their uniforms, and sometimes served as household servants for high-ranking officers in shore establishments. They were not, of course, wanted for actual combat duties, the navy refusing to accept blacks on any basis whatsoever except for the handful needed as servants. Buttressing the policy and representing a major roadblock to any diminution of the navy's Jim Crow practices was its cabinet secretary, Frank Knox. Though hardly untypical for his time, Knox was convinced African-Americans were inferior beings and saw civil rights agitation as counter to the best interests of a nation at war. The secretary believed that stewarding represented the most appropriate duty for blacks because it "avoided the chance that Negroes might rise to command whites."

With the services in desperate need for men in the months following Pearl Harbor, black leaders tried hard to get the navy to end its policy of excluding African-Americans. Under this intense pressure, in January 1942 the president finally weighed in on the issue. Suggesting to Knox that he was "certain" blacks could successfully accomplish something besides steward duties, Roosevelt ordered the secretary to direct the navy's General Board to see what could be found. The board's answer was music. Inspector General Rear Admiral Charles Snyder suggested putting some blacks in the Musicians' Branch because, as he viewed it, "the colored race is very musical and they are all versed in all forms of rhythm." He also suggested that some berths might be found in the Aviation Branch and on a few minor vessels, but that any such effort was going to be "troublesome and require tact, patience, and tolerance."

The navy's commanding officers routinely ignored the entire exercise. The spokesman for the Bureau of Navigation wrote that if "they [African-Americans] are not satisfied to be messmen, they will not be satisfied to go into the construction or labor battalions." The commandant of the Marine Corps referred to any change in existing naval policy regarding the enlistment of blacks as "absolutely tragic," since blacks had the opportunity "to satisfy their aspiration to serve in the Army." In spite of Roosevelt's admittedly mild urging, the navy initially continued to see to it that virtually none of its race policies changed. Only after the president pushed a little more did Knox begin to get the message. In April 1942, the secretary agreed that the three branches under his control—the navy, the Marine Corps, and the Coast Guard—would in fact accept 277 black volunteers each week, and not in messmen's duties but in regular enlisted positions.

The navy predicted it would have fourteen thousand African-Americans in general service within a year (this when millions of white Americans were in, or about to be in, uniform). Despite this jump in black enlistment, in all cases these men would serve in segregated units. The

NAACP scorned the plan as unacceptable tokenism, A. Philip Randolph charging that it merely "consolidated the naval policy of Jim Crowism as well as proclaims it as an accepted, recognized government ideology that the Negro is inferior to the white man." Randolph was absolutely right. When the new policy failed to attract many enlistees, the service absurdly attributed the problem to blacks' "relative unfamiliarity with the sea or the large inland waters and their consequent fear of the water" rather than seeing that African-Americans shunned the navy because of the stunningly obvious bigotry inherent even in its "new and improved" racial policies. Volunteer naval enlistments came to about 5 percent of its wartime strength, though blacks represented about 11 percent of all men drafted into that service.

With blacks being inducted principally for shore duties, the concern arose that disproportional concentrations of African-Americans at shore stations would be detrimental to efficiency. This thinking led to proposals that at least small numbers be allowed to serve on ships in other than mess duties and servant roles, specifically as firemen and ordinary seamen on the large carriers then being built in high numbers. Still the service rejected any such integration. What was more, naval Jim Crow meant that no black could aspire to commissioned rank and that black women would not be accepted into either the Waves or the Naval Nursing Corps. In the end, African-Americans—all of them male—served the nation's seagoing service during World War II almost exclusively as servants, as stevedores in overseas Seabees outfits and laborers at overseas bases, and as cooks and guards at shore stations, as well as in a few billets available in harbor defenses such as small-craft service. Since until mid-1944 there was no such thing as a black officer, all were at first commanded by whites. (The Seabees got their first black commissioned officer—an ensign—in March 1945.)

When by early 1944 the concentrations of shore-based blacks were beginning to cause significant public relations problems for the navy, Admiral Ernest King finally decided to give African-Americans a chance to go to sea in nonservant roles. Consequently, two small ships—the USS *Mason* and a patrol boat—were assigned all-black crews, officered by whites, of course, although black officers served in junior positions on both vessels.

Mounting complaints from both Congress and civil rights organizations finally prodded the navy into commissioning black officers. More than two years after Pearl Harbor, the first class of sixteen candidates entered Great Lakes for training—training that was, almost needless to say, segregated. All sixteen made it through, but the navy decided twelve black officers was more than enough, resulting in the return of three to the ranks while one was made a warrant officer. The twelve winners got their ensign stripes on March 17, 1944, but were designated as "Deck Officers Limited—Only" to ensure that they didn't get into line duties and thus find themselves in the position of commanding white line officers. By the end of the war, sixty African-Americans would serve as commissioned officers in the navy.

Black women finally made their way into the Waves when in 1944 Thomas Dewey, the Republican presidential candidate, charged the administration with discrimination against female African-Americans, a charge that couldn't have come as much of a surprise to anyone. In the event, Roosevelt ordered the navy to quickly enlist a few black women to head off a Republican campaign issue. Headlines from black newspapers throughout 1944 chronicled the story of how black women gained admittance to the women's services: March 18—"Navy Promises Action on Waves"; June 6—"Navy Tells Why No Negro Waves"; August 19—"Navy Considers End of Wave Ban"; October 27—"Two-Year Fight Won at Last"; October 28—"Waves, Spars to Admit Negroes." At the beginning of 1945, two black Wave officers graduated from training, and the enlistment of black women at long last got under way. Seventy-two made it into the service before the war ended in August. The era's profoundly ingrained white supremacy was hardly ever beaten back quickly.

On Frank Knox's death in 1944, Roosevelt appointed the more enlightened James Forrestal to head the Navy Department. Though not considered notably progressive even by the standards of the day, Forrestal had served on the board of the Urban League and was at least sensitive to the widespread national disgust with the armed forces' Jim Crow practices felt by many whites and almost all blacks. What was more, he believed segregation actually hindered military efficiency, the one argument that might resound favorably in an atmosphere where winning the war was more important than was meaningfully addressing a domestic social disaster. Another factor pushing for a new agenda was that one of the new secretary's most influential aides was Adlai Stevenson, a liberal who repeatedly counseled his boss to direct the navy toward greater racial integration.

Forrestal dropped no bombshells of opportunity for blacks, but he quietly told his service to eliminate race barriers wherever possible, initiating what he characterized as "a start down a long road." In March 1945 he prodded the surgeon general into accepting black women into the navy's nursing corps. Most important, three months later he ordered segregation ended in the training of recruits, a move that didn't halt the practice aboard ships but did send an important signal to the navy's white supremacist culture. By that summer—the war's last—blacks were assigned to submarines and to aviation training, theretofore lily-white departments that segregationists believed would be destroyed if forced to accept blacks. On V-J Day, the African-American numbers in the navy were still pitiable: some 60 officers altogether, 6 of whom were women (4 nurses and 2 Waves), 68 enlisted Waves, and the 165,000 black enlisted male sailors, almost all of whom remained physically segregated.

The wartime racial policies of the Marine Corps and the Coast Guard were even more egregious than those of the army and the navy. As would later be the case with Jim Crow in general, so, too, did Jim Crow in the armed services diminish in close proportion to the amount of pressure brought against it. And because the nation's major civil rights organization made the integration of the army their highest priority in the war, that branch in fact achieved the best record. The navy came in a distant second, and the ending of segregation in that service came later in the war and with more modest achievements than what was achieved in the army. Statistically, the Marines and the Coast Guard hardly show up on the graph.

During the war, both services were components of the Navy Department, and thus under the executive direction of its secretary, Knox at first, then Forrestal. Both branches theoretically followed the racial directives of their parent organization. In fact, their commandants were left pretty much free to handle personnel policies as each saw fit. The Marine Corps' commandant at the war's outset, Major General Thomas Holcomb, told the navy's General Board in April 1941 that "if it were a question of having a Marine Corps of 5,000 whites or 250,000 Negroes, I would rather have the whites." More circumspectly, and for public consumption, his rationale for excluding blacks centered on the "impracticality" of forming separate units in so small a service, with actual integration itself, of course, not even an issue. In fact, any proposal for including blacks that would "prevent the maintenance of *necessary* segregation," as it was phrased, remained out of the question.

In June 1942, a few blacks were allowed to enlist in the Corps. But none could be sent to specialist schools because no segregated schools were available. By the war's end, just under twenty thousand African-Americans had been inducted under the Selective Service requirements, about 4 percent of the service's enlisted force. Since many were the product of inferior segregated Southern schools, the upshot was that the black units as a whole performed below marine standards. As with the army's experience, though, this outcome told a skewered tale: since the better-educated blacks couldn't be dispersed around the entire Corps, as lower-performing whites were, this blanket aspersion on black abilities was patently unfair. Even when black marines were eventually assigned to integrated units, General Holcomb saw to it that no black NCOs were ever senior to white men in the same units, a logistical nightmare and an extraordinarily heavy brake on black advancement.

Since the Corps was primarily a Pacific-war force, a great deal of anxiety was experienced over the placement of black marines in that theater. A senior combat commander absurdly warned that African-American troops were not to be stationed in the Polynesian areas of the Pacific because "Polynesians were delightful people" and "primitively romantic" and their women would have sex with any comers. He explained that this would be acceptable if white troops fathered their children since "a very high-class half-caste would result," and even if whites mixed with Chinese "a very desirable type would come of the union." But mixing with blacks would "produce a very undesirable citizen." Much the same concern was directed toward American Samoans, for whom General Charles Price professed a special moral obligation to keep from intimacy with blacks. He urged the Corps to send Pacific-bound blacks to Micronesia where they "can do no harm"—presumably meaning no genetic harm.

The story of the Coast Guard in terms of its wartime racial policies is a dreary variation on that of the navy and the Marine Corps. This branch inducted about fifteen thousand blacks through the draft. At first the Coast Guard tried to use all African-Americans in its stewards department, but its decision makers realized that so many couldn't be absorbed in so small a service. Consequently, many ended up being assigned to general service, which again because of the small size of the Coast Guard necessarily meant serving in integrated units, and in the end, about thirteen hundred of the Coast Guard's fifteen thousand blacks did serve in integrated units. But like the Marine Corps, the Coast Guard commissioned extremely few blacks into its officer ranks. The first two were authorized in 1944 and remained almost the last throughout the war. The Coast Guard's record was, however, proportionately better than the navy's in regard to black petty officers. And in late 1944 it accepted black enlisted women in token numbers in its female auxiliary, the Spars. Unlike in the marines, black coast guardsmen were allowed to advance to petty officer rank and to serve as superiors over white enlisted men.

The bitterness caused blacks by the official and pervasive racism of the armed forces during World War II culminated in a double disaster that brought the issue to a wide national audience. The tragic incident accounted both for the greatest loss of life of any American home-front accident in World War II and for one of the most notorious injustices ever perpetrated on American servicemen of any color.

Today the facility exists only in memory. But at the height of the Second World War the navy's ammunition base dominated Port Chicago,

California, a small Sacramento River town almost within sight of San Francisco Bay. On a July evening in 1944, hundreds of black enlisted men were hard at work in the base's segregated labor battalions, that night loading ammunition onto a pair of Liberty ships, the cargo carriers *E. A. Bryan* and *Quinalt Victory*. Suddenly and utterly without warning, a massive explosion rent Port Chicago, the blast nearly vaporizing the seven-thousand-ton *Bryan* along with the six thousand tons of ammunition and explosives tightly packed inside it. Within seconds a cloud of smoke and debris rose nearly two miles above the town. A moment later, the heat reached the nearby *Quinalt*. Filled with the same deadly cargo, the ship was thrown up over the middle of the river in its own violent explosion, settling into the muddy bottom in gigantic chunks of twisted and charred steel, some as big as houses. The glare was visible thirty-five miles away in San Francisco. All 320 ammunition handlers and loaders and their officers working on the pier that evening were killed, as were the entire crews of both ships. Included in the total, every one of the 202 black enlisted men present was killed. Beyond these dead, another 390 men in the vicinity of the base, a few whites but mostly black, were injured, many maimed for life. Though never proven, the explosion was likely touched off by a roughly handled depth bomb made of a new explosive material called Torpex and whose dangerous fragility wasn't yet entirely understood by the navy. But thirty-nine days after the disaster, a navy inquiry reported the cause was due to incompetence on the part of the black sailor-stevedores, "rough handling [of munitions] by . . . individuals," as the report put it. The service would formally absolve all the white officers involved.

The consequences for the surviving sailor-stevedores were nearly as catastrophic as had been the explosion itself, though reflecting perfectly the bottomless racist mind-set in which the armed services were locked during the Second World War. Some four hundred African-American sailors from Port Chicago, many still in shock, were transferred across the delta to another ammunition-loading facility at nearby Mare Island and there ordered by their white superiors to resume precisely the same kind of work in which they had been engaged at Port Chicago. Still traumatized from the Port Chicago disaster, 258 men—all black sailor-stevedores—flatly refused to work.

If the explosion that had destroyed two ships and killed scores of men had in fact been caused by the loaders' lack of knowledge, it was hardly the fault of the sailors themselves: all had been put to work without any training in the dangerous job of explosives loading, and all had been told by their white officers that the bombs they were handling couldn't explode because those weapons were "unarmed." In actuality, the navy had no clear plan for loading munitions aboard ships and, as we've seen, did not yet appreciate the dangers of Torpex. The now-chary men at Mare Island said they would not continue loading until the navy instituted safety measures to prevent another explosion.

It was wartime, and the nation was engaged in a two-front conflict in which thousands of American men were dying, factors that undoubtedly led to the navy's hasty and ill-judged response. But it is impossible to view the navy's reaction to the men's refusal in terms that exclude racism directed at blacks. The 258 sailors who refused to work were rounded up and placed on what was, in effect, a prison ship, a barge tied to the pier. They were told they faced mutiny charges, for which offense in wartime the penalty was death by firing squad. At that dramatic point, all but fifty of the men agreed to return to work. Nonetheless, even these 208 sailors were handed bad-conduct discharges for disobeying orders. Meanwhile, the remaining fifty—the navy called them the "ringleaders"—were formally charged with mutiny in wartime. After thirty-two days of hearings, the verdicts came following a mere eighty minutes of court deliberations. Even though white naval officers conscientiously represented the sailors in the docket, all were found guilty of mutiny. Ten men were sentenced to fifteen years in prison, twenty-four men to twelve years, eleven men to ten years, and five men to eight years. All were to be dishonorably discharged from the navy.

The black press immediately and vigorously criticized what it held to be a railroading of the sailors. Legal appeals by the NAACP's Thurgood Marshall were turned down. Finally recognizing something approaching common sense, the navy released the fifty from prison. But one final humiliation was laid on these men: before being allowed to return home, all were shipped to Pacific islands in small groups for a year's "probation."

As for the dead of the Port Chicago explosion, Congress proposed awarding each man's family $5,000. When segregationist congressman John Rankin from Mississippi realized that most of this money would be going to black families, he talked his House colleagues into reducing the amount to a more "sensible" $3,000 per dead man.

Late in the war, the War Department finally began to challenge Jim Crow in the nation's scores of army posts. In July 1944 every army station received an order directing that "all personnel regardless of race would be afforded equal opportunity to enjoy recreational facilities on each post." The directive did nothing to stop segregated training or segregated units, but at least set out to ban discrimination in post exchanges and theaters and in government transportation hauling soldiers around posts and into adjacent towns, the latter humiliation premised on "local civilian custom."

Predictably, the South raised a wounded cry even at this tokenism, the region's editorialists particularly feverish with rage that the federal government would tamper with local usage. The *Montgomery Advertiser* thundered that "Army orders, even armies, even bayonets, cannot force impossible and unnatural social race relations upon us. It has been tried before and failed." The writer, perhaps recalling Reconstruction, ended by noting that "it will fail if tried again." Joined by several Southern congressional delegations, Alabama's governor wired President Roosevelt in an attempt to stop the order. The army stood fast, but its reply to criticism was low-key and bereft of any sense that it held the high ground on the morality of the issue. In fact, the order had been disseminated with a "restricted" classification and wasn't made widely known on the army's posts until the black press publicized the issue.

Without the strong moral support needed to ensure compliance with what at the time amounted to social experimentation that was widely regarded as revolutionary, local commanders believed themselves free to regard the secretary's communiqué as more a "directive" than an actual order.

In some places, commanders did enforce it: for example, when a group of black officers at Tuskegee Army Air Field walked into a white section of the base restaurant and cited the new order as their justification in doing so, they were, after some argument, served—even though a few whites conspicuously left the room. In answer to the disgruntled whites' complaints, the base commander explained he could do nothing about the order and told all officers they'd have to live with it. It wasn't a ringing endorsement for this modicum of long-delayed racial justice, but at Tuskegee the order was at least followed. And throughout at least one entire theater of operations the commander followed his superior's directive: in England, General Dwight Eisenhower let it be known that the new arrangements would be strictly carried out.

Other commanders responded that they could indeed do something about it, which was usually simply to ignore it. The Fort Benning commander refused to implement it and warned blacks against any efforts to take advantage of it. The order was also dismissed at Northern army posts in which Southern-style Jim Crow prevailed. In a case at Selfridge Field in Michigan, the commander fully upheld existing Jim Crow custom segregating use of the post's facilities. Where commanders did choose to disregard the anti–Jim Crow order, the Army Department seemed unable or unwilling to do very much about it.

With a hundred thousand African-American soldiers sent to the United Kingdom during World War II, maintaining American-style Jim Crow policies and practices there was the unexceptional expectation of most American commanders. From the president down, efficient operation of the army and prosecution of the war was held to entirely overshadow any overseas efforts to moderate—let alone resolve—issues that were seen as purely America's own domestic social problems.

At the war's outset, Britain was virtually entirely white, and in consequence a nation in which American-style racial discrimination remained almost unknown. Had large minority communities lived in prewar Britain, discrimination *would* probably have been all too common, as the country's postwar history suggests. But, as black Americans began in 1942 to appear in large numbers, the British people found themselves profoundly shocked at the discrimination blacks suffered from official U.S. army policy mandating Jim Crow practices, as well as unofficially from the ill treatment directed at them by individual white GIs.

Foreign Secretary Anthony Eden, Winston Churchill's most important wartime subordinate, suggested in a cabinet meeting that to avoid problems black American soldiers should simply be kept out of the country or, at most, be received only in strictly limited numbers. It likely seemed to Eden that Americans wouldn't care much one way or the other what policy Britain took on the matter. But in fact the United States government understood the impracticability of severely limiting blacks in the European theater. Roosevelt himself demanded that black troops be sent to Europe, even while admitting that it would cause "many complications," the president obviously judging that it was politically and logistically impossible not to utilize African-American troops in the European theater. What *was* possible was to make sure stateside-style Jim Crow was enforced, and U.S. commanders made clear that such was the army's intention.

British war minister James Grigg, who believed that "colored troops themselves probably expect to be treated in [the UK] as in the United States, and a markedly different treatment might well cause political difficulties at the end of the war," candidly spelled out the difficulties he saw arising from black troops being stationed in Britain. He worried Americans would lose respect for Britain if they witnessed Britons "drawing no distinction between blacks and whites" and further believed the morale of British troops would be injured if they suspected intimate relations between black GIs and the women the British were leaving behind as they themselves went to war around the world, a view that suggests these same troops might not have been so aggrieved to hear that their women were being unfaithful with *white* GIs. The desire to placate white Americans' racial sensibilities must have seemed paramount to many British officials, as well as to ordinary civilians, when most of the country understood that the nation's survival depended on the United States and its participation in the war.

Another sensitive issue between the two governments concerned the racial slurs, discrimination, and outright battery white American GIs directed toward Britain's own blacks, as when two U.S. marines assaulted a West Indian with a knife in a London restaurant. British blacks had come mostly from the empire and still represented only a small proportion of the population. But this group had not hitherto been subjected to any structured kind of British-style Jim Crow. One politician thought it might be a good idea for his country's blacks to wear special badges so they could be distinguished from black Americans, but the idea wasn't adopted. Neither, though, did the British government ever unequivocally tell the American military authorities that U.S. troops must treat *all* its citizens with respect, regardless of color.

In many ways, the British simply went along with America's race "sensibilities." Britain saw to it that black GIs were placed in segregated wards in British hospitals, just as they were treated in American military hospitals as the latter sprang up all over the country. More obvious to Britain's own citizens was the segregation of recreational clubs set up for Allied soldiers. Blacks' own segregated facilities were called Silver Birch Clubs.

On American military bases throughout Britain, Jim Crow operated fully as freely as if those posts were located in the Mississippi Delta instead of the middle of Cornwall or Cheshire or Lancashire. In many cases, entire villages were designated either "black" or "white" for GIs' recreational purposes. The army would simply put one off-limits to whites, another off-limits to blacks. Furthermore, military police wouldn't hesitate to arrest soldiers found outside their own respective racial reservations.

By early 1944, an American officer in the army's Historical Section commented that American-imported racial tensions had become so acute throughout the island that "if the invasion doesn't occur first, trouble will." In fact, by that time race relations had already degenerated to such a volatile state that mini-riots between black and white American GIs had begun to seriously mar official Anglo-American relations. Watching all this were German fifth columnists, who forwarded information on these conditions back to the Reich for subsequent reportage in Nazi newspapers charging America with hypocrisy over its vaunted "democratic" principles.

(The Japanese exploited American racism in much the same way on its Radio Tokyo broadcasts throughout Asia, telling audiences that "Americans periodically will run amok to lynch Negroes individually or to slaughter them wholesale . . . in race wars," an observation demonstrated in the 1943 Detroit riots to be essentially correct.)

Nazi "condemnation" of American racism represented, of course, some pretty serious hypocrisy itself, but Britons' disgust with U.S.-imported Jim Crow was genuine and widespread. The majority view in Britain held black American troops in the same regard as any other Allied troops. In fact, some Britons regarded blacks more favorably than they did the many white Americans with whom they came into daily contact. For example, young British women, most of whom had never met nor even seen a black before, and who were free of racial prejudice, found the African-American troops attractive enough to date, have sex with, and even marry. This unquestionably caused consternation among many of their elders, but not generally the kind of rabid anger or disgust it would have elicited from Americans. After the invasion of France, the black American presence—along with white American racism—became visible to many more Europeans. It is impossible to measure the damage this inflicted on the United States in the eyes of Europeans, but it was a considerable factor in Europe's and Asia's postwar regard—or lack of—for America's values and America's claim to international moral leadership.

One small advance was made in the U.S. Congress in the field of civil rights during the war. Though Southerners held any tampering with the notorious poll tax—a device designed almost solely to keep blacks from the ballot box—to be an assault on the "Southern way of life and on white supremacy," the federal legislature passed the Soldier Vote Act in September 1942, giving service members an absentee ballot and the right to cast it without having to pay any tax. For the first time since Reconstruction, voting had been made easier or freer for African-Americans, even though the right was of proportionately greater benefit to the 90 percent of servicemen and servicewomen who weren't black and many of whom would have had to pay the tax before being allowed to cast their ballot at home. When that same year congressional liberals tried to eliminate the poll tax in all federal elections—New York congressman and bill supporter Emanuel Celler called suffrage "the greatest weapon of democracy"—the Senate killed the House-passed measure with a filibuster that ended any congressional hope for voting reform on the home front. Two years later, though, the Supreme Court struck down the "whites-only primaries" that had kept blacks from Southern polls, a tool the African-American statesman Ralph Bunche had called "the most effective device for exclusion of Negroes from the polls in the South and, therefore, the most effective political instrument for the preservation of white supremacy."[4]

During the war years, beyond the military yet another American institution was steeped in Jim Crow, a part of the national life that filled a vital role in the maintenance of wartime morale: the entertainment industry. From vaudeville to radio to Broadway and from executives to performers to clerks, the constraints of racial intolerance covered that enterprise as neatly as a well-tailored glove covers a hand.

Dismal is as fair a term as any to describe the state of black participation in America's performing arts during World War II. *Negligible* or *marginal* or *superficial* would also serve. When African-American entertainers performed outside the limits of their own segregated communities, it was all too often as jiving, joking, simpering representations of a black world that existed in few places other than the imagination of whites. Hardly any parts of the white performing-arts spectrum could be found wherein blacks were depicted as responsible, educated, intelligent adults whose lives were seen to be spent as they really were, which was, ironically, to a tragic degree in getting around barriers put in their way by whites.

Probably the most popular rendering of any kind of black American life during the war was radio's *Amos 'n' Andy* show. Ironically, its stars were not black nor did blacks contribute to its scripts, facts that mattered not

[4] Klinkner, 193.

a tittle to its white listeners, legions of whom had been devoted to the program since it had gone on the air in Chicago in 1926. Over its nearly four decades on radio and (starting in 1951) on television, it became the longest-running program in broadcasting history. Two of the show's most dedicated listeners were also its most influential—Franklin and Eleanor Roosevelt. At its wartime peak, no other program on radio came close to the popularity of *Amos 'n' Andy*, cities across the country coming to a near standstill during the half hour it was being broadcast six nights a week at its peak.

Set in Harlem, the serial featured three principal characters. Amos, generally the narrator, was the philosophical cabdriver. Andy was Amos's blowhard and scheming but well-meaning friend. The Kingfish was the conniving head of the Mystic Knights of the Sea Lodge and a man forever on the lookout for a way to cadge a quick profit on preposterous schemes. The Kingfish's mirth-stirring (among whites) catchphrase—"Holy mackerel, Andy!"—was heard at least once on every broadcast. The two white actors who played all three roles, Freeman Gosden and Charles Correll, did so in broad dialect, a kind of Negro-talk manqué that vast numbers of white Americans of the era found hilarious and probably believed incapable of giving offense to blacks.

Many African-Americans were themselves torn by the dilemma the program brought their community. In its way, *Amos 'n' Andy* was sympathetic toward a part of America that was unrepresented—not *under*represented, but totally *non*represented—on network radio at the time when that medium was the only broadcast game in town. The show almost always portrayed its characters in a loving manner. And until 1943, when the serial structure was switched to a dumbed-down sitcom format, it had its cast interested in and seriously discussing the issues of the day, sometimes even hinting at the racism besetting America and the 13 million blacks who lived here. The African-American *Kansas City Call* admiringly wrote that the show had "all the pathos, humor, vanity, glory, problems, and solutions that beset ordinary mortals—and therein lies its universal appeal."

But few would deny that the characters—Amos; Andy; the Kingfish; Andy's girlfriend, Madame Queen; the Kingfish's wife, Sapphire; the slow-moving janitor, Lightnin'—were, particularly in the show's sitcom years, not very bright and as often as not shiftless and flimflamming, rarely venturing outside the routines of uncomplicated or childlike creatures, a stereotype that didn't dangerously conflict with white notions of black lives. In direct opposition to the *Call*'s admiration, another African-American newspaper, the *Pittsburgh Courier*, mounted a long and heartfelt campaign to get the program off the air because, it editorialized, *Amos 'n' Andy* "undermined the self-respect and general advancement" of America's blacks.

Correll may have hit closest to the mark when he remarked late in life that "if they [Amos and Andy] had been any more positive, they wouldn't have been allowed on the air." In truth, had the show been only one of a spectrum of portrayals of the era's black life, it might have been easier to overlook its flaws. But, to repeat, *Amos 'n' Andy* was the *only* broadcast-network portrait of black life in the war years. Elizabeth McLeod Post noted that the "only way for a black-themed program to get on the air [then] was for it to be strained through a white filter." And, she added, the real blame lay more with the times than with *Amos 'n' Andy*.

Unlike radio, Jim Crow's grip on the Broadway stage wasn't so tight during World War II, likely because Broadway wasn't beamed in a southerly direction. Blacks participated in what were then moderately prevalent all-black productions, but dozens of other plays featured racially mixed casts, as for example such hit shows as *Othello, On the Town, Strange Fruit,* and *Show Boat*. Many famous blacks refused to appear in road productions of these plays if they were to be presented before segregated audiences, which was, of course, almost invariably the case in the South. Among the most famous actors taking this stand were Lena Horne, Paul Robeson, and Hazel Scott, all three of whom were adamant in their refusals to play stereotyped roles that demeaned African-Americans.

The most important entertainment medium and the one that might have weaned America from its symbiosis with Jim Crow was the movies.

The forties were still years of studio control over film production, a time in which Hollywood failed miserably to exploit its potential power to lessen the depth of American race hate.

Jim Crow had gotten its grip on the movies from their very beginning as flickering images in nickelodeons. Since film so closely reflected society, there is, it follows, nothing particularly odd about the medium's immersion in racism. The tragedy was how strongly the film industry affirmed white Americans' already entrenched racist beliefs, and how unwilling the industry was to use its unique pulpit to nobler-minded ends, an admittedly high expectation when it would undeniably have adversely affected the filmmakers' financial bottom line.

The industry didn't create the white popular image of African-Americans as dim-witted dolts or neutered mammies or sex-crazed beasts lusting after white women, but it cashed in on it with enthusiasm. In the book *Hollywood Goes to War,* the authors noted that the movies made "tarts of the Negro's daughters, crapshooters of his sons, obsequious Uncle Toms of his fathers, superstitious and grotesque crones of his mothers, strutting peacocks of his successful men, psalm-singing mountebanks of his priests, and Barnum and Bailey sideshows of his religion."[5] The misfortune of film and America's black experience was how widely and deeply the black stereotype was cast and how egregious was its impact on African-Americans' hopes for social and political change.

We've already looked at the effects on American racism of David Griffith's *Birth of a Nation.* That film spread the Southern justification for Jim Crow and for keeping blacks in tight political check to every corner of the country, with President Wilson's praise for Griffith's toxic account of Reconstruction confirming in many Americans' mind the picture's supposed historical correctness, in reality a faulty analysis of history that few other than African-Americans took to task for poisoning the national well. With the picture setting the industry's racial standard at so early a point in film history, serious analysis of the African-American experience, the white

[5] Klinkner, 185.

supremacist view or otherwise, never really reached the nation's screens throughout the entire Jim Crow epoch.

But blacks did slowly begin to gain a hold in mainstream film. In the early 1930s the most successful black actor was Lincoln Perry, who comically and self-patronizingly called himself Stepin Fetchit after his own earlier minstrel act. From 1927 through the war years, Perry appeared in more than forty films, including comparatively big-budget pictures like *Judas Priest* and *Stand Up and Cheer*. In most of his movies he played the slow-witted servant or lackey who provided comic relief for the films' "real" white characters. His groveling humor unquestionably reinforced white notions about black inferiority, yet with his considerable acting skills he stole many of the scenes he appeared in. In fact, he generally stole the films themselves. Eventually his sloppy shuffle, bugged-out eyes, and excruciatingly slow drawl came to be seen as an embarrassment even to the black supporters who had earlier believed that his portrayals, though humiliating, at least kept a black presence in mainstream film. The movie parts made Perry rich: he reportedly earned $2 million during the 1930s, allowing the actor to maintain six houses, employ sixteen Chinese servants, and attach his name in neon to the side of his champagne-pink Cadillac. Another black actor became famous for the same kind of characters played by Perry—Mantan Moreland, also bearing an unbecoming double-entendre name, who acted in more than a hundred films in the forties, generally as a scared and wide-eyed servant whose moronic antics in the Charlie Chan films delighted white audiences while reinforcing their low opinions of black intelligence.

Where the establishment film industry—the white filmmakers—failed to portray blacks on the screen in any serious way, African-Americans themselves provided for black audiences eager to see anything other than whites or stereotyped blacks. What they brought forth were "race films," movies that instilled pride in blacks who were everywhere else treated so shabbily by the industry. The best known of the race filmmakers was Oscar Micheaux, a onetime Pullman porter and novelist whose *Within Our Gates* from 1919 is the oldest surviving film of this genre. Made for black audiences and almost never shown in theaters that whites attended, these films were, perforce, low budget and therefore generally crude compared to what Hollywood was able to produce. But they gave African-American audiences real black people on the screen rather than the black bumbling idiots of Hollywood. While whites watched the derring-do of Tom Mix, blacks cheered on their own cowboy hero, the great rodeo star Bill Pickett, who starred in *The Bull Dogger* and by doing so provided a black-oriented Wild West mythology for his own audiences. Micheaux's greatest star was athlete and singer Paul Robeson, who after working in race films crossed over into the mainstream white industry in *The Emperor Jones, Othello,* and *Show Boat.*

During this era best-selling books were routinely transferred to the screen, as is the custom today. The most renowned of them all, *Gone With the Wind,* became the highest-earning movie in the medium's history. The film's representation of blacks in the Civil War and Reconstruction era wasn't viciously racist, thanks mainly to producer David Selznick's efforts to eliminate the most stereotyped aspects of Margaret Mitchell's novel. But it nonetheless mirrored Hollywood's sentimentalized vision of slaves as without intellectual depth and needing little in life other than to be of service to their masters and mistresses. The dilemma in *Gone With the Wind* was that its most beloved character, Mammy, beautifully portrayed by Hattie McDaniel (who was rewarded with a Best Supporting Actress Oscar for her efforts, the first African-American to win an Academy Award for acting and the last to do so for another twenty-four years), was sexless and, except for her relationship to the family that owned her, without any interests whatsoever in life, except possibly a desire to someday possess a red silk petticoat. The actress played the role much as the book's author had created it, though, and white audiences loved it. Yet that portrayal nonetheless suffused the film in the most sinister way with the whole garbage tip of white supremacism, which was to make white audiences happy to see a black man or woman happy just to make white people happy.

In its wartime musical films, Hollywood would use extraordinarily talented African-Americans, knowing that for Southern showings the black performances could quickly and easily be edited out. Dramas couldn't utilize this technique of course, and consequently the studios refused major dramatic roles to African-Americans because a film with blacks risked being banned in theaters south of the Mason and Dixon Line.

Partly at the urging of the Office of War Information, the Hollywood studios began to cautiously integrate the story lines of a few productions. Pictures such as *Bataan*, *Crash Dive*, and *Sahara* told stories using casts made up of black and white actors, the African-Americans playing not servants or comedy relief but characters on the same level with the rest of the actors. Shortly after the war, dramatic films with blacks in major roles or with black-accented story lines began to come out of the studios in a significant stream. *Pinky* (about a light-skinned black woman who passed for white in the North and comes home to her black grandmother in the South), *Home of the Brave* (a black soldier endures racism from whites in his unit), and *Intruder in the Dust* (an elderly black man is accused of killing a white neighbor) would at the end of the 1940s begin to substantively part with the Jim Crow monopolization of America's movies.

The singer's gesture was magnificent, in its simplicity condemning both Nazi racism and its American cousin, Jim Crow. The setting was a prisoner of war camp for captured Germans, one of the first to be set up by the victorious Americans in the closing months of the war. The occasion was a camp show, and the entertainer was Lena Horne. The camp's commander had neatly arranged the German POWs in the front-row seats. Behind the Germans stood a contingent of American guards, all blacks from a segregated unit.

As Miss Horne appeared before her audience, she looked at the position of the guards vis-à-vis their former enemies. The singer slowly stepped down from the stage and walked up the aisle to where her fellow Americans, her fellow *black* Americans, were standing. With her back to the Germans, she sang the songs she had brought from America.

7

GETTING TO THE END

We people of the South must draw the color line tighter and tighter, and any white man or woman who dares to cross that color line should be promptly and forever ostracized. No compromise on this great question should be tolerated, no matter who the guilty parties are, whether in the church, in public office, or in private walks of life. Ostracize them if they cross the color line and treat them as a Negro or his equal should be treated. . . . It is imperative that we face and frankly the conditions which confront us. We must not sit idly by, but we must ever be on guard to protect the southern ideals, customs, and traditions that we love and believe in so firmly and completely. There are some issues that we may differ upon, but on racial integrity, white supremacy, and love of the Southland we will stand together until we pass on to another world.[1]

—Delivered on March 22, 1944, to a joint session of
the Mississippi legislature by Theodore Bilbo
and later published in his book,
Take Your Choice: Separation or Mongrelization

Seventeen months after these words were spoken in an American legislative chamber, the war against the German and Japanese versions of tyranny was completed, the United States and its allies having con-

---

[1] *Congressional Record.* 78th Cong., 2d sess. Vol. 90, pt. 9.

quered a pair of regimes that each murdered countless human beings solely for their having been racially unworthy of life. In achieving its part in this triumph America had spent a quarter million of its own warriors' lives and in the doing gained a moral eminence as high as it had ever known. But in that season of its success, the tenth of America's own people whose skin was black remained, almost bottomlessly, discriminated against. The paradox of this abyss between the heights and depths of American morality did not, amazingly, weaken by even a trace the resolve of those who defended the white supremacism that was so devastating to America's image abroad and its progress at home. The point of view expressed by Senator Bilbo was by no means that of a lone, or even lonely, fanatic.

Yet Jim Crow would be far from unaffected by what had happened during World War II. The horror of the Holocaust exposed as frauds concepts like the social Darwinism that had long underpinned notions of white supremacy and the eugenics that had supported with superficial rationality the theories of racists. On America's home front the social structure—between classes and between the sexes—had as a result of such exposure changed substantially, and some of these changes went straight to the heart of black-white relationships. The laws that underlay race discrimination did, sadly, remain in place at the war's end, particularly in the South, where the entire Jim Crow canon still stood virtually unchecked. But widening hopes for racial justice were beginning to illuminate other corners of American life, and this time—unlike after the First World War—they weren't going to be extinguished.

To win the war, the United States had embarked on the greatest spending binge in its history, a matériel and manpower investment that has not in real terms been exceeded to this day. And at long last, the color of its manpower began to lose its relevancy. Almost anyone, white or black, male or female, had been able to find a job in the war plants that arose almost overnight in every region of the country, and generally these workers earned more than they had ever before been paid. Most of the work was to be found in the North, where most of the plants were located. And because the great majority of African-Americans still lived in the South at the war's onset, that had translated into a reenactment, albeit a much larger one, of the 1917–18 black migration northward to jobs. Again African-Americans relocated to industrial centers, this time to Detroit and Los Angeles, Denver and Seattle, places where race discrimination had admittedly never been in short supply but where Southern-style Jim Crow hadn't poisoned every facet of life. The result was a new and unprecedented empowerment for African-Americans, vast numbers of whom had never before known anything but the old social conditions that characterized the South. With change came a new understanding that existence was possible without the humiliation of a system that had constricted and debased virtually every public aspect of black life in America's Southern states.

When the fighting ended in 1945, this transplanted multitude of civilian blacks was joined by a flood of young African-American veterans, men and women then in the prime of their lives. Nearly a million had served in the military from the Pearl Harbor attack to the atomic bombing of Japan, and the experience energized many of them beyond anything that America's white supremacists could have imagined—or could have prevented. Though Jim Crow was practiced by the armed services with a doctrinaire punctilio throughout almost the entire war, these blacks nonetheless interacted with whites on a basis other than servile, many seeing a North in which Southern-style racial dogma was, if not unknown, at least far less rigorous than in their own homes. Even more experienced European and Pacific theaters of wars that were simply too busy to attend to the thousand details of Jim Crow that held sway in America. As the war wound down and the services slowly began to break apart their segregationist structures, soldiers and sailors black *and white* witnessed an emerging world in which the old standards of white supremacy and habits of black submissiveness were peacefully being overcome.

The experience gained by civil rights leaders, again both black and white, who had been persistently pressing for greater African-American inclusion in the war effort found new uses when the conflict ended. The NAACP vigorously pressed the courts and legislative bodies to end racial discrimination, playing off prewar legal victories that had begun to crack a then-monolithic Jim Crow. Especially important as a precedent-setting wedge amongst these groundbreaking advances had been the well-publicized case of *Gaines v. Missouri*, the first real reconsideration of the issues that had been so damaging to black civil rights in *Plessy v. Ferguson* half a century earlier.

Lloyd Gaines was a young African-American who in the mid-1930s hoped to become a lawyer. But because of his black skin, Gaines had routinely been denied admission to the racially segregated law school of the University of Missouri. He therefore sued the state on the Fourteenth Amendment's grounds of denial of his civil rights. Missouri's response was to tell Gaines he had to wait until the state's black college, Lincoln University, built its own proposed law school, and in the meanwhile he should start his legal schooling in the law school of some adjacent nonsegregated state, for which tuition charge Missouri would be willing to provide a grant. The Missouri Supreme Court found this solution acceptable, which is to say constitutional, and denied Gaines's lawsuit. With every other avenue of redress blocked, Gaines took his grievance to the U.S. Supreme Court, whose justices agreed to hear the case.

Chief Justice Charles Evans Hughes delivered the court's opinion. In an 8–1 decision, the court found the state of Missouri in the wrong, affirming that Lloyd Gaines's constitutional rights had indeed been violated. Gaines's lawyer had based his case on the grounds that anything other than a *Missouri* legal education could be unfair and unequal for a future Missouri attorney, but the court importantly ignored that argument. Speaking for the majority, Chief Justice Hughes explained that since "the white resident is afforded legal education within the State . . . the Negro resident having the same qualifications is refused it there and must go outside the State to obtain it. That is a denial of the equality of legal right to the enjoyment of the privilege which the State has set up, and the provision for the payment of tuition fees in another State does not remove the discrimination." Missouri therefore was instructed to admit Gaines to its law school, a sharp legal jab at state-mandated racism and a serious blow to the "separate but equal" logic on which de jure Jim Crow had been built. The decision did not, however, force the opening of Missouri's other segregated schools to blacks.

Throughout the war, similar kinds of legal decisions—particularly in the areas of higher education, interstate (not at first in*tra*state) commerce, and residential segregation—had begun to be constructed into an ever more solid legal base from which civil libertarians attacked Jim Crow and from whose rationales other judges found precedents to pare back the edges of statutory racial discrimination. What was more, and of greater long-term importance, were legal decisions refranchising Southern blacks, particularly the ruling that found whites-only primaries illegal. Even the insidious "social" variants of Jim Crow came under fire and were in some places found illegal or else quietly dropped: a few public parks and libraries discreetly opened their gates and doors to African-Americans in the upper South, and even the odd Southern newspaper began to report on blacks and their activities in a manner more substantial than the sidebars to which nonwhites had traditionally been relegated.

But over the ten-year period following the end of World War II, the South remained an exceedingly long way from anything even remotely approaching authentic racial justice, which meant that the vast majority of Southern blacks were unable to see in any part of their lives where tangible progress was being made. Ominously, as more gains against white supremacism were made—even minor gains or those that were largely symbolic—Southern whites now began to sense change and thus take close notice of what was happening. What they saw scared them, to the degree that a backlash set in. But what these whites *hadn't* anticipated was the opposite reaction, a commensurate and new resolve from blacks, who, even though gingerly at first, began to resist the whole cartload of Jim Crow baggage with a vigor neither the South nor the nation had ever before witnessed.

Of nearly inestimable importance to the young African-Americans whose military experiences had opened new possibilities in the way they would live their lives were the character and actions of the man who succeeded Franklin Roosevelt as president. In fact, Harry Truman just barely made it to the Oval Office. By 1944, Franklin Roosevelt had, physically, become a walking dead man, as sick a president as the nation had ever known—though the nation at large, of course, did not realize the extent of Roosevelt's infirmities. The president was debilitated by a dozen years in the presidency and the literally overwhelming burden of leading the Western alliance to victory in a worldwide war, not to mention the wear and tear from crippling polio, from too many cigarettes and too little sleep and a body racked with cardiovascular disease and exhaustion, and a small group close to the Oval Office knew he could not last through another four-year term. The man most intimately aware of this reality—Roosevelt's personal physician—understood beyond any real doubt that the president wouldn't likely live another four years under any circumstances, as president or otherwise. Whether Roosevelt himself was aware of the true state of his health isn't clear, but in any case he determined to run for a fourth term, evidently certain that no one but himself knew enough to get the war ended in the country's best interests. The Democratic nomination was incontestably Roosevelt's to command, and the country's Democratic voters assumed he wouldn't leave his office until the war was won. These circumstances made whoever was going to be his vice president a man of some very considerable importance.

Since the beginning of FDR's third term, Henry Wallace had occupied the number two position. By training a plant geneticist and by profession a millionaire hybrid corn grower before becoming Roosevelt's agriculture secretary in 1933, Wallace was chosen by the president as his running mate in 1940 because of his popular New Deal political views. But by 1944 it had become clear to Roosevelt and most of the Democratic Party that Wallace was in reality far to the left of the American electorate and thus too liberal to remain in an office that could well result in his unelected ascendancy to the presidency. Though his pro-Soviet stand was seen as a political liability even as the war and the U.S.-Soviet alliance were both still going strong, Wallace's brand of liberality by the standards of the mid-1940s might have been acceptable if it hadn't been quite so left-leaning in terms of civil rights and his regards for African-Americans. Thus by early 1944 Roosevelt had begun to think seriously about getting Henry Wallace off the fourth-term ticket.

The favorite to replace him was James Byrnes. A Southerner, Byrnes was a racist of unshakable conviction, a senator who in 1938 had been in the forefront of a congressional fight against a federal antilynching proposal and a man who had preposterously charged that blacks and the NAACP had "come into control of the Democratic Party" by the mere fact that the antilynching measure had ever reached the Senate. Fortunately for the future of a civil rights agenda, Byrnes was kept off the ballot not only for his over-the-top racism that by 1944 had become embarrassing, but also because he was unacceptable to organized labor. When he married, he deserted his Roman Catholicism for his wife's Episcopalianism, which breach party leaders feared would cost the Democrats the Catholic vote.

There weren't a lot of other obvious or even suitable choices to replace Wallace. In the end, it looked to come down to finding the man who would likely do the ticket the least harm in the November election. As names were eliminated, one doggedly remained in the hopper, that of the junior senator from Missouri. Harry Truman was probably best known nationally for the widely viewed dishonor of having been sent to the Senate in 1935 as the handpicked choice of Kansas City's venal but powerful political boss, Tom Pendergast. But since the beginning of the war, Truman had awed the party and a fair slice of the electorate with his proficient service as the chairman of the Senate committee—the famous Truman Committee—that had investigated graft and corruption in the purchase of military matériel. With no better option, Roosevelt let it be known at the convention that his choice as running mate might as well be Truman.

Characteristically, the senator was genuinely reluctant to leave the Senate for what he figured amounted to a demotion to a ceremonial office with virtually no power—"the vice president . . . sits around hoping for a funeral" was how Truman pictured the offer and the new job. What he wasn't intimately aware of was the precarious state of the chief executive's health. As it turned out, he would actually *be* vice president for only eighty-two days after Roosevelt's inauguration in January 1945, FDR's fourth. On April 12, 1945, the unassuming but far from simple little Missourian lost forever his last vestiges of anonymity when Franklin Roosevelt died from a massive stroke. As understudy, he was swept into power as the most consequential human being on the planet.

Like pretty much every white person of his time and, especially, from his part of the country, Harry Truman had accepted the inferiority of the African-American as simply a kind of "that's the way it is" truth. The politics and social views of small-town Missouri often leaned more in the direction of Southern populism and white supremacism than they did toward the more cosmopolitan bearings of the North. In private, Truman had since childhood spoken of African-Americans as "niggers" and "coons,"[2] more as routine references to their perceived inferiority than from personal animosity. Yet irrespective of his conviction that blacks weren't and would never be on an equal social or intellectual footing with whites, Truman's mature views on civil rights differed radically from those of the segregationists and run-of-the-mill racists of both Southern *and* Northern stripe. As a senator, he spoke out in what was for the times a radical declaration that legal and civil rights were every bit as much the birthright of black Americans as they were of white Americans. "If any class or race can be permanently set apart from, or pushed down below, the rest in political and civil rights," Truman affirmed in a 1940 speech, "so may any other class or race when it shall incur the displeasure of its more powerful associates, and we must say farewell to the principles on which we count our safety."[3] Few national politicians of stature were making such declarations of equality for the uncomplicated reason that they often amounted to political suicide. What Truman possessed, and what was then and is still the exception in public life, was the ability to grow, at least to grow in his power to think.

After three years as president, at the beginning of 1948, Truman announced in his State of the Union address that he planned to send the

---

[2] McCullough, 247.
[3] Ibid.

Congress a bill on civil rights. True to his word, within three weeks the first special message on this neglected subject arrived on Capitol Hill. In Trumanesque language as plain as the president's Missouri roots, the ninety-six senators and 435 members of the House of Representatives were reminded that in America not everyone was "free to live and work where they please" nor were all free to "enjoy the full privileges of citizenship." Though Truman noted that the duty to ensure such rights was shared by all three of the branches of government, it was the responsibility of Congress to pass comprehensive civil rights laws "adequate to the needs of the day, and demonstrating our continuing faith in the free way of life."[4] Specifically, he wanted antilynching legislation passed, poll taxes abolished, interstate travel desegregated, and segregation in the military ended "as soon as possible." The president would quickly find out that his then-revolutionary requests would translate into a potentially disastrous Southern revolt against himself and against the national Democratic Party.

One impulse behind Truman's efforts to improve America's racial dilemma was a series of horrendous outrages committed against soldiers—some while they were actually wearing their uniform—and which were shocking even to people who had grown accustomed to racists' depravities. In Liberty, Mississippi, a mob lynched an ex-GI named Eugene Bells for not returning to his former employer after his discharge. In another incident, a young soldier named Isaac Woodard, only days out of the army after having served fifteen months in the South Pacific, was blinded by the tips of billy clubs wielded by policemen after heated words had been exchanged with a South Carolina bus driver, the argument apparently resulting from the driver's belief that the black sergeant had spent too much time in the station's bathroom; later, the police terrorism was not even remarked upon, while "charges" against Woodard were magnanimously dropped.

But in terms of carnage from a single incident, the worst of these outrages and one that especially disgusted the president and—at last—much of the rest of America was a quadruple lynching in Georgia. The

---

[4] McCullough, 587.

victims were four young black people in their twenties: two men, one of whom was a veteran just returned home from the Pacific war and four and a half years of service in the army—his discharge button had shortly before been delivered to his mother's home—and the men's wives, who were sisters and one of whom was six months pregnant. On July 14, 1946, one of the men, a tenant farmer, got into an argument with the son of the white man who owned his farm. The heated words ended in a knife fight in which the white man was stabbed. The black knife wielder was taken that afternoon to the county jail. Meanwhile, the other black man asked his own white boss for help in getting his friend released on bail. The boss agreed, and he and the two men's sister-wives found enough money for the bond, securing the arrested man's release.

The day of the bond posting—a week after the knifing—the white benefactor arrived at the jail and offered to drive the two black couples home. Instead, he drove them to his own farm. There about fifteen white men awaited them. Realizing the men meant to lynch them, the women began to scream for mercy. Ignoring their pleas, the white men shoved the two couples down a path to a river. There the lynchers started pumping shots into the four African-Americans, the fusillade of bullets so great that the upper parts of the victims' bodies were rendered unrecognizable.

A young boy witness, on his way that afternoon to take a cow to pasture, came forward years later to say that after the firing stopped smoke and bubbles rose from the corpses. He said one of the men he had seen firing was the white man who had driven the blacks to the farm. He also said he saw that among the automobiles at the slaughter was a black-and-white state police car. The now-grown witness, who recounted the events to "get it off [his] conscience" and after the men whom he named as having committed the massacre were dead, said he understood even as a boy the way the black men were viewed: the dead soldier may have fought for his country in the war, but when he came back home to Georgia, he was to whites "just a nigger." Although a hundred witnesses had been heard by a grand jury in the immediate wake of the slaughter, no indictment was ever issued. At the funeral, close relatives of the victims failed to show up, telling friends that they had been "too frightened" to attend, that they thought it had been "too dangerous." Instead, they simply said a prayer over the yet-unburied bodies, put them in the ground, and finally just walked away without further words.

When a Missouri friend wrote to Truman advising him not to go too fast on civil rights, the president answered with his own letter, an explanation of how he viewed his responsibilities: "I am not asking for social equality, because no such things exist, but I am asking for equality of opportunity for all human beings. . . . When the mob gangs can take four people out and shoot them in the back, and everybody . . . is acquainted with who did the shooting and nothing is done about it, that country is in a pretty bad fix from the law enforcement standpoint."[5] It may be that these deaths contributed materially to Harry Truman's growing conviction that Jim Crow could no longer operate unchecked in America. But what did for certain happen to this president was that he never looked back to his Missouri roots to find answers to this most terrible of the nation's problems.

Truman would continue to argue for black civil rights and against violence directed at the nation's 13 million African-Americans, and he would do so because he believed such rights were the inalienable birthright of all Americans. Addressing the NAACP (he was the first president to speak publicly before the organization), he said—and here again as no president had before him—that he could find "no justifiable reason for discrimination because of ancestry, or religion, or race, or color." It may be the case that Truman's strongest personal justification for racial justice in America was based on how the world viewed—and rightly denounced—America for its race iniquities, particularly since America's condemnation of communism was predicated on that system's indifference to civil rights on its own turf. Irrespective of the motives, it bears repeating that Truman's pursuit of civil rights would far exceed that of any previous president.

While the Truman administration was on its way to deciding how to end Jim Crow in the nation's armed services, it paused long enough to lend its power to one other great civil rights cause. Earlier we've seen how white

[5] McCullough, 589.

Americans kept black Americans out of their neighborhoods through attempts at zoning and, more successfully, through economic means and unadorned terror. After the Supreme Court had declared that white attempts to impose segregation by street or district were unconstitutional, a new device—the "restrictive deed covenant" we looked at in chapter 3—had been found by whites to work well in effectively separating themselves from blacks. The device was, in reality, far from being just another piece of Southern Jim Crow; in fact, by the 1950s it had come to be employed in every state in the country.

Thanks in large part to these covenants, in virtually every city in the nation blacks lived here, whites lived there, and rarely did much question arise as to where the line between here and there lay. Blacks stayed in inner-city apartments, collecting rent receipts while their landlords were collecting tax breaks on their apartment buildings. Whites moved to new neighborhoods and into the suburbs, where they bought houses with mortgages and wrote the mortgage interest off their income taxes, meanwhile becoming owners of nearly the entirety of the nation's stock of decent housing. The situation amounted to one more way of enriching white America while impoverishing black America, not to mention keeping the two from getting close to one another and possibly learning to live together. The NAACP designated one of its chief aims to be the ending of legally restricted covenants, a large number of which contracts, incidentally, ran into "perpetuity." At the end of the 1950s, 40 million dwelling units in America—covering about 90 percent of all housing built in the country since 1945—were by such methods rendered off-limits to nonwhite purchasers.[6]

For many years courts had upheld the validity of the restrictive covenants. Occasionally legal decisions hemmed in the device, as when California ruled that covenants barring selling and renting to minorities were illegal but at the same time upholding those barring occupancy, which meant that a black could buy a house where he wasn't wanted, but he couldn't actually live in it. Challenged by the NAACP, the legality of

[6] Stetson Kennedy, 75.

covenants was to be considered by the Supreme Court in 1948. President Truman directed the attorney general to file a brief with the court supporting the NAACP, the first time the government had ever intervened in such a case before the nation's highest court. The decision came down in May of that year in a case known to history as *Shelley v. Kraemer*. The justices unanimously affirmed that restricted covenants were not enforceable by any court, state or federal. This wasn't, unfortunately, quite the same thing as declaring them invalid—which it did not do. Nor did it stop them from being written by private homeowners, as witnessed by the fact that 40 million covenants still existed a decade later, when much of the enforcement clout attached to them had disingenuously been transferred to banks and loan institutions, who wielded discriminatory power by refusing to offer mortgages to blacks on houses outside of their racial preserves. Probably the most important element of the *Shelley* case was the administration's involvement in it, the government (or, at least, this administration) at last having given a powerful signal to the nation that it would proceed similarly in future civil rights cases.

By far the most important blow struck against Jim Crow during the Truman years was against racism in the military. Vastly consequential to the course of American race progress, the ending of segregation in the armed forces did not come about, however, purely from Truman's altruism, regardless of the way in which many Americans today regard its origin. We cannot know that Truman would not at some point have desegregated the armed forces—he had, after all, voiced a deep concern about such racism early in his presidency—but we do know that the celebrated act was taken *after* black leaders' threats left him little choice but to issue the order that would begin to end Jim Crow in the uniformed services.

After only a few months in office, Truman had authorized a general policy review of how best African-Americans could be integrated into the armed forces. The committee he appointed to come up with answers took only a short time to study the issues before delivering a recommendation. Foremost, it declared that black Americans had a "constitutional right to fight, and the Army had an obligation to make the most effective use of every soldier." The committee members frankly admitted the problems with black troops during the war—that their skills generally ranked below those of whites—but acknowledged that rather than "race deficiencies" these difficulties were rooted in poor leadership and bad training, tacitly blaming segregation rather than denigrating the innate abilities of the black servicemen. In calling for an immediate end to segregation in the services, the chairman of the American Veterans Committee echoed this view, saying that it was Jim Crow, not the enemy, that had "defeated" the underperforming black combat units. Truman's advisers recommended using black personnel in integrated work units, but added that some segregation, primarily social—barracking, dining, officering—be maintained. The War Department essentially agreed, stating that the army "should never be ahead of popular opinion on this subject: otherwise it will put itself in a position of stimulating racial disorders rather than overcoming them."[7] This state of affairs in early 1946 clearly portended a long struggle ahead to reach the genuine break with military Jim Crow sought by black leaders as well as by progressive whites.

For a while, Truman was content to maintain the status quo. But by 1948, civil rights activists had brought the issue to a place in American society where the president was forced to make hard decisions as to how America was going to face and resolve its race problems. For one thing, since most of the country's editorialists had already written him off to his probable Republican opponent, New York's Governor Thomas Dewey, Truman believed he would desperately require every vote he could find in the upcoming election. The president increasingly appreciated that his already demonstrated racial liberalism, tepid though it may seem to today's sensibilities, was going to cost him the South's electoral votes, and as a result there didn't seem to be a lot of use in trying to placate that region's sensibilities on the issue. On the other hand, Truman was being pushed hard by black leaders and Democratic Party liberals to do something substantive in furthering the democracy that America had just waged a war to preserve for the *rest* of the world. The hardest push was coming from

[7] MacGregor, ch. 2, p. 3.

A. Philip Randolph, the president of the Brotherhood of Sleeping Car Porters, Roosevelt's onetime bane, and still the nation's most powerful African-American.

Aware of Truman's revulsion over the crimes committed by racists against black veterans, Randolph likely judged the time was at hand to push the president for a genuine civil rights triumph, which in his view was what ending segregation in the armed forces would represent to black America. The civil rights leader was also aware of the president's vulnerability on how American racism was seen abroad and how the Soviets were using it to castigate the United States in its propaganda directed to the third world. Randolph and other civil rights leaders met with the president in the Oval Office and told Truman what they thought he ought to do about Jim Crow in the military. The president didn't particularly like what he heard.

The black leadership believed and so stated that a postwar continuance of the military color line would result in young black men refusing induction, a potential disaster in light of the renewed draft act that Congress had just passed. They further informed the president that that was precisely how they would counsel prospective black inductees to act. Randolph told Truman that he had just returned from a fact-finding survey around the country, and with shocking bluntness, he assured Truman that "the mood among Negroes of this country is that they will never bear arms again until all forms of bias and discrimination are abolished."

The furious president, interpreting the civil rights leader's statement as a threat and almost on par with treason, icily ended the meeting. But seeing Truman's reaction evidently strengthened Randolph's resolve, and the seeds of the tactic of civil disobedience, one of the most effective weapons deployed in the war against Jim Crow, began to sprout.

Truman might have treated Randolph's remarks as a bluff. There was, of course, no irrefutable evidence that black men would in fact massively resist the draft. What was more, the criminal penalties for refusing to respond to an induction order were not insignificant. But the NAACP's own polling of draft-age college students showed that almost three-quarters favored such civil disobedience if the military wasn't desegregated.

The poll was obviously imperfect since noncollege black males weren't included, but the figures were still high enough to indicate that a significant, and embarrassing, number of blacks would support the leadership's new tactic. A real possibility existed that Randolph's promised League for Non-Violent Civil Disobedience Against Military Segregation was going to happen unless Truman used his presidential authority to end segregation in the military and abandon the administration's preferred policy of gradual integration for one of immediate action.

In the election Truman was facing in the fall, ample intelligence existed indicating that both the left and right flanks of the Democratic Party would defect if Truman was the party's candidate for another term. Both defections did indeed take place—the political left to a radical splinter under Henry Wallace called the Progressives, which was likely to draw away from Truman much-needed black votes, and the political right to Southern segregationists under Strom Thurmond, which would undoubtedly siphon off white votes from the mainstream Democrats. The president's ultimate decision on military segregation was likely based on a combination of factors: how he saw the three-way division in the Democratic Party affecting his chances of reelection, what the rest of the world would make of the specter of America jailing thousands of young black men for refusing to be inducted into a segregated military, and clearly disgusted himself with the excesses of domestic racists, his own basic determination to give African-Americans a future that would be a lot better than their past.

Truman acted as Randolph hoped he would. On July 26, 1948, the president signed Executive Order 9981. The crucial words lay in the first sentence of the first paragraph: "It is hereby declared to be the policy of the President that there shall be equality of treatment and opportunity for all persons in the armed services without regard to race, color, religion or national origin." There was no "immediate" in it, but only a statement that the order should be "put into effect as rapidly as possible," such wording included at James Forrestal's insistence, the defense secretary judging that a deadline would work against the ability of the service chiefs to implement the order as harmoniously as could be managed. Nor were the words *desegregation* or *integration* found in Executive Order 9981, since the president hoped that by not specifically rejecting Jim Crow he would soften the blow for Southern consumption. But when asked by a reporter in a press conference the following day whether his order meant the end of segregation in the military, Truman unambiguously replied, "Yes," even though he admitted that a time limit had purposely been omitted.

The presidential mandate did not result in the immediate, or even a quick, end to segregation in uniform. It did, however, end Randolph's threats of inciting widespread black disobedience to the draft. The goal of many civil rights leaders—the complete end to official military Jim Crow—took another half decade to achieve. But if the real goal of the executive order had been to lay the groundwork for equality of opportunity irrespective of race rather than to implement the immediate racial balancing of individual units in the armed services, Truman's feat was unquestionably successful. The newly constituted independent air force had already established an integrated service from its own foundations as a separate branch—before Truman's directive was issued. The other branches were slower, but the navy and the army (the latter's chief of staff, Omar Bradley, continued to openly doubt the wisdom of military integration, saying it deviated from the "national pattern" of black-white relations) did begin to re-form with blacks and whites in the same units. And critical for the services' future, Annapolis and West Point undertook to admit African-Americans and thereby establish a professional black regular-commissioned-officer presence for the nation's future. And finally, the move did *not* lose Truman the election. (If it had, a President Dewey would likely not have rescinded his predecessor's directive, but given Dewey's higher regard for states' rights, the chances of his enforcing it with Truman's steady vigor would probably not have been great.)

In Korea, uniformed Jim Crow got its back broken for good. Though Truman's order laid the necessary and important groundwork for military desegregation—which, it must be remembered, at the time deviated by a long distance from the race relations obtaining over a huge part of America's civilian life—it was simple battlefield need in this Asian "police action" that fully tipped this country's official military segregation into history's garbage bin. In simplest terms, the commander in Korea, General Matthew Ridgeway, faced a severe shortage of (white) manpower, which he rectified by calling for all possible replacements, *irrespective* of the skin color of those replacements. In 1954, a year after the Korean War ended, the secretary of defense announced the disbanding of America's last all-black unit. Isolated acts of discrimination would still occur in the services, but they would do so in contravention of policy and, eventually, result in severe penalties for the wrongdoers. By the latter part of the 1960s, civilian desegregation even brought a halt to off-base or off-post discrimination in civilian housing and public accommodations. Hidden or sotto voce private hate unquestionably festered in uniform much as it did in all of American society, tragically right up to the present day. But Jim Crow was gone, and the resonance of its leaving would help destroy what remained of it *outside* of America's military community.

Away from the federally controlled world of the military, though, Jim Crow continued nearly unabated in its polluting of the nation's social well. Like a man who sees the only reality he has known beginning to be seriously eroded, white Southerners—not all, but most—dug in their heels and resisted. They resisted every court decision that chipped away at the structure of Jim Crow, and they resisted the common sense that should have told them that their region's intolerance was holding the South ever further behind the rest of the country. They were angry at every black American who demanded the rights assumed as a patrimony by every white American. They hated any notion that their schools, their restaurants, their stores, their neighborhoods, would ever be forced to open to the black tenth of the nation that had always been kept away from these reserved bastions of their white world. And their backlash made this the last generation before blacks gained their due—the two decades following the end of World War II—as bad as any time, perhaps even the worst of all times, since the end of slavery itself.

In this last generation of Jim Crow, the South's white supremacists—a term that justly applied to the vast majority of the region's population—

saw little reason to let go. Looking at the situation today, it would seem that at midcentury the Southerners who defended white supremacy *should* have realized that the old norms could not continue to stand. Yet most remained convinced their race-determined way of life would somehow last, if not forever, then at least until a day in a far-off future. The postwar court decisions that were beginning to limit Jim Crow hadn't yet pierced the heart of the system, and in truth, most were bereft of any real sting in their tentative sanctions. African-American leaders were still seen as distant and ephemeral black intellectuals, allied with their (mostly) Northern liberal white supporters. No Southern grassroots organizer had yet midwifed a real movement. And in Washington the federal government was doing comparatively little to battle discrimination, a bleak realization that for African-Americans grew even bleaker when in January 1953 the mildly progressive Truman administration turned the country over to a new and, to all appearances, less sympathetic regime.

Dwight Eisenhower's prepresidential record on race had not been one to overly encourage optimism in African-Americans. During his years of high military command in World War II and immediately after the war in NATO, Eisenhower in racial matters had largely advocated the status quo. He was essentially against integrating the armed forces, on the grounds that the military's proper role should be as a fighting machine, not a social laboratory. He further believed that civilian advances in civil rights must lead the military rather than the other way around. When he was elected president, many thought his view of America's racial landscape hadn't changed a great deal since his days as an immensely successful military leader, a time when his major contribution to increased rights for blacks had come because a severe shortage of white troops had necessitated the integration of formerly segregated units.

If Eisenhower had never pushed for civil rights for African-Americans because it was the right thing to do, another external factor *would* move him in that direction when he became president. The world was clearly no longer going to give America a pass over its appalling hypocrisy apropos human rights. If it were still the Nazis reproaching the United States for such abuses, it would have been painless to ignore a government that was doing far worse to people under its own control. Even in the postwar world, it wasn't much harder to ignore Soviet taunts directed at America's racial iniquities when Stalin's attention to civil rights in his own country was nonexistent. But when a large percentage of the members of the United Nations—countries that America considered its allies—berated the United States for its racial discrimination, the president realized that change was overdue.

At the outset of his administration, Eisenhower's United Nations representative clearly warned him that America's notorious racist practices amounted to a "diplomatic Achilles' heel." While Washington ceaselessly sought support from new and third world member states against Soviet-backed initiatives, those countries had a hard time offering sympathy for a nation in which black and brown diplomats couldn't sit at a lunch counter or rent a hotel room in its capital. In the early days of his presidency, the strongest factor in Eisenhower's order to desegregate Washington's public accommodations was likely not that black *Americans* had for so long suffered the indignity of Jim Crow in the nation's capital, but that important black *foreigners* were now being humiliated.

In fact, life in 1953 for African-Americans in the District of Columbia was a long way from the horror it remained over large parts of the Southeast, especially in rural areas and small towns where white treatment of blacks was in some ways worse—given white lawlessness—than the Nazi treatment of Jews in prewar Germany. As World War II approached its end, an African-American soldier was asked what he thought ought to be done with Hitler if he was captured alive. His answer was as searing an indictment of American racial injustice as has ever been spoken: "Paint him black and sentence him to life in Mississippi."[8]

Through the 1950s, the lives of black men in the American South were as danger-filled as any in the Western world. A black man put his situation plainly when he said, "It is reason enough to at least pretend you respect

---

[8] Stetson Kennedy, 229.

white folks when you know they will get you killed for disrespecting them."[9] This was neither hyperbole nor self-pity. As we've seen throughout this book, the danger was especially acute in an encounter between a black male and a white female—almost any age of either sex was irrelevant. If a white female felt, merely *felt*, she had been given a look or a glance or a smile from a black male that implied familiarity, or if she was accidentally bumped or brushed on the sidewalk, or if, God forbid, she was shown any actual sexual interest, the black male's life was liable to forfeit in expiation for his sin. For example, in August 1955 fourteen-year-old Emmett Till looked at the white wife of a grocer with a degree too much familiarity in Money, Mississippi. If one could in that year have pinpointed America's ground zero for intolerance and danger for black males, Money would surely have been within hailing distance of it. Till paid for his "crime" with his life. Though witnesses identified two white men as the boy's killers, an all-white jury predictably acquitted the pair on state murder charges. When the federal government later charged the men with kidnapping, the U.S. attorney couldn't persuade a Mississippi grand jury to indict them.

Life in the South of the fifties encompassed a dearth of justice for African-Americans far beyond white paranoia over black male sexuality. The inevitable consequence of Jim Crow was the enormous economic disparity it created and maintained between black and white. Not only did whites ensure that blacks not participate in their social world, they saw to it that blacks were equally frozen out of most of their work world. African-American poverty rates in the South were everywhere double and triple what they were for whites. The "last hired, first fired" rule for blacks meant that even making a marginal living was all but impossible for African-Americans during times of job scarcity or economic downturn. The vaunted "upward mobility" of the 1950s meant little for the vast majority of black workers. Whereas whites could learn and be promoted, blacks were because of their color frozen onto the lowest rungs of the job ladder, the nonfarming majority most often toiling as laborers or domestic work-

[9] Stetson Kennedy, 206.

ers. Inferior schools contributed to an unknowable but doubtless huge degree toward keeping this situation unchanged. So did the unions, which in the South (as well as in much of the North) saw to it that blacks did not participate in their apprenticeship programs and wherever possible denied them membership. Throughout the 1950s South, civil service or government jobs for blacks were also exceedingly rare: the police and fire departments remained almost entirely white in every Southern city and town, and Southern city halls and county governments invariably hired whites only except in the most menial jobs. Some white hospitals hired blacks for unskilled positions, but black doctors and nurses rarely received invitations to join their staffs. Moreover, black patients knew that their chances of being treated at white hospitals were slim. Even Southern libraries, institutions supported by the combined tax dollars of whites and blacks, remained no more welcoming to black patrons in the fifties than they had been throughout the earlier decades of the century. When blacks wanted books in most Southern communities, they might find one or two branches that allowed African-American patronage or one that had set up a Colored room somewhere in some inconspicuous cranny—but this only if they were lucky enough to live in either a city or in a relatively "liberal" town.

As an example of Nuremberg-like race controls over American society that existed during the first two postwar decades, one of the most bizarre spectacles is New Orleans' Bureau of Vital Statistics registration rules. Amazingly, one person kept the city's venomous system in effect until 1965.

Reigning as head of the bureau that decided the race of generations of New Orleans babies was Naomi Drake. To Ms. Drake's way of thinking, her department could commit no greater sin that to get a baby's race wrong on the birth registration documents. The great majority of such babies were, of course, either obviously black or obviously white. But as a consequence of this bureaucrat's zeal, the race of an untold number of those born in the city was *changed* on official records from white to black (hardly ever was a change made the other way around). Rather than duly register as white a newborn whom she suspected of having black ancestry—under the one-drop rule, a single black ancestor, no matter how far distant in the past, meant a baby was legally black—Drake would use her official position to institute an "investigation." What piqued Drake's suspicions about a baby's race were small things, such as bearing a family name known to be held by African-American families, ordinary names such as Adams and Charles and Olsen. Even if the parents asking for the registration were themselves patently white, Drake often pressed ahead with an inquest. By the time she was finally fired in 1965, a backlog of 4,700 birth certificates clogged her office. Indeed, rarely were Drake's findings successfully challenged. In one of Naomi Drake's cases, a parish district attorney in 1956 indicted a woman for filing a false document: the mother had considered herself white and thus registered her newborn as white, but Ms. Drake found out otherwise.[10]

On May 17, 1954, the most important legal social ruling in American history was announced to a nation many understood was approaching the edge of a racial abyss. The highest court in the land said that instead of remaining a society governed by caste and *Plessy* in the schooling of its youth, Americans would now have to—*at least in law*—make good on the nation's egalitarian principles. The nine justices, all white, all men, spoke words that the black tenth of the American people had waited their entire lifetimes to hear, words many had believed would never be uttered. That decision was named for one of the complainants, an African-American girl who because of segregation laws was forced to ride a bus five miles to a black school instead of being free to attend a white school only four blocks from her house. The larger issue was the damage perpetrated in the name of white supremacy against millions of American children: damage from ill-trained teachers, from lack of school libraries, from patently inferior school buildings to which black children were required to walk great distances rather than being permitted to attend nearer white schools, from being made to sit in classrooms far more crowded than those used

[10] O'Byrne, *Times-Picayune*.

by their white contemporaries—and mostly, from being saturated with the belief that they weren't good enough, clean enough, or smart enough to join the 90 percent of children whose skin was not black.

If any one element of Jim Crow supremely represented the damage racism inflicted on American society, it was Southern education—the region's withholding from African-Americans an equal opportunity to learn and the concomitant forbidding of whites from sharing their education with blacks and by so doing discovering firsthand over the years of schooling a common humanity. (There is undeniable irony in the fact that Linda Brown's case originated in Kansas, one of the few non-Southern states in which school segregation was mandated by state law.) So crucial to white supremacism was the maintenance of the South's whites-only schools that no realistic hope existed for the eventual death of this system as long as change was left to the volition of segregationists themselves. After World War II, a growing number of Americans cognizant of the ideals for which the country had been founded and for which the recent war had been fought came to understand that the nation could not morally tolerate the ignoring of those principles. Exclusion of blacks from white schools was predicated on the entire catechism of black inferiority, but it was centered squarely on the perceived need to prevent miscegenation and the mixing of the races—what many white Southerners saw as the unavoidable outcome of allowing black and white children to grow up and be educated under the same school roof.

The legal tide had begun to turn on segregated education at the college level. We've already looked at the Missouri law school case. In 1949 another court required Oklahoma to provide an equal legal education for African-Americans, specifying that if the state was unable to do so in racially segregated facilities it must provide such an education in its white law school. In 1950 the University of Texas was ordered to admit blacks to its law school since "in terms of the number of faculty, variety of courses and opportunity for specialization, size of the student body, scope of the library, availability of law review . . . the University of Texas Law School is superior" to any state law school that had been established for blacks only. That same year, the state of Oklahoma was held in violation of the

Constitution when it required a black student to use an isolated seat in classrooms and the library and a separate table in the cafeteria, the court unanimously finding such treatment unconstitutional in its violation of Fourteenth Amendment guarantees of equal protection under the law.

But where segregated *higher* education was being slowly and case by case attacked and beaten back by civil rights organizations, their attorneys, and sympathetic judges, the far larger field of primary and secondary education—the learning place of students in their formative years, years during which Southerners believed children required immersion in the region's racial ethos—was through the early 1950s as rigidly segregated as it had ever been. The NAACP, the principal organization dedicated to ending Jim Crow, had favored tackling segregation on the grounds of state failure to provide an *equal* education for blacks, which is to say failure to uphold the standards of *Plessy v. Ferguson.* But in 1949 the organization changed its tack when a group of black parents—including those of Linda Brown—asked for help. Representing four states in which children were required to attend segregated schools, the plaintiffs were supported by chief NAACP counsel Thurgood Marshall, the lawyer who would set the stage for what would be the most important face-off with segregation since *Plessy* itself half a century earlier.

By the time Marshall took on this task—what was called the School Segregation Cases—the NAACP's top legal strategist had become one of the most influential civil rights lawyers in America. Marshall had hewed to one overriding objective throughout his legal career, which was simply to end legal racial discrimination. In the upcoming battle over school segregation, this grandson of slaves would be tilting his lance at the very platform that had supported Jim Crow's growth and prosperity. Victorious in a number of segregation cases through his tactics of demonstrating that *Plessy*'s separate-but-equal formula was unavoidably bathed in inequality, in the matter at hand—the School Cases—he would instead show that racial segregation in schools should end because it inherently and compulsorily violated America's fundamental social morality. He had to prove to the justices sitting on the high bench half a century after *Plessy* that the matter of equality or inequality of facilities—the keystone of the 1896 decision—was immaterial. Marshall reasoned that the nation could not wait until every case of racial inequality was fought on the grounds of inequality and won individually. Instead, segregation *in and of itself* had to be felled in a single massive judicial stroke.

If the majority of the American people in 1954 were of a mind that school segregation was morally wrong, a large part of the country fervently believed precisely the opposite. Even if all nine justices could be made to say that such segregation had to go, Chief Justice Warren knew the court could not go beyond the point where its decision would simply be ignored in the South. In fact, every one of the justices understood that a finding for the plaintiffs could result in massive civil disobedience in the South. A decision framed in language effectively declaring race immaterial in American law would, most explosively, be presumed to affect the nation's marriage laws, and that would amount to the worst fear of many Southerners coming true: namely, that antimiscegenation statutes would be rendered unenforceable. And *that*, it was feared, would overshadow the issue of school desegregation, perhaps even pushing the South to armed resistance to the will of the federal government, if not to another attempt at outright secession.

The decision handed down by the court under Chief Justice Earl Warren in May 1954 did not speak directly to the law behind school segregation nor did it declare the Constitution color-blind. And surprisingly, neither did the justices specifically renounce the reasoning behind *Plessy* that related to the Fourteenth Amendment. Instead, the nine men chiefly based their unanimous decision on the testimony of social science—on psychologists' findings that education under segregation was *inherently* unequal and thus created unavoidable mental harm to black schoolchildren, that it "retarded" the emotional and mental development of the plaintiffs.[11] At bottom, psychologists said, *nothing* could make the "separate" part truly "equal."

Though the decision ended the legality of school segregation in America, at the same time it gave notice to the nation of the wider moral

[11] Kull, 154.

bankruptcy of Jim Crow, even though not yet declaring other forms of segregation illegal. To stress the point, the ruling did *not* maintain that the Constitution was color-blind, which was and still is widely believed, or at least *supposed,* to have been one of the justices' core intentions in *Brown.* Warren's predecessor as chief justice, Fred Vinson, had succinctly summed up his and his colleagues' dilemma with the comment that "however we construe it, *Congress* [emphasis added] did not pass a statute deterring or ordering no segregation."

The decision delivered in May 1954 was not the entirety of the court's action regarding the School Cases. Rather than wait until it had worked out a specific (and unquestionably complicated) remedy for the *Brown et al.* plaintiffs, Chief Justice Warren divided the case. What became known as *Brown II*—the concluding remedy phase—took nearly a year more of the court's time. In 1955, *Brown* was again argued before the court, the lawyers for both sides contending what should specifically be done to actually end segregation in public schools, as mandated by *Brown I.* The issues were immensely difficult, especially regarding exactly *who* was entitled to relief, how such relief would be carried out, and what time frame would be allowed the seventeen affected states to undo their school segregation. Marshall argued that race should simply be forbidden as a factor in setting school assignments for students. But the justices clearly understood that many, probably most, Southern school districts would use every kind of obfuscation at their imagining to keep schools virtually the same as they had forever been, which was either all-white or all-black—and utterly separate. In fact, some of the states had already made it clear that they intended to close public schools rather than integrate them.

Brown II essentially shifted the burden from the Supreme Court to local courts to find answers to these questions. In fairness to the states affected by *Brown,* the Supreme Court had not at any time given specific guidelines as to what constituted impermissible school "segregation," at least not in terms that later courts would adopt in their efforts to, for example, use busing to try to end it. To indicate a timetable for legal compliance, the high court used the famous phrase "with all deliberate speed"—which, of course, meant almost nothing in terms of an actually measurable time frame. Desperately attempting to avoid riling the South so that it would show "restraint" rather than unlawfully flouting the law of the land, Warren and his associates gave the region all the time it appeared it could possibly need to desegregate—very nearly "forever" it seemed to many African-Americans. And as the years went by with, at best, token compliance, it indeed looked as though white Southerners were going to take every bit of that "forever." For a long time, vast numbers of the region's white population judged that all that was needed to effectively sweep *Brown* under the rug was to vigorously oppose the decision as being too "complicated" to implement.

In 1954 and for some years after, most liberals and probably nearly every African-American would have regarded a specific Supreme Court dictum declaring the Constitution "color-blind" a triumph for right and fairness. But what would soon appear on the legal horizon was a realization that color-consciousness in law would actually be a necessity—so realized, in any case, by those same liberals and minorities. Which is precisely what happened. The system of granting preferences under the designation of "affirmative action" meant to remedy or make up for past injustices of both a social and an economic nature could not later have passed constitutional muster had the Constitution been declared in 1954 to be "color-blind." And in which case the post-*Brown* history of American civil rights would have turned out very differently.

Regardless of the court's politically tortuous formulations for over-turning school segregation—formulations fundamentally meant to see to it that Southerners opposed to integration weren't unduly offended—the decisions following *Brown I* ignored the issue of equality of treatment as commanded by the Fourteenth Amendment and the *Plessy* decision that flowed from it. In a stream of cases after *Brown*, the high court simply struck down without explanation segregation statutes that truculently continued to be upheld by state courts, the justices' explanation resting on the illegality of discrimination that flowed from the *Brown* mandate. With some exceptions (for some years more miscegenation was the main one), from 1954 the American people would see the Supreme Court as consistently asserting segregation as immoral, thus wrong, thus illegal, and thus "foreclosed as a litigable issue."[12] From 1954 on, the nation's segregation-ists would be all but deprived of the boat that had kept them afloat, the court pulling out from under their oars *Plessy*'s long-lived blessing that Jim Crow was okay.

Of course, not *all* Americans, it goes without saying, took the matter as "foreclosed." A large majority of those living in the Southeast would continue to view school integration as very much an open matter, an out-look in which their elected representatives at every level of government joined them. Of the 128 men representing the South in Congress, 101 signed a "Southern Manifesto" attacking *Brown* and urging their states to ignore it. Southern whites also took comfort from what they saw as Northern hypocrisy regarding the civil rights of African-Americans, a view containing more than a little merit. Everywhere in America, many kinds of racial discrimination in other than statutory guises continued after the *Brown* decision, just as if nothing had transpired in the white marble Supreme Court temple in Washington to change the race realities of American life. Unions and employers continued to keep blacks out of their ranks and their shops and their factories, and landlords and home sellers and real estate agents entrenched the residential apartheid that had long since ghettoized almost every American city. Blacks in America still found discrimination everywhere in the media and the arts—television, movies, theater, news, journalism, publishing—all of which fields openly practiced de facto black exclusion with almost no sanctions worthy of the name.

But in the South the reaction to *Brown* was visceral, and it looked for a long time to stay that way. In 1954 school segregation was legally man-dated in seventeen southeastern states and the District of Columbia, and it was optional—though not observed—in four other states. The practice kept 12 million black and white schoolchildren apart from each other. But along the edges of the segregationist region—the border states and the upper South—it did look at first as though moderation might carry whites through whatever social "trauma" school integration would bring them.

[12] Kull, 161.

The court had, after all, in avoiding deadlines or specific penalties for failure to comply, signaled mile-wide moderation.

Allan Shivers, Texas's governor, announced that his state would comply with the court's directive—though adding that it might "take years" for results to be achieved. Virtually the same words popped up in many places. In the months following the decision, several Southern states did begin to integrate their schools; 350 school districts in Oklahoma, Texas, Kentucky, West Virginia, Maryland, Tennessee, Arkansas, and Delaware decided to obey the court sooner rather than later, though in many cases the degree of compliance could most charitably be described as token. In fact, only one Jim Crow stronghold obeyed the court without dragging its feet: though President Eisenhower after the *Brown* decision remarked that Earl Warren's appointment to the high bench was "the biggest damn fool mistake" he had ever made, the nation's chief executive knew the law had to be obeyed and consequently immediately ordered the integration of every school in the District of Columbia, territory that the federal government controlled and in which it could call the shots. Eisenhower also directed an immediate cessation to all remaining vestiges of segregation, of any nature, in the armed services.[13]

What Eisenhower would not do, however, was personally urge the South to comply with *Brown*. He remarked with questionable moral logic that "extremists on both sides" of the issue should remain calm, as though African-Americans eager to attend decent schools represented "extremists" as much as did the die-hard segregationists.

A great part of the official reaction in the lower South sounded practically insurrectionary. South Carolina's Governor James Byrnes—the man who had come within shooting distance of being named FDR's vice-presidential running mate in 1944 and, had he been, would have become president in April 1945—threatened to abandon his state's public school system rather than comply with the court's "edict." The reaction in Georgia, Mississippi, and Alabama followed roughly the same tack: typical of

---

[13] Manchester, 903.

the utterances coming out of the Deep South was Governor Herman Talmadge's threat that Georgia would "map a program to insure continued and permanent segregation of the races."[14] Virginia floated the tactic of "interposition," a highly suspect flouting of the Supreme Court's writ based on a state's supposed right to ignore a federal court's "usurpation" of its sovereignty by using the tactic of somehow "interposing" the state between the federal government and the citizens of the state; interposition actually amounted to little other than fancy lawlessness. Beyond such quasi-legalistic devices, Southern politicians reviled a post-*Brown* America as one in which a new racial order would destroy life as Southerners had always known it, a nation in which the specter of "equalization" for African-Americans would translate into mobs of black men targeting white women for sex.

Efforts to undo *Brown* had begun almost the moment the decision came down. The more sophisticated segregationists quickly seized on the legal front as the most vulnerable to an attack on the court's decision. That the justices had lent substantial weight to the nonlegal testimony of social scientists and those scientists' views concerning the damage caused by school segregation to black children inevitably led to the court's being accused of "substituting psychology for law."[15] What was more, given the anticommunist political temper of the time, charges flew out of the South that sociologists were "left-wingers of the first order." A Montgomery newspaper editorialist wrote that "deprived of the strength of character of its people by racial mongrelization, the United States would be stripped of the national strength to permanently keep up a successful resistance against the battering ram of Communist infiltration forces." In fact, the Supreme Court justices had not been able to find specific wording in federal statutes or law that prohibited school segregation, their decision instead the result of their personal interpretation of Fourteenth Amendment violations and their consensus that segregation itself was immoral and at odds with American notions of liberty and equal rights.

---

[14] Manchester, 902.
[15] Newby, *Challenge to the Court*, 186.

From the emotional heights experienced by black Americans on the day *Brown* was announced, the journey to justice seemed at first as if it might be short. But such was not to be the case. Though some jurisdictions undertook important measures—however resentfully—toward obedience to the court, the progress made by the states of the old Confederacy for the next decade and more was paltry at best: by 1965, only 6.5 percent of black children living in the South attended school with white children. A great many white Southerners simply didn't see "liberty and equal rights" as having anything at all to do with schooling their children with black children. What percentage of white Southerners held these views in 1954 is unknowable; nothing like a plebiscite was taken on the issue. But what *is* beyond question is that a huge majority of those in positions of political and social power either believed wholeheartedly in segregation or at least felt themselves bound by community standards to behave as though they did. And the voters continued to return these same legislators or else elect new ones who believed the same way, with an individual lawmaker's approval of segregation a key factor—likely *the* key factor—in winning voter approval. And the techniques, excuses, and obfuscations by which such titanic disobedience to the law would be achieved were ingenious, indeed often legally brilliant.

The South, eventually including even its geographical fringes, undertook massive efforts to thwart the Supreme Court's decision, efforts that eventually reached a point of near insurrection with concepts like "state sovereignty," "nullification," and "interposition" expressing Southern resistance to the will of the federal government. With belligerence openly and proudly expressed by the South's political leaders, editorial writers, and a large part of its clergy and academicians, those further down the social and intellectual ladder quickly assumed free license to form resistance organizations. Typical was a reinvigorated Ku Klux Klan, which used terror to keep schools segregated, as well as the somewhat better-mannered but no less dedicated civil resistance groups calling themselves White Citizens Councils, composed of marginally better-mannered elements of the middle-class white community than was the Klan.

The latter phenomenon evolved into an unofficial layer of government across the South in the region-wide drive to nullify *Brown*. Begun in Mississippi in July 1954, the White Citizens Councils dedicated themselves to maintaining both segregation and white supremacy. Within three months of the first council's founding, twenty-five thousand people had joined these organizations, and the idea spread to other states like a steamroller, with councils garnering one hundred thousand members in Georgia and South Carolina alone. In addition to its Citizens Councils, Mississippi, the most reactionary Jim Crow stronghold, came up with the Sovereignty Commission, later described as a sort of Southern KGB. Created by the state legislature in 1956 and hanging on until it was defunded twenty-seven years later, this taxpayer-financed agency existed for the sole purpose of defending segregation and white supremacy in every quarter of Mississippi, and doing so through means often as much outside the law as within. To discharge its secret mission, the commission investigated and spied on scores of people, both black and white, basically keeping its collective eye on anyone who espoused or promoted racial equality. It infiltrated most of the state's major civil rights organizations and passed its findings to employers and, more dangerously, to the Klan. Because of the commission unknown numbers were fired from their jobs, many were beaten, and even a few were thought murdered by the Klan based on the commission's recommendation. The commission was also responsible for thwarting black voter registration and for intimidating black children attempting to attend white schools, and some fourteen hundred documents regarding murdered civil rights leader Medgar Evers were found in its files after its demise. One of its more farcical efforts was to encourage locals to boycott organizations sponsoring entertainer Lena Horne.

White supremacists were not, however, the only Americans to be inspired to action by the *Brown* decision. The NAACP's Roy Wilkins weighed in on the opportunity given African-Americans by the Supreme Court's blow to Jim Crow: "This great day is ours, upon us depend the speed, the order, and the completeness of the victory. In fashioning the new era we shall use all the weapons at our disposal." And writer James Baldwin gave courage to black men and women even while he warned white Americans to heed the will of African-Americans to end the centuries of racism, warned that now was the nation's last chance to bring about peaceful change. Baldwin eloquently wrote: "We may be able, handful that we are, to end the racial nightmare, and achieve our country, and change the history of the world. If we do not dare everything, the fulfillment of that prophecy, re-created from the Bible in song by a slave, is upon us: *God gave Noah the rainbow sign, no more water, the fire next time!*"[16]

What is now regarded as the opening salvo in America's civil rights revolution as well as the first great personal blow struck against Jim Crow came late in the year following the *Brown* decision. On the evening of the first day of December 1955, a Montgomery, Alabama, municipal bus driver named James F. Blake ordered a forty-two-year-old African-American woman to give up her seat on his bus to a white man. Rosa Parks's refusal to follow the demand unleashed a torrent of indignation that would never again be dammed, even though the scene in Montgomery that evening in 1955 was such a commonplace in the universe of Southern racism that no one then could have imagined its consequences. Not only did Mrs. Parks's action inspire worldwide admiration and nationwide emulation, it led to a desperately needed voice being given to African-American aspirations, the eloquent, passionate, and reasoning voice of the man who would lead the war against Jim Crow to victory. As the sides fought it out over the next ten years, the whole structure of America's race relations changed and in doing so transformed American society into something far closer to its avowed ideal.

---

[16] Baldwin, *The Fire Next Time*, 141.

8

THE LAST YEARS

oday it seems fantastic, as if from a thing imagined, that the seats on the buses of an American city could ever have been assigned by the color of the passengers' skin, that passengers of one color would be made to stand rather than occupy empty seats assigned to those of another color, that members of the so-called inferior race would be made to stand for members of the self-styled superior race when the latter's predetermined seats filled up, that members of the inferior race would not even be allowed to board the bus through its front door but would instead be made to pay up front and then get off and run to the back door and there reboard. But this grotesque farce of racial etiquette was the way it was in Montgomery, Alabama, in 1955, and so far as anyone could remember, it had always been that way, and by God and His saints, if the majority of the white citizens of Montgomery had anything to say about it, it was always going to be that way.

For decades, the Montgomery City Lines had humiliated the black citizens of Alabama's capital, not only with ironclad segregation on its buses but also with the brutal way it wielded its power. About fifty thousand strong in 1955, the city's African-American community counted for about three-quarters of the bus company's clientele. Notwithstanding, every one of the company's drivers was white, and not a few were petty tyrants who used their policing authority to intimidate, humiliate, and sometimes even physically attack black riders, shouting such epithets as "heifers" and "whores" and "black bitches" at African-American women who in any way breached the Jim Crow rules governing the buses. On rainy days, many drivers simply passed by black passengers waiting at bus stops, believing wet blacks gave off an odor offensive not only to the drivers themselves but also to their other passengers—the white ones. African-Americans clearly understood their vulnerability to arrest at a driver's whim for such transgressions as "sassing"—talking back—when ordered to vacate a seat for a white, or for showing the slightest irritation when an operator refused to make change for the fare box. Some drivers would not even hand a black person change or even a transfer—it being socially taboo for Southern whites to touch black skin except that of a mammy or a servant—instead throwing the coins or the slip of paper on the bus's floor for the African-American passenger to have to bend down to pick up. Drivers occasionally even refused to allow the target of their wrath to escape by getting off the bus, instead summoning a police officer to take the offending black into custody, such requests always being promptly carried out by Montgomery's entirely white police force.

One such outrage especially scandalized the city's African-American community. A black mother had boarded a Montgomery bus with her two babies in her arms. As always, the front four rows of seats were "reserved" for whites, meaning they were off-limits to blacks under any circumstances, even when all the white seats were unused on runs into black neighborhoods. Seeing that all the front seats were empty, the woman placed her babies on the first of the seats so she could get her fare money out of her purse. Instantly, the driver screamed at the woman to remove her "black, dirty brats" from the "white" seat. The horrified woman managed to drop her coins into the fare box, but when she tried to grab for her infants, the operator jammed the accelerator down to cause the bus to lurch, throwing both infants into the aisle. Though a few passengers tried to help the young mother, the crying and humiliated woman instead got off at the next stop, undoubtedly to the driver's smug satisfaction.[1]

The operators worked with the knowledge that they were not only obeying their employer's orders, but were also managing their buses

[1] Robinson, 33.

according to the letter of the city's segregation ordinance. Even the least offensive drivers—those who might, if feeling kindly disposed, wait an extra moment for a black man or woman who was running to catch the bus—could not at the risk of breaking the law set aside any of the minutiae of Jim Crow governing how the races must comport themselves on the city's buses. Especially infuriating to Montgomery's African-Americans was the practice of maintaining inviolate the front white seats on all buses when they were empty, yet this rule was never set aside.

Rosa Parks had just left her workplace that Thursday evening in December 1955. Her working days were spent as a seamstress at the Montgomery Fair, the city's biggest department store, a job for which she was paid $23 a week. Parks didn't look in any way unusual, but in fact her attainments were highly singular. Because the city of Montgomery had not provided a high school for African-Americans during her youth, Parks had attended the black Alabama State College's laboratory school and become one of the relatively few members of her community to earn a high school diploma. She had long belonged to the NAACP and had completed a course in race relations at Myles Horton's nationally respected Highlander Folk School in Monteagle, Tennessee, where, in violation of that state's segregation ordinances, blacks and whites had worked and studied together since the early 1930s in a setting designed to help both groups learn to break the barriers of segregation. The school was where some of the best-known leaders of the civil rights movement learned the skills of political organizing. Parks's standing and reputation amongst Montgomery's progressives, both black and white, was, in a word, impeccable. She was, in fact, just about the perfect person for the events that were about to flow from her act of criminal civil disobedience on the Cleveland Avenue bus line.

Parks's bus picked her up at a stop close to the Montgomery Fair, at the bottom of Dexter Avenue in the heart of the city that ninety-four years earlier had served as the first capital of the Confederacy. She quickly found a seat in the fifth row, the first row available to blacks. The first four rows completely filled with whites after two more stops. At the third stop after Dexter, a white man boarded. According to the rules, the driver told Parks, the black man sitting next to her, and the two blacks sitting together directly across the aisle to give up their seats (blacks and whites were forbidden from even sitting in the same row abreast of each other). Not only did he *tell* them, but he barked it in the tone many whites with a little power loved to use against blacks who had no power at all. The operator was, she would later recall, the same one who a dozen years earlier had threatened to have her arrested when she balked at having to reboard by the rear door, and when recounting this evening's incident, she joked that he had still been "mean-looking."

On the driver's demand, the other three blacks in her row stood up and moved toward the rear of the bus. But a day of hard work and a lifetime of disgust with Jim Crow overtook Rosa Parks in that instant, and she stayed seated, calmly telling the driver that she would *not* get up. In turn, the driver told her she would be arrested if she refused. She was, of course, already well aware of that, yet still she refused. The driver pulled his bus over to the curb, got out, and phoned for a police officer. Within minutes one arrived at the scene of the "crime." He arrested the criminal, put her in the police cruiser, and took her first to city hall and then to the city jail, where she was fingerprinted and photographed for a mug shot.

After her husband, Raymond, and a white civil rights lawyer and his wife named Clifford and Virginia Durr bailed her out of jail that evening, Parks, her husband, the Durrs, and the Reverend E. D. Nixon, head of the local NAACP chapter, talked into the night about the arrest. The group understood it would make an excellent case on which to test the Jim Crow bus law. Rosa Parks agreed, despite the obvious danger to herself from violence-prone white racists. It was decided to ask for financial help from the NAACP's Legal Defense and Education Fund. Without in any way diminishing Rosa Parks's courageous role in the city's drama, it was the man who was contacted the day after the arrest who transformed the incident from a local occurrence into one of international notoriety.

After the Reverend Ralph Abernathy, a prominent black Montgomery minister, joined the about-to-be protesters, he contacted the twenty-six-year-old pastor of the city's Dexter Avenue Baptist Church, the still largely unknown Reverend Martin Luther King Jr., who quickly pledged he would help in any way he could. Later that evening the city's black leaders met at King's church, a stone's throw away from the state capitol, to discuss Parks's plight. All immediately understood that the soft-spoken but imposing woman would indeed represent a stunningly effective defendant on whom to base a lawsuit. And fortunately, Parks had, despite her husband's misgivings, already agreed to be the guinea pig. Also fortunately, the soft-spoken but passionate Reverend Mr. King knew that the time for their actions was long past due.

The first item of business would be to organize the African-American community in a boycott to protest the transit company's policy. King and Nixon thought it should begin the following Monday. Jo Ann Robinson, a black college professor and local activist who would be as much responsible for the planning of the coming boycott, and for its success, as any other person—a recognition later supported by King himself—mimeographed handouts that her students carried around to African-American households throughout the city, distributing altogether fifty-two thousand copies of the hurriedly written message. The instructions were brief but the words were ardent:

This is for Monday, December 5, 1955. Another Negro woman has been arrested and thrown into jail because she refused to get up out of her seat on the bus for a white person to sit down. It is the second time since the Claudette Colvin case that a Negro woman has been arrested for the same thing. This has to be stopped. Negroes have rights, too, for if Negroes did not ride the buses, they could not operate. Three-fourths of the riders are Negroes, yet we are arrested, or have to stand over empty seats. If we do not do something to stop these arrests, they will continue. The next time it may be you, or your daughter, or mother. This woman's case will come up on Monday [in court]. We are, therefore, asking every Negro to stay off the buses Monday in protest of the arrest and trial. Don't ride the buses to work, to town, to school, or anywhere on Monday. You can afford to stay out of town for one day. If you work, take a cab, or walk. But please, children and grown-ups, don't ride the bus at all on Monday. Please stay off of all buses Monday.

King hoped for 60 percent compliance, a degree of participation that he believed would send a strong anti–Jim Crow message as well as ensure the boycott ended in success. Instead, on Monday morning, virtually the city's entire black community stayed off the buses, an outcome he later called "a miracle." Though some of the black ministers thought the boycott should end that day in light of this apparent success, King and the rest of the leadership decided to press for a permanent boycott until the black community's demands were met. These entreaties were modest: only that drivers treat blacks with courtesy and that black sections of the buses be reserved for blacks even if whites completely filled their own seats; the end of bus segregation was not demanded. But the bus company refused even this, and so the boycott continued.

Montgomery's African-American community organized itself brilliantly, with the charismatic King the leader of the boycott group, which group was formally named the Montgomery Improvement Association. Thousands had relied on the buses every day, most often for commutes to jobs downtown or to domestic work in homes far out in the city's all-white suburbs. During the boycott African-American car owners picked up many of these people, stopping at a network of designated locations and delivering them to jobs in the mornings and back home again in the evenings. Drivers of the taxicabs, a form of transportation as segregated as any other in the city, charged boycotters cut rates for their services. Black Montgomery's compliance was spectacular. Almost no African-Americans were seen on the buses, which severely cut into the transit company's revenues.

Not unexpectedly, whites almost immediately began to retaliate. The profoundly offended White Citizens Council saw its membership increase handsomely, with white fears stoked by such comments as that made by the segregationist city commissioner Clyde Sellers: "If we grant the Negroes [their] demands, they would go about boasting of a victory that they had won over the white people, and this we will not stand for."[2] Under its taxi ordinance, the city prosecuted cabbies who charged less than the minimum fare. White insurance companies canceled coverage on those black policyholders who were using their cars to ferry boycotters. Black drivers were taken to jail for minor offenses, including King himself, who was charged with "speeding"—traveling at thirty miles per hour in a twenty-five-mile-per-hour zone. All of this came to the boil in February 1956 when the boycott leaders were arrested for violating a long-unused Alabama ordinance prohibiting boycotts. The arrest was the second for King, and the increasingly respected minister was convicted on the charge and ordered to pay $500 plus $500 court costs in lieu of spending 386 days in the state penitentiary.

But in bombing King's home, the reactionary whites blundered fatally: seeing the opposition's intransigence, the black leadership gave up on their mild demands and filed a federal lawsuit charging that the Montgomery segregated-bus law was unconstitutional. From that point on, King and his associates would no longer settle for *milder* segregation on the buses, but would instead demand an end to any form of racially discriminatory practices on the part of the Montgomery City Lines.

The bus boycott went on, with great sacrifice on the part of the thousands who were forced to get to work by whatever means the boycott committee could provide. Happily, both riders and organizers performed nobly. One black man who did board a bus found out how one member of his community regarded such disloyalty. Letting the black man off at his stop, the white driver saw in his rearview mirror an elderly black woman racing down the sidewalk, trying to catch the bus, he thought. When she got near the door, he said, "You don't have to rush, auntie. I'll wait for you." The woman answered, "In the first place, I ain't your auntie. In the second place, I ain't rushing to get on your bus. I'm jus' trying to catch up with that nigger who just got off, so I can hit him with this here stick."

Two converging streams simultaneously made the boycott a success and brought it to a halt and put a monumental psychological foot in the

---

[2] Brinkley, 144.

door of racial justice. First, Montgomery's white business leaders realized that the boycott was hurting *them* badly, both because black shoppers couldn't easily get downtown and because many African-Americans had extended their personal bus boycott into a pledge to stay clear of white businesses. Though the businessmen were not in the least sympathetic with black demands for equality, they were decidedly in sympathy with each other's loss of income. Calling themselves the Men of Montgomery, they at first tried to negotiate an end to the struggle by agreeing to the original demands of the black leaders, though by that time the black leadership understood it could not waste this opportunity to attempt to achieve true desegregation of the city's buses. Nonetheless, the white business leaders began to work with rather than against the African-American community, a significant omen for the city's future.

The real breaching of the dam of Jim Crow came, of course, via the law rather than from the actual boycott itself. Though the city diligently fought the blacks by claiming desegregation would result in violence—meaning white violence against black bus riders—a white federal judge spoke with pointed logic: "Is it fair to ask one man to surrender his constitutional rights, if they are his constitutional rights, in order to prevent another man from committing a crime?" The federal judge, Frank Morrison, a thirty-seven-year-old white Alabamian put on the bench by President Eisenhower only a year earlier, obviously believed it wasn't, in effect ruling for the boycotters by declaring bus segregation illegal. The city duly appealed to the Supreme Court of the United States. But the high court upheld the lower court. Segregation was broken on Montgomery's buses, and the boycott finally came to a victorious end.

The importance of the struggle was not in the sweet gain that came for Montgomery's bus-riding black public, though that victory represented a great symbolic justice. What Rosa Parks's simple act of disobedience led to was the opening of the floodgates of black anger. It inaugurated the first real African-American cohesion as a community fighting white supremacism. It showed that sympathetic and fair-minded white judges and white sympathizers would play a major role in helping African-Americans achieve civil rights. It showed that the struggle to strike Jim Crow dead was going to be played in the streets by organized action and in the courts—largely federal and Northern courts—by judges who understood that America could not survive with unequal levels of justice and rights and notions of decency. And it made a national figure of Martin Luther King, a man who would take the movement for African-American equality to heights undreamt of by those who had toiled before him. It was an American analogy to the storming of the Bastille, which ended France's ancien régime. But, like the French nobles, much of the white South would continue to resist—and resist mightily.

Even after Montgomery's morally exhilarating victory against Jim Crow, the remaining machinery of discrimination would continue to cheat death in the South for another decade before being incontrovertibly destroyed. As the years of statutory segregation went on, many, not least in the North, wondered why Jim Crow zealots doggedly refused to accept that statutory segregation had contracted a fatal disease, why those so obsessed continued to dig in ever more fiercely against a ballooning of national sympathy for African-American goals and for concrete gains in civil rights, why what appeared to be such unambiguous portents of white supremacism's defeat seemed invisible to so many who would continue so hard to sustain it.

In reality, millions of people in Jim Crow territory believed right up to the end of the system in the mid-1960s that fundamental and lasting change in the South's racial relationship would not occur, that white supremacy would in the end prevail despite the wider American disgust and frustration that became increasingly obvious in the civil rights battles that followed Montgomery, that a system that had lasted so long, in which so much money and energy had been invested, could not fail, could not have been *wrong*. But most important to the continuation of Jim Crow was that the law remained on the side of segregation. Though the direction of court decisions had clearly swung against segregation—most important, of course, being the Supreme Court decisions that tore great chunks out of the flanks of Jim Crow—the courts had not yet made truly comprehensive civil rights decisions nor had overarching civil rights legislation passed in Congress. Thus each piece of Jim Crow, large or small, had to be attacked frontally and individually. Even against the growing army of protesters and lawyers battling segregation—a body that included many white Southerners—in the last years of Jim Crow the race supremacists still commanded the overwhelming support of the Southern law enforcement and justice establishments, both of which bodies invariably lent their weight to the status quo while fighting those who sought any wider casting of civil rights protections and the abandonment of discrimination. The predominant Southern mind-set remained firmly that African-Americans were inferior beings, a conviction mortared by dead but still honored generations that had to their dying breath upheld white supremacy. Furthermore, most Southerners believed that the Northern liberals and "do-gooders" still had neither an understanding of how to "handle" the African-American, as did the Southerner, nor as "outsiders" were entitled to dictate how the region's affairs should be conducted. Finally in those years, the federal government itself comforted and supported the white South's racism: President Eisenhower withheld what would have been prestigious support where the *Brown* decision was concerned, and even Adlai Stevenson, the 1956 Democratic presidential candidate, remarked (with uncharacteristically clumsy grammar) that "you do not upset habits and traditions that are older than the Republic overnight."[3]

Close on the heels of the *Brown* decision and of the Montgomery bus battle, African-Americans did gain yet another victory, though one whose value proved more symbolic than substantial in increasing rights. Despite a filibuster mounted by Southern segregationists, Congress passed and the president signed into law the Civil Rights Act of 1957; for an unbroken twenty-four hours Senator Strom Thurmond of South Carolina energetically but, in the end, unsuccessfully spoke against the bill. The act created a Civil Rights Division in the Department of Justice, one designed to seek injunctions against those who would violate another's voting rights, African-Americans obviously being the primary recipients of such protection. Even though a new Civil Rights Commission came along with it,

---

[3] Palmer, 258.

this weak 1957 law unfortunately lacked strong enforcement provisions. (Another civil rights act, passed in 1960, dealt with, among other issues, violence carried out interstate; it was generally regarded to be as weak as the 1957 measure.)

Despite Congress's tepid efforts, the war against any expansion of black rights unsurprisingly went on. After Montgomery, the next major battlefield for the newly regrouped forces would be Little Rock, Arkansas, where the moral poverty of the Southern obstructionists' efforts to block black rights first widely came to the electronic attention of not only America but of the world. The outcome of this encounter inflicted deep damage on white supremacy and, more specifically, on white-engineered resistance to school integration. Support for such integration, most of which of course came from African-Americans themselves, had largely been unfocused before Little Rock, but coming out of this clash in Arkansas would be the unmistakable message that the authority and power of the federal government had, three years after *Brown* and in spite of the president's lassitude, settled decisively on the side of justice and the law.

The confrontation at Little Rock was, at bottom, a crisis wholly set up by Orval Faubus. For a few weeks in 1957, that Southern-inflected name became intimately familiar to an international newspaper-reading, television-watching public. In even the remotest corners of the world, Faubus's actions made a bitter brew of America's self-congratulatory assertions of moral superiority. In America itself, his actions offended millions of people who watched with repugnance as the Little Rock race drama played out. The plot was the attempted introduction of African-American children into this sleepy city's thus far all-white schools, the community's first effort to do so since the *Brown* decision. The chief antagonist was Arkansas's Governor Faubus. The chief protagonist, albeit a clearly reluctant one, was President Eisenhower. In the background waited nine high school freshmen, all black, and all of whose lives were to be put at risk by Governor Faubus's crack at preserving Jim Crow against the onrush of changing times.

Though three years had passed since the Supreme Court had told the nation that statutorily segregated education violated the Constitution, in

1957 only a few places in the South were school boards obeying the court. In most cases, what movement toward integration did exist was purposely slow and tentative, largely designed to forestall violence and generally succeeding thus far. This kind of relatively peaceable change was also expected in Little Rock, the capital of a state that thought itself almost as much Western as Southern. The NAACP had gone to court demanding the integration of the city's schools, and the white citizens of Little Rock had to date made no threats of violence to resist the action. The governor even sounded different from his counterparts in Alabama and Mississippi in that he didn't indulge in grandstanding over the oncoming change in how the people of Little Rock were going to educate their children. But events conspired against peaceability, specifically the unfortunate timing of an election: that fall Orval Faubus was already gearing up for reelection the following year. He tragically concluded that if he didn't make a point of forcefully resisting racial integration in the schools, he would open the door for overtly segregationist opponents to wipe him off the polling-booth floor.

Unaware of what was coming, the Little Rock school board went ahead with its integration plans, having chosen the downtown high school as the single school in the city with which to kick things off. The targeted facility, Central High School, was a handsome, even noble, building, rising a few blocks from the capitol like a latter-day Babylonian palace. Obviously though, Central had been chosen for reasons other than its physical stateliness. It was the city's working-class high school, and that meant that the influential white parents who enrolled their children in the tony suburban high schools wouldn't be facing the possibility of their own offspring getting involved in whatever racial turbulence might attend desegregation. The white officials who ran the public schools had reasoned that integration must come slowly, certainly no faster than the nebulous "all deliberate speed" formula handed down by the Yankee Supreme Court. The idea was that after all the city's high schools had peacefully settled into the realities of mixing whites with blacks, then the elementary schools could be seen to, at the rate of a class a year, starting with the eighth grade and working down. That would stretch things out to the point where it was hoped that whites would accept the "shock" of the mixing. Such, at any event, was the plan.

It might just have worked, except for the governor's anxiety over getting reelected. Instead, on the day before school was to open for the new term—Wednesday, September 4, 1957—Faubus announced to a surprised city that he intended to call out the Arkansas National Guard to "maintain order" (read: stop integration) in a community that he said stood on the "brink of riot." In fact, the image of armed troops symbolically holding back the black tide gave tremendous comfort to those parents who quietly but intensely loathed the prospect of African-American children fouling their white schools. Equally overjoyed was the local Ku Klux Klan and its attendant groupies of Central's own teenage segregationist thugs.

Nine ninth-grade black students—six girls and three boys—had been chosen by the school board as a vanguard to integrate Central. The morning they were to commence their attempted journey through Faubus's troops and into the schoolhouse—Thursday the fifth—eight of them approached Central in the company of NAACP safety monitors. As scripted by the governor, the Arkansas Guard turned these black youngsters back, literally at the school door. Asked by a monitor what their specific orders were, one of the soldiers simply said, "To keep the niggers out." The young African-Americans retreated.

But the ninth student, a girl named Elizabeth Eckford, somehow hadn't heard that she was supposed to have been accompanied by adult monitors that morning. After she stepped off her bus a block from Central, dressed in a new black-and-white outfit she had sewn herself, the about-to-be freshman walked the final few yards alone. As she neared the school building, entirely unprotected and sickeningly vulnerable to the taunting, hate-filled protesters attracted by Faubus's military circus, the mob reckoned it had a victim within its reach. "Here she comes. Here comes the nigger. Lynch her. Lynch her." Elizabeth barely managed to escape, helped by a *New York Times* reporter named Ben Fine and a white woman who got her back on a bus and out of reach of the hooligans, who might well have killed her if they had been able to reach her. The entire episode was broadcast nationally and internationally to an incredulous television audience, viewers that included the president of the United States.

Regardless of his posture on integration, which was in the main unsympathetic to forced mixing of the races, Dwight Eisenhower well understood his responsibility to the Constitution, to uphold it. As fuzzy as the Supreme Court had been in the matter of solutions, it allowed no uncertainty as to how that document was now to be interpreted in regard to school segregation itself. Eisenhower thus had to make certain Faubus was aware that the authority of the president of the United States would be exercised to carry out the high court's mandate. Within days, an emergency meeting between the two men was called at the summer White House in Newport, Rhode Island. After his discussion with Faubus, Eisenhower believed he had persuaded the governor to go home and get the black children safely and expeditiously enrolled in Central High School. Alas, such was the last thing on Faubus's mind.

Following his return to the Arkansas capital, the governor instead simply continued stonewalling both the Supreme Court and the president. Left with little choice, Eisenhower then made one of the most famous and portentous decisions of his eight years in the White House: he ordered the 101st Airborne Division to Little Rock to do what the governor refused to do. A fascinated nation was watching even while Little Rock was forced to share the headlines with the sensation of the Soviet Union's recently launched *Sputnik*. Thus when federal troops took up their positions around Central High School to see to it that nine kids got a chance at their long-deferred promise of an equal education, those schoolchildren stepped into a spectacle in which they were escorted to their classes by bayoneted and helmeted troops acting under the direct aegis of the federal military and its commander in chief, a real-life passion play instantaneously being broadcast into millions of homes via the shiny new medium of television. In fact, during those Little Rock days the networks' evening news programs irreversibly became a national institution while they monitored America's civil rights revolution getting well and truly under way.

Relatively little attention has been paid to what happened to the nine kids of Little Rock in the weeks following their military-backed insertion into Central High School. All acquitted themselves as heroes in the truest sense of the attribution. All were subjected to every kind of vile treatment that their white classmates could devise. They were called niggers—one white girl said it was her perfect right to use the epithet, and in those days, not much could be done to stop her—and each of the nine was abused in the halls and classrooms and cafeteria of Central High, so much so that one or another of them was often on the verge of breaking down. But only one child left, a girl who was unable to stand the torment for the entire year and who struck back at a taunter who called her a "nigger bitch"; she was expelled for what can only be considered the most human reaction imaginable. After she left, signs immediately went up on the campus: One Down, Eight to Go. But the other eight didn't go. And by the start of the *next* school year, Little Rock's Central High School was indisputably integrated, despite a feeble and short-lived effort by the governor to simply close down the city's high schools.

Eisenhower was widely vilified for his actions. Practically every Southern official—senator, representative, governor, dogcatcher—directed unconscionable rhetoric against the chief executive. Richard Russell of Georgia compared the president's actions to Nazi storm trooper behavior, and Mississippi's archsegregationist senator James Eastland preposterously charged Eisenhower with lighting "the fires of hate." What was more, the nation's enemies abroad covered America in humiliation throughout the episode and long afterward, despite the reality that after centuries of white-on-black discrimination the American government had finally taken measures to stop it. But Little Rock seemed to make black America—especially *young* black America—come alive with purpose and strength and indignation. In the turbulent wake of the Central High spectacle, African-Americans, in the company of countless thousands of like-minded whites, turned their energies toward eradicating, once and for all, the nightmare of Jim Crow.

* * *

White resistance stiffened as all over the South cities and towns closed public schools rather than even begin a token accommodation toward integration in primary and secondary education. In Virginia, Alabama, and Georgia, white parents enrolled their children in private "academies," while legions of black children went without public schooling of any kind. In places where integration was attempted, whites rioted: when New Orleans admitted four young black girls to a white public elementary school, white supremacists took to the streets in fierce protest.

Even before Little Rock, the Southern contingent to Congress had made clear to the nation its intent to preserve Jim Crow. On March 11, 1956, ninety-six Southern congressmen presented a joint declaration challenging the right of the Supreme Court to "encroach" on their region's educational system. Citing *Plessy* for their authority, and noting that the Fourteenth Amendment was silent on education, these men served notice that they would "use all lawful means to bring about a reversal of this decision [*Brown*] which is contrary to the Constitution and to prevent the use of force in its implementation." For the next decade they and their Senate colleagues made it their primary order of business to obstruct any legislation designed to further civil rights for African-Americans, school-related or not.

But while Southern politicians focused their professional lives on the preservation of Jim Crow, the groundswell of black resistance initiated a new technique to further *their* ends. The unlikely new battleground would be the lunch counter, the ubiquitous restaurant that in those years served essentially the same role that would in later years be taken over by McDonald's-style fast-food emporiums. But if lunch counters were a commonplace for most Americans four decades ago, for Southern blacks most represented forbidden territory, officially off-limits because the creed of segregation forbade blacks and whites to sit under a common roof to eat together. On February 1, 1960, the new tactic designed to break Jim Crow began in earnest in Greensboro, North Carolina.

The day before, four college freshmen had attempted to buy a cup of coffee at the rigidly segregated city's Greyhound bus station lunch counter.

They failed because these young men—Ezell Blair Jr., Franklin McCain, Joseph McNeill, and David Richmond—were African-American, and the law forbid any of them to eat at the Greyhound lunch counter and forbid any of the lunch counter's waitresses to sell anything to any of them. Ironically, the waitress that winter day was black, yet she showed little sympathy for what the four were attempting. "You are stupid, ignorant!" she yelled at them. The men remained seated, undisturbed by the police, until the counter closed for the day.

That night as the four discussed their mission, one they had of course known would end in failure (although in the past two years a few students in Miami and Tulsa had managed to get themselves served at similar lunch counters, the tactic hadn't caught on in any organized way), they decided to dip a little deeper into the Greensboro waters, the four North Carolina Agricultural & Technical College undergraduates hoping they might succeed in a city where it had seemed impossible that they would be able to break Jim Crow. The next day—February 1—they went to the town's Woolworth store and, neatly dressed and conspicuously carrying their schoolwork, sat at the counter. As at the Greyhound station, here, too, the waitress refused to serve them. This time, though, the police were summoned. In many parts of the South, the police would simply have charged them with civic misconduct and likely bashed their impertinent heads with billy clubs. But in the comparative moderation of Greensboro, they were left alone—unarrested but still unserved.

But the four returned the next day, this time in the company of twenty-three of their friends, like themselves all black. They went unserved again that day. The following day they came yet again—with sixty-three others, all black, and this time enough to fill every seat. And still they went unserved. On Thursday, even more joined them, including for the first time a few whites. They went unserved. And on the next day, there were a thousand, most of course spilling out of Woolworth's and onto the sidewalks of Greensboro's main street. Their demands were simple: they wanted an end to segregation, specifically at the Woolworth stores and, more broadly, *everywhere*.

The tactic of young, well-mannered, well-dressed, courteous blacks being refused food had turned into a spectacle. White hoodlums who had smelled an opportunity to put their bigotry on show roamed the aisles behind their seats, heckling the blacks and their white compatriots, throwing food on them, spitting at them. Yet any one of these bullies could have sat down at the Woolworth counter and would instantly have been served. The contrast was stunning and, most important, enormously effective. The tactic of the *sit-in*—a newly coined term that became a verbal icon of the civil rights revolution—eventually spread to fifty-four cities in nine Southern states, with seventy thousand students, all of whom were trained in the same peaceful tactics like those employed by the first four students—"sit tight and refuse to fight"—all the while risking injury and incarceration in their effort to bring an end to at least one form of Jim Crow.

The tactic did end in victory. Within three months of the first use of this new weapon, Woolworth's and other chain stores integrated their lunch counters in 114 cities where they had been segregated, now all finally open to the entire "public"—a term that had up to then meant something quite different. What was more, many other kinds of public services also began to bend to the changing winds, finally discarding Jim Crow barriers and opening their doors and services to everyone: hotels, libraries, amusement parks, movie theaters—many recognizing justice, and likely economic gain, in for the first time accepting an African-American clientele.

But not everything, everybody, everywhere. Jim Crow grimly hung on in hundreds of thousands of places, still stunting Southern society and still injuring millions, especially in the Deep South, in Mississippi and Alabama and Georgia and South Carolina, where progress came most slowly and most painfully. The students who marched and sat in and began to register black voters pricked America's conscience, but the *segs* (a term of opprobrium that was beginning to be used nationwide) *still* had the law to fall back on. And the tactics of protest continued to demand enormous bravery in a region where racial violence and murder could still strike the unwary, the defenseless, the vulnerable—and as often as not, without warning.

As obvious as the impending fall of Jim Crow in the late 1950s and early 1960s seems to contemporary sensibilities, countless white Southerners still clung ferociously to the hope that the old ways could, somehow, endure. Buoying last-ditch segregationists' hopes was the belief that sympathy in the rest of the country for the African-American's plight did not run especially deep. As keepers of the myth that they and they alone understood the race problem and the impossibility of social equality between blacks and whites, many segregationists hoped the disturbances in the South would frighten Northerners and dampen white Northern support for black gains in civil rights. In fact, as television news programs beamed pictures of civil disobedience into Northern homes every evening, many in the North did wonder if such disturbances would migrate northward, to a region still mired in its own kinds of racial inequality. The message that Southern politicians weren't in the least hesitant to cast as widely as possible was that if the South could be flooded with black "disorder," then precisely the same could happen in the North.

In the face of these dispiriting realities in the final years of Jim Crow, the fight to end it nonetheless grew by the month, seeming to double and redouble in energy even while most of the American people sat watching from the safety of their living rooms. To end Jim Crow discrimination on the South's public transport, the Congress of Racial Equality—CORE, one of the most important of the era's civil rights organizations—undertook a region-wide attempt to break the back of this form of segregation, specifically that which persisted on the interstate buses serving the South of the Trailways and Greyhound companies. In theory, the effort shouldn't have been necessary: in 1946 the Supreme Court had declared such segregation on interstate buses unconstitutional, then in 1960 had also ruled segregation for interstate passengers in the bus terminals unconstitutional as well. But both rulings had widely been ignored in the South, and CORE decided to attack the problem headlong.

What the organization devised was something called a Journey of Reconciliation, soon popularly rechristened the Freedom Rides. The plan was that racially mixed groups of riders would board buses in Washington, travel through the South, and end their journeys in New Orleans. White participants would sit in back of the buses, blacks in front. At rest stops, blacks would try to use the whites-only restaurants, toilets, and waiting rooms, while the whites used those designated for blacks. Fully aware that they would meet resistance, the CORE volunteers intended to utilize white racists to create a crisis, into which emergency the riders would summon the federal government to uphold their constitutional rights. CORE director James Farmer said, "When we began the ride, I think all of us were prepared for as much violence as could be thrown at us. We were prepared for the possibility of death."

That expectation was almost realized. The riders split themselves into two groups—half boarding a Greyhound liner heading for Anniston, Alabama, the remainder getting on a Trailways bus bound for Birmingham. Arriving in Anniston, the Greyhound bus encountered a mob of two hundred white racists waiting at the station, where the vehicle was stoned and its tires slashed. Though the bus and its riders escaped the station, just outside town the bus broke down. There the mob that had chased it from the station set it on fire. The passengers miraculously escaped through a gauntlet of blackjacks and clubs, helped by a rescue party of civil rights workers.

Later that day the Birmingham-bound Trailways liner pulled into the state's largest city. It was Mother's Day, and though Birmingham was unusually quiet as the bus drove through, the reception at the terminal would be anything but subdued. There a throng descended on the riders as they tried to disembark, beating and seriously injuring a number of the volunteers. No police had been dispatched to the station, the commissioner—the notorious and pathologically racist Eugene "Bull" Connor—later explaining that his officers had been "visiting their mothers." Nor did Alabama governor John Patterson apologize for the terror: "When you go somewhere looking for trouble, you usually find it."

Badly mauled by their experiences, the nonhospitalized CORE riders flew to New Orleans. But a group of sit-in students from Nashville who were affiliated with the Student Nonviolent Coordinating Committee decided to complete the original itinerary, taking up anew the ride from Birmingham. When they arrived in the city that Martin Luther King called the most segregated in America, the Birmingham police quickly arrested them and drove them to the Tennessee state line, where they were unceremoniously dumped beside the border marker on the highway. Undeterred, the riders all went straight back to Birmingham.

At this point the Justice Department intervened as the situation was becoming deadly dangerous for everyone involved. The Alabama highway patrol director promised Justice officials that protection would be provided for the bus with the Freedom Riders during its ninety-mile drive from Birmingham to Montgomery. But when that bus reached the city that had recently become world famous for Rosa Parks's heroism, it was greeted at the bus station by yet another mob of white thugs. This time a government official riding with the students was beaten nearly to death and left lying in the street, the city's police prominently absent. Even Southern editorialists were appalled at the treachery: the *Atlanta Constitution* wrote that "if the police . . . refuse to intervene when a man—any man—is being beaten to the pavement of an American city, then this is not a noble land at all. It is a jungle." It had taken the *Constitution* a long time to come to that conclusion, but even in Atlanta it was understood that the South was being internationally viewed as a place where justice remained utterly confounded.

Finally leaving Montgomery, the riders continued on to Mississippi. Though Attorney General Robert Kennedy had made arrangements with Mississippi authorities to protect the riders' safety, when the youths arrived and attempted to use facilities forbidden to their race in that state, they were promptly arrested. At their trial, the judge turned his back to the wall as their defense attorney spoke. When the lawyer finished, the judge swiveled around to face the riders and sentenced them to sixty days in the Mississippi State Penitentiary.

Though three more Freedom Rides spread out over the South that summer, and more young people were arrested, and some were beaten and some scarred for life from their physical injuries, their results justified the costs. Humiliated, in September 1961 the Kennedy administration ordered the Interstate Commerce Commission to prosecute any kind of segregation in interstate bus travel.

After the Freedom Rides, civil rights workers both black and white would be subjected to many more blows from the defenders of the South's "heritage." In Albany, Georgia, African-Americans attempting to end discrimination in that small city's public facilities would for their efforts pass long and ugly days in jail. In Oxford, Mississippi, James Meredith would show to a watching world indelible courage in the face of campus protesters (most of whom were not even students) as he tried to integrate the University of Mississippi's all-white student body. In Selma, Alabama, civil rights activists encountered a phalanx of Jim Crow defenders. "They literally whipped folks all the way back to the church," a young man recalled. "They even came up in the yard of the church, hittin' on folks. Ladies, men, babies, children—they didn't give a damn who they were." The same evening that Selma was being racked, the film *Judgment at Nuremberg* was being broadcast on ABC television. When the network interrupted it with news scenes of the violence at Selma, some viewers thought they were part of the motion picture.

And in Birmingham . . . In Birmingham the violence, sickening in scope, was, many believed, the worst, more disgraceful than all that had gone on before it. The then mordantly graceless city, called by the civil rights revolution's leader the most racist in the nation, was chosen by King for a direct confrontation of all the shadows in all its corners. Determined to end segregation in Birmingham's businesses and schools and public recreational facilities, as well as to publicize demands for the hiring of blacks by the city's segregationist employers, King and his lieutenants were facing a municipal commission implacably opposed to any substantive lifting of the constraints of Jim Crow. The civil rights leaders decided to create a civic disturbance that they knew would embarrass the city and, it was hoped, lead to a breaking of the racist grip holding back rights for Birmingham's black citizens.

King and a group of ministers at first tried a march through the city, but the man who had by now become almost as much symbol as flesh and blood was arrested for those efforts and jailed. King then decided on the potentially dangerous and morally delicate tactic of using schoolchildren to force the city's hand. On May 2, 1963, the forces arrayed against Jim Crow had gathered seven hundred eager black youngsters to march out to meet a police force led by Safety Commissioner Bull Connor. As the mass of schoolchildren stepped from the Sixteenth Street Baptist Church, the city's premier black temple of worship and a building that stood just a few blocks from the heart of Birmingham's downtown, Connor's waiting officers arrested the young demonstrators, threw them in paddy wagons, and took them to a detention facility. That ended the day's demonstration. But King's most dramatic act would come the next day.

On May 3, a thousand *more* children gathered at the same Sixteenth Street church. To block their planned march into the downtown core, Connor's men unleashed their German shepherd police dogs against the demonstrators even while they randomly beat the children as they tried to flee the yapping animals. Adding to the chaos, the police turned high-powered fire cannon on both the marchers and the spectators, sweeping many down sidewalks turned into rivers, the force of the water tearing the clothing off the demonstrators. The spectacle on that evening's television news both in America and abroad was simply beyond the pale, giving the Soviet Union enough propaganda material to last through countless of its anti-American diatribes.

When President Kennedy ordered federal troops into the brutalized city, Birmingham's business leaders agreed to a truce with King rather than face what they feared would end in race riots should concessions be refused. The agreement required the city to remove the thousands of Jim Crow signs that had segregated everything in town from the toilets to the bus stops, as well as to desegregate lunch counters, and finally, to guarantee to hire more African-Americans to work in downtown stores. Though Connor himself was livid with the compromise, the city carried out its end of the bargain.

And still Jim Crow hung on. A few months after King and the white elders of Birmingham worked out their settlement, the most unregenerate of the white supremacists struck this same city a blow that even hardened segregationists knew would leach away much of whatever sympathy remained with the cause of racial separation. In the same church from which King had sent his squadrons of schoolchildren out to face Bull Connor's policemen, hate-filled men planted a bomb on a Sunday morning just before worship services were to begin. When it went off, it took the lives of four young girls who had gathered in the Sunday-school room. When people sought the identity of the culprits, one man said, in effect, that they already knew who it was, that the bomber was "every little individual who . . . spreads the seeds of his hate to his neighbor and his son."

Over the following summer, murderers took the lives of three young civil rights workers in Mississippi for having committed the crime of helping African-Americans register to vote. The killers, who included law enforcement officials, were widely known to their community, but it was still too early to expect white-controlled Mississippi justice to punish the guilty.

Just as Martin Luther King and the other civil rights leaders had hoped would happen, John Kennedy and his administration had finally become embarrassed by the revolution that had turned much of the South into a battlefield. Since his election, the president had believed that easing relations with the Soviet Union in an attempt to stand down from nuclear confrontation should be his administration's highest priority, with stopping Soviet influence in the developing third world a close runner-up. The ending of segregation had remained, in comparison, a relatively distant domestic concern for Kennedy. But what was happening in the South was dangerously depleting the United States of its authority in the United Nations, of its ability to lead world affairs, and finally, of the moral high road from which to deal with a bellicose Soviet leadership. The cost of segregation was proving enormous, not merely in the dollars wasted by upholding the separate-everything apparatus of Jim Crow but also in the international loss of American prestige. The events in places like Birmingham were increasingly circumscribing the nation's freedom to act with certainty and resolve in the rest of the world. And at long last, Kennedy understood that he had to take real, measurable, and swift steps toward a resolution to this home-front crisis. To do it, he would employ his brother's Justice Department as his primary tool.

More than any other aspect of the growing crisis, it was Birmingham—the fire hoses, the children, the dogs, the bombs—that led the president to demand Congress pass a new civil rights bill, one that would end legal racial segregation in America once and for all. In June 1963, Kennedy spoke to a nationwide television audience to tell the nation why this was needed. In reference to the humiliating dispatch of federal troops to Southern cities, he said that "it ought to be possible . . . for American students of any color to attend public institutions they select without having to be backed up by troops." Noting that the issue wasn't merely about the reputation of the United States abroad, he came down eloquently and unequivocally on the side of justice when he said America was confronted "with a moral issue . . . as old as the Scripture and as clear as the American Constitution. The heart of the question is whether all Americans are to be afforded equal rights and equal opportunities, whether we are going to treat our fellow Americans as we want to be treated." The "we" seemed, of course, to make it clear he was speaking to *white* Americans, Americans who were not subjected to the Jim Crow faced every day by the most direct beneficiaries of his proposed bill.

It took a single sentence to get to the heart of America's abiding moral dilemma. Talking to tens of millions of people in words such as they had never before heard from the nation's chief executive, Kennedy said, "We preach freedom around the world, and we mean it, and we cherish our freedom here at home, but are we to say to the world, and much more importantly, to each other that this is a land of the free except for the Negroes; that we have no second-class citizens except Negroes; that we have no class or caste system, no ghettos, no master race, except with respect to Negroes?" The following week he sent a bill to Congress outlawing discrimination on grounds of race in America's public accommodations.

Five months later this voice was stilled forever in Dallas. Over those five months Southern senators had seen to it that the president's bill hadn't even been raised in Congress. But less than a week after Kennedy's murder, addressing Congress for the first time, the new president—with spectacular irony, a Southerner—asked it, almost *ordered* it, to immediately pass his predecessor's bill as a "monument" to the fallen leader. A master politician and parliamentarian who was riding a wave of public sympathy supporting any action that would honor Kennedy, Johnson spent every ounce of his power and prestige in aid of the bill, one he had in fact strengthened far beyond what Kennedy had proposed.

Six weeks later, it passed by a lopsided 290–110 vote in the House of Representatives, a chamber in which the filibuster was not allowed. But a filibuster *was* used in the Senate, and Johnson conjured every trick, called in every marker, and put every scrap of pressure at his command on Southern senators to forgo a filibuster and thus to get the "Kennedy" bill passed. Yet even Johnson's magic wasn't enough to convince every senator to bow to the inevitable. Richard Russell of Georgia characterized the bill as a "vicious assault on property rights and on the Constitution," while others warned of "quotas" in the bill's section on hiring. A filibuster ensued that lasted eighty-two days. Finally, in June 1964 the Senate voted to impose cloture on filibustering senators for the first time in that body's history, after what had been one of the longest Senate deliberations ever. The Senate voted 73–27 for the far-reaching civil rights bill, the most sweeping social legislation since Reconstruction, and on July 2 President Johnson signed it into law. To forestall any effort to have it declared in violation of the provisions of the Fourteenth Amendment (the last such bill had in 1883 been overturned by the Supreme Court on the constitutional grounds that it was beyond the scope of Congress's power), the high court immediately agreed to test it by an accelerated review of two pertinent cases. The court unanimously upheld both.

The heart of the act was in its Title II. In a handful of paragraphs enumerating those practices no longer legal in the providing of public accommodations, statutory Jim Crow was delivered a mortal wound. The law would now require that every American be entitled to the "full and equal enjoyment of the goods, services, privileges, advantages, and accommodations of any place of public accommodation ... without discrimination or segregation on the ground of race, color, religion, or national origin." It went on to clearly define those accommodations: the inns, hotels, and motels, the restaurants and cafeterias and lunchrooms, the theaters and concert halls and sports arenas, that had barred blacks would no longer hold any legal right to do so. The law now forbade racial discrimination in transportation, finally dropping the essentially spurious "states' rights" distinction between interstate and intrastate travel by specifically outlawing discrimination on transportation between points within the same state. It also importantly prohibited discrimination related to voter registration, as well as creating an Equal Employment Opportunity Commission to help ensure nondiscriminatory job opportunities for African-Americans—and for that matter, for anyone else subject to racial or ethnic discrimination.

Though many tried to circumvent the 1964 Civil Rights Act by ruses involving "private" facilities and other such devices, the full weight of the federal government stood behind the act, and this time the law would not be, as its predecessors had so often been before, ignored. Almost overnight the Jim Crow signs came down from thousands of the South's walls and stanchions and doors and barricades. And almost overnight tens of thousands of restaurants and theaters and skating rinks and nightclubs and bowling alleys opened their doors to blacks, almost invariably without serious incident. In many places recalcitrance to obey the law had to be addressed by judges, who affirmed where the law now stood, and such last-ditch attempts to protract Jim Crow were almost uniformly condemned. No one suggested this fall of Jim Crow was done out of the goodness of anyone's heart. Rather it was because people unmistakably understood that to discriminate meant to risk substantial fines and even imprisonment. If hearts and minds hadn't necessarily changed, consequences had.

One more legal barrier stood in the way of finally pronouncing statutory Jim Crow dead. Though the 1964 Civil Rights Act addressed and prohibited some of the discriminatory issues affecting voting, it did not effectively end such abuses. Neither had the bill's two predecessors addressing voting, the 1957 and 1960 Civil Rights Acts that had been bereft of effective enforcement provisions. Riding the crest of his 1964 victory in civil rights, President Johnson pressed to close this remaining loophole.

The civil rights leadership had spent the summers of the early 1960s organizing voter registration among African-Americans in the South, meeting failure as well as success. Aware that the entire structure of Jim Crow could never be genuinely torn down until African-Americans effectively and without fear used their constitutional right to vote, the major organizations had sent thousands of workers, black and white, into the South to correct this situation. Yet voter registrars still wielded sufficient power to prevent blacks from either registering or voting. Southerners had for the hundred years since emancipation regarded polling stations as exclusively white territory: for blacks to be allowed this ultimate privilege of citizenship would signify in racist terms an unacceptable political equality between black and white, and as long as whites held the power to decide who could and who could not vote, the situation would not change of its own accord. Polling officials remained within their legal writ to demand that prospective voters be able if called on to explain esoteric constitutional questions, most of which would, of course, have stumped most whites had the tests been fairly applied irrespective of race; the correctness of a prospective voter's explanation remained solely within the discretion of the white polling officials' judgment, the outcome of which was obvious.

To dramatize black disfranchisement, Martin Luther King decided in early 1965 on a protest march to publicly voice African-American grievances. Dallas County in Alabama had long been a particularly notorious locale for white disregard for black civil rights, a place where activists accompanied many blacks to the courthouse in the county seat at Selma, but where registrars exploited the old but still highly effective registration tactics that had kept African-Americans voteless. King and his compatriots would march to the state capital in Montgomery with their demands, and with rich symbolism, they would set off from Selma.

On a Sunday morning in late winter, some six hundred demonstrators had gathered outside the small Alabama town to begin their march. They knew they were doing so in contravention of the county sheriff's explicit order barring what he called an "illegal demonstration," an order fully backed in Montgomery by the governor, George Wallace. As the protesters of both races crossed the Edmund Pettus Bridge spanning the Alabama River and headed directly into Selma's compact downtown, Dallas County sheriff James Clark and his deputies, backed by a brigade of two hundred state troopers, all of whom were heavily armed with bullwhips and nightsticks and wearing gas masks over their helmet-protected faces, ordered King and the six hundred marchers to halt. When the latter nonetheless pressed forward, the enforcers of Alabama's law plowed into the marchers, often delivering their worst savagery to the whites, at whom they screamed "nigger lover" even as they brought down leaded batons on their heads. Seventeen of the demonstrators were hospitalized.

More than anything else, this crisis led President Johnson to send to Congress a bill specifically ending the voting abuses that had given rise to the violence at Selma—and in countless other places over so many decades. For emphasis, Johnson decided to address Congress himself, the first time since 1946 that a president would personally speak to that body on any domestic issue. In laying out to the legislators his reasons for a voting rights bill, in a televised address on the evening of March 15, 1965—a week after Selma's "Bloody Sunday"—Johnson's voice assumed the tone and language of the civil rights movement itself. He acknowledged that "rarely in any time does an issue lay bare the secret heart of America," hitting squarely on the often-buried but omnipresent nature of prejudice in the nation's life. "There is no Negro problem," the president continued, "there is no Southern problem, there is no Northern problem. There is only an American problem." Though not quite accurate in asserting that keeping blacks from the polls wasn't a *Southern* problem, which it certainly was, the president appreciated the political necessity to try not to offend Southerners any more than necessary. But getting to the heart of his task of convincing Congress to pass this bill, the president stated the cardinal national birthright in irrefutable language: "Every American citizen must have an equal right to vote. There is no reason that can excuse the denial of that right. There is no duty which weighs more heavily on us than the duty we have to ensure that right."

Never before, and never since, has a president spoken so forthrightly, or so courageously, in addressing the need to end race discrimination in America. He ended what was in effect a peroration by refraining the emblematic dictum of the civil rights revolution: "It is the effort of American Negroes to secure for themselves the full blessings of America. Their cause must be our cause, too. Because it is not just Negroes, but really it is all of us who must overcome the crippling legacy of bigotry and injustice. And we shall overcome."

With Martin Luther King Jr. at his side, Lyndon B. Johnson signed the Voting Rights Act into law on August 6, 1965. It was subtitled, "An act to enforce the Fifteenth Amendment to the Constitution of the United States," the latter a law that had been ratified in 1870. It had taken ninety-five years for America to meet its promise.

Bibliography

Appiah, Kwame Anthony, and Henry Louis Gates Jr. *Africana: The Encyclopedia of the African and African-American Experience*. New York: Basic Books, 1999.

Applebome, Peter. *Dixie Rising: How the South Is Shaping American Values, Politics, and Culture*. San Diego: Harcourt Brace, 1997.

Ayers, Edward L. *The Promise of the New South*. New York: Oxford University Press, 1992.

Blair, Lewis H. *A Southern Prophecy: The Prosperity of the South Dependent Upon the Elevation of the Negro*. New York: Little Brown and Company, 1964 (originally published 1889).

Brinkley, Douglas. *Rosa Parks*. New York: Viking, 2000.

Brundage, W. Fitzhugh, ed. *Under Sentence of Death: Lynching in the South*. Chapel Hill: University of North Carolina Press, 1997.

Carnes, Jim. *Us and Them: A History of Intolerance in America*. New York: Oxford University Press, 1996.

Cash, W. J. *The Mind of the South*. New York: Vintage, 1941.

Cashman, Sean Dennis. *African-Americans and the Quest for Civil Rights, 1900–1990*. New York: New York University Press, 1991.

Clark, Thomas D. *The Emerging South*. New York: Oxford University Press, 1968.

Conrad, Earl. *Jim Crow America*. New York: Paul S. Eriksson, Inc., 1947.

———. *The Invention of the Negro*. New York: Paul S. Eriksson, Inc., 1966.

Cox, Oliver C. *Caste, Class and Race*. New York: Monthly Review Press, 1948.

Davis, F. James. *Who Is Black? One Nation's Definition*. University Park, Pa.: Penn State University Press, 1991.

Dees, Jesse Walter, Jr., and James S. Hadley. *Jim Crow*. Ann Arbor: Ann Arbor Publishers, 1951.

Delaney, David. *Race, Place, and the Law, 1836–1948*. Austin: University of Texas Press, 1998.

Dollard, John. *Caste and Class in a Southern Town*. New Haven: Doubleday Anchor, 1937.

Doyle, Bertram Wilbur. *The Etiquette of Race Relations in the South: A Study in Social Control*. Port Washington, N.Y.: Kennikat Press, 1937.

Dye, Thomas R. *The Politics of Equality*. Indianapolis: Bobbs-Merrill, 1971.

Eaton, Clement. *A History of the Southern Confederacy*. New York: The Free Press, 1954.

Egerton, John. *Speak Now Against the Day: The Generation Before the Civil Rights Movement in the South*. Chapel Hill: University of North Carolina Press, 1994.

Finkelman, Paul, ed. *The Age of Jim Crow: Segregation from the End of Reconstruction to the Great Depression*. New York: Garland, 1992.

Fishel, Leslie H., Jr., and Benjamin Quarles. *The Negro American: A Documentary History*. New York: William Morrow and Company, 1967.

Fraiser, Jim. *Mississippi River Country Tales: A Celebration of 500 Years of Deep South History*. Jackson, Miss.: Persimmon Press, 1999.

Franklin, John Hope, and Alfred A. Moss Jr. *From Slavery to Freedom: A History of African-Americans*. New York: Alfred A. Knopf, 2000.

Frazier, E. Franklin. *The Negro in the United States*. New York: Macmillan, 1949.

Fredrickson, George M. *White Supremacy: A Comparative Study in American and South African History*. New York: Oxford University Press, 1961.

Gatewood, Willard B. *Aristocracy of Color: The Black Elite, 1880–1920*. Bloomington: Indiana University Press, 1990.

Gillon, Steven M. *That's Not What We Meant to Do: Reform and Its Unintended Consequences in 20th Century America*. New York: W. W. Norton, 2000.

Ginzberg, Eli, and Alfred S. Eichner. *The Troublesome Presence: American Democracy and the Negro*. New York: Mentor Books, 1964.

Goldfield, David R. *Black, White, and Southern: Race Relations and Southern Culture 1940 to the Present*. Baton Rouge: Louisiana State University Press, 1990.

Gossett, Thomas F. *Race: The History of an Idea in America*. Dallas: Southern Methodist University Press, 1975.

Graham, Lawrence Otis. *Our Kind of People: Inside America's Black Upper Class*. New York: HarperCollins, 1999.

Gray, Fred. *Bus Ride to Justice: Changing the System by the System—the Life and Works of Fred Gray*. Montgomery: Black Belt Press, 1995.

Griffin, John Howard. *The Church and the Black Man*. Dayton: Pflaum Press, 1969.

Guelzo, Allen C. *Abraham Lincoln: Redeemer President*. Grand Rapids: W. B. Eerdmans Publishing Company, 1999.

Gunther, John. *Inside U.S.A.* New York: Harper & Brothers, 1946.

Hale, Grace. *Making Whiteness: The Culture of Segregation in the South, 1890–1940*. New York: Pantheon Books, 1998.

Hall, Kermit L., ed. *The Oxford Guide to U.S. Supreme Court Decisions*. New York: Oxford University Press, 1999.

Haywood, Harry. *Negro Liberation*. New York: International Publishers, 1948.

Higginbotham, A. Leon, Jr. *Shades of Freedom: Racial Politics and Presumptions of the American Legal Process*. New York: Oxford University Press, 1996.

Hilliard, Sam B. *The South Revisited: Forty Years of Change*. New Brunswick, N.J.: Rutgers University Press, 1992.

Jacobson, Matthew F. *Whiteness of a Different Color*. London: Harvard University Press, 1998.

James, C. L. R., et al. *Fighting Racism in World War II*. New York: Monad Press, 1980.

Johnson, Charles S. *Backgrounds to Patterns of Negro Segregation*. New York: Thomas Y. Crowell Company, 1943.

Jones, Claudia. *Jim Crow in Uniform*. New York: New Age Publishers, 1940.

Jordan, Winthrop D. *The White Man's Burden: Historical Origins of Racism in the United States*. London: Oxford University Press, 1974.

Kantrowitz, Stephen. *Ben Tillman & the Reconstruction of White Supremacy*. Chapel Hill: University of North Carolina Press, 2000.

Katz, William Loren. *Eyewitness: A Living Documentary of the African-American Contribution to American History*. New York: Touchstone Books, 1995.

Kennedy, David M. *Freedom from Fear: The American People in Depression & War, 1929–1945*. New York: Oxford University Press, 1999.

Kennedy, Stetson. *Jim Crow Guide to the U.S.A.: The Laws, Customs and Etiquette Governing the Conduct of Nonwhites and Other Minorities as Second-Class Citizens*. London: Lawrence and Wishart, Ltd., 1959.

Kisch, John, and Edward Mapp. *A Separate Cinema: Fifty Years of Black Cast Posters*. New York: The Noonday Press, 1992.

Klinkner, Philip A. *The Unsteady March: The Rise and Decline of Racial Equality in America*. Chicago: University of Chicago Press, 1999.

Kull, Andrew, *The Color-Blind Constitution*. Cambridge, Mass.: Harvard University Press, 1992.

Latham, Frank B. *The Rise and Fall of Jim Crow, 1865–1964: The Negro's Long Struggle to Win "the Equal Protections of the Laws."* New York: Franklin Watts, Inc., 1969.

Levine, Matthew. *Social Issues in American History Series*. Phoenix: Oryx, 1996.

Lincoln, C. Eric. *Race, Religion, and the Continuing American Dilemma*. New York: Hill and Wang, 1984.

Litwack, Leon F. *Trouble in Mind: Black Southerners in the Age of Jim Crow*. New York: Alfred A. Knopf, 1998.

Loewen, James W. *Lies My Teacher Told Me: Everything Your American History Textbook Got Wrong*. New York: Touchstone Books, 1995.

MacGregor, Morris J., Jr. *Integration of the Armed Forces, 1940–1965*. Washington, D.C.: Center for Military History, 1985.

McCullough, David. *Truman*. New York: Simon & Schuster, 1992.

McGuire, Philip. *Taps for a Jim Crow Army*. Santa Barbara: ABC-Clio, 1983.

McMillen, Neil R. *Dark Journey: Black Mississippians in the Age of Jim Crow*. Urbana: University of Illinois Press, 1989.

McNeil, Genna Rae. *Groundwork: Charles Hamilton Houston and the Struggle for Civil Rights*. Philadelphia: University of Pennsylvania Press, 1983.

Manchester, William. *The Glory and the Dream*. Boston: Little Brown, 1973.

Marable, Manning, and Leith Mullings, eds. *Let Nobody Turn Us Around: Voices of Resistance, Reform, and Renewal—An African American Anthology*. Lanham, Md.: Rowman & Littlefield, 2000.

Massey, Douglas S., and Nancy A. Denton. *American Apartheid: Segregation and the Making of the Underclass*. Cambridge, Mass.: Harvard University Press, 1993.

Miller, Elizabeth W., and Mary L. Fisher, comps. *The Negro in America: A Bibliography*. Cambridge, Mass.: Harvard University Press, 1970.

Murray, Florence, ed. *The Negro Handbook, 1942*. New York: Wendell Malliet and Company, 1942.

———. *The Negro Handbook, 1946–1947*. New York: Current Books, 1947.

Myrdal, Gunnar. *An American Dilemma: The Negro Problem and Modern Democracy*. New York: Harper & Brothers, 1944.

Nearing, Scott. *Black America*. New York: Schocken Press, 1929.

Newby, I. A. *Jim Crow's Defense: Anti-Negro Thought in America, 1900–1930*. Baton Rouge: Louisiana State University Press, 1965.

———. *Challenge to the Court: Social Scientists and the Defense of Segregation, 1954–1966*. Baton Rouge: Louisiana State University Press, 1967.

———, ed. *The Development of Segregationist Thought*. Homewood, Ill.: The Dorsey Press, 1968.

Nieman, Donald G., ed. *African-Americans and the Emergence of Segregation, 1865–1900*. New York: Garland, 1994.

O'Byrne, James. "Together Apart: The Myth of Race." *New Orleans Times-Picayune*, 15 Aug. 1993.

Palmer, Colin A. *Passageways: An Interpretive History of Black America, Volume Two: 1863–1965*. Fort Worth: Harcourt Brace College Publishers, 1998.

Pettigrew, Thomas F. *Epitaph for Jim Crow*. New York: Anti-Defamation League of B'nai B'rith, 1964.

Ploski, Harry A., ed. *The Negro Almanac*. New York: Bellwether Company, 1971.

Powe, Lucas A., Jr. *The Warren Court and American Politics*. Cambridge, Mass.: Harvard University Press, 2000.

Rabinowitz, Howard N. "From Exclusion to Segregation: Southern Race Relations, 1865–1890." In *African-Americans and the Emergence of Segregation, 1865–1900*, ed. Donald G. Nieman. New York: Garland, 1994.

Rasmussen, R. Kent. *Farewell to Jim Crow: The Rise and Fall of Segregation in America*. New York: Facts on File, 1997.

Reader, John. *Africa: A Biography of the Continent*. New York: Vintage Books, 1997.

Robinson, Jo Ann. *The Montgomery Bus Boycott and the Woman Who Started It*. Knoxville: University of Tennessee Press, 1987.

Roche, John P. *The Quest for the Dream: The Development of Civil Rights and Human Relations in Modern America*. New York: Quadrangle Books, 1963.

Roper, John Herbert. *C. Vann Woodward: A Southern Historian and His Critics*. Athens, Ga.: University of Georgia Press, 1997.

Russell, Francis. *Confident Years*. New York: American Heritage Publishing Company, 1969.

Segal, Geraldine R. *In Any Fight Some Fall*. Rockville: Mercury Press, 1975.

Segal, Ronald. *The Race War*. New York: Viking Press, 1966.

Silberman, Charles E. *Crisis in Black and White*. New York: Vintage, 1964.

Smith, Graham. *When Jim Crow Met John Bull: Black American Soldiers in World War II Britain*. London: I. B. Taurus and Company, Ltd., 1987.

Sprigle, Ray. *In the Land of Jim Crow*. New York: Simon and Schuster, 1949.

Stephenson, Gilbert T. *Race Distinctions in American Law*. Appleton, N.Y., 1910.

Sternsher, Bernard, ed. *The Negro in Depression & War: Prelude to Revolution, 1930–1945*. Chicago: Quadrangle Books, 1969.

Stewart, Jeffrey C. *1001 Things Everyone Should Know About African-American History*. New York: Doubleday, 1996.

Talmadge, Herman E. *You and Segregation*. Birmingham: Vulcan Press, 1955.

Thernstrom, Stephan, and Abigail Thernstrom. *America in Black and White: One Nation, Indivisible—Race in Modern America*. New York: Simon and Schuster, 1997.

Williamson, Joel. *The Crucible of Race: Black and White Relations in the American South Since Emancipation*. New York: Oxford University Press, 1984.

Woodward, C. Vann. *The Strange Career of Jim Crow*. 3rd rev. ed. New York: Oxford University Press, 1974.

Wright, Richard. *Black Boy*. New York: Perrenial Classics, 1993.

Index